STEADY WORK

BOOKS BY IRVING HOWE

The U.A.W. and Walter Reuther (with B. J. Widick)

Sherwood Anderson: A Critical Biography

William Faulkner: A Critical Study

A Treasury of Yiddish Stories (edited with Eliezer Greenberg)

Politics and the Novel

The American Communist Party: A Critical History (with Lewis Coser)

Modern Literary Criticism, an Anthology

A World More Attractive

The Basic Writings of Trotsky (editor)

The Radical Papers (editor)

Once in Chelm, the mythical village of the East European Jews, a man was appointed to sit at the village gate and wait for the coming of the Messiah. He complained to the village elders that his pay was too low. "You are right," they said to him, "the pay is low. But consider: the work is steady."

IRVING HOWE *Steady Work*

Essays in the Politics of Democratic Radicalism 1953 - 1966

HARCOURT, BRACE & WORLD, INC.
New York

First edition

Library of Congress Catalog Card Number: 66-22275
Printed in the United States of America

Some of the essays in this book previously appeared in *Dissent, The New Republic, The New York Review of Books,* and *Partisan Review.* "Berkeley and Beyond" is reprinted from *Revolution at Berkeley,* edited by Michael V. Miller and Susan Gilmore, with an introduction by Irving Howe. Copyright © 1965 by Michael V. Miller and Susan Gilmore, and is used with the permission of the publishers, The Dial Press, Inc. This version of "Leon Trotsky: The Costs of History" is from *Basic Writings of Trotsky,* edited by Irving Howe, © Copyright 1963 by Random House, Inc., and is reprinted by permission. "This Age of Conformity" and "Images of Socialism" also appeared in Irving Howe's *A World More Attractive,* © 1963 by Irving Howe, and are reprinted by permission of The World Publishing Company.

FOR *Lewis Coser, Manny Geltman,*
AND *Stanley Plastrik*

☼ CONTENTS

Introduction

This book brings together a selection of political writings from the years 1953–1966. It records an effort to develop a politics of democratic radicalism that would be relevant to American life, and it offers a history—personal, informal, fragmentary—of the radical mind in this country, or at least one sort of radical mind, as it has tried to grapple with political-intellectual problems in a time of difficulty and disintegration. The modes of writing included here are various, ranging from the formal essay to the brief review, from the topical comment to the polemical attack. I should like the reader to feel not merely that he is being addressed directly, but also that he is overhearing someone, a man of the left, in a dialogue with himself, asking which of his earlier ideas should be preserved, which modified, which discarded. After a time the reader may care to amend or interrupt.

The period of time covered in these essays is relatively brief, but the experiences touched upon are numerous: the dismal McCarthyite years of the early fifties, the prolongation and distension of the Cold War, the new conservative moods among American intellectuals, the crack-up of domestic Stalinism, the hopes raised by the Negro liberation movement, the accomplishments and fanfare of student rebellion, the crisis in Vietnam. Despite this span of topics and the variety of expository forms through which I approached them, I claim for this book a firm unity. It is the only kind of unity that matters, the unity of a mind steadily and intensely engaged with a complex of problems, struggling in behalf of and sometimes in opposition to its own premises, turning repeatedly to the themes of its commitment.

Reading through these essays once again, I have been struck not only by their persistence of concern, but also—to be candid with both the reader and myself—by the fact that not many of them deal with specific problems of domestic or foreign policy. Such analyses have been attempted by writers of my political outlook, most recently in *The Radical Papers*, a group of studies composed by a number of close political collaborators and edited by myself. In this present book, however, the recurrent focus of interest seems to be: from which premises, by which methods, and in behalf of which values can such specific analyses of American society be undertaken? Were the phrase not so hopelessly pompous, I would say that this book consists of "position papers"—with the somewhat wry amendment that my "position" is by no means fixed but, like all other efforts at political thought aspiring to seriousness, is entangled with difficulties, problems, crises. For obviously the essays in this book have been shaped and colored by the fact that in the last few decades we have been experiencing a major crisis in socialist thought, not only in America but everywhere else in the world. And far from presuming to improvise a surrogate ideology—Humpty-Dumpty can't be put together again, and even if he could be, I should not care to do it—I have tried to see how far we could go in reconstructing a politics for the democratic left with fragments of ideology, a complicated and chastened sense of history, a sharp concern for the actualities of immediate social life, intuitions of fraternity and freedom, and a rigorous commitment to democratic values.

About radicalism itself there is nothing to say here that does not appear in the book itself, except this: Being a socialist in the mid-twentieth century means, to serious people, a capacity for living with doubt, revaluation and crisis; a capacity for living, as all truly modern men must live, by the style of the problematic. But if the ideal of socialism is now to be seen as problematic, the problem of socialism remains an abiding ideal. I would say that it is the best problem to which a political intellectual can attach himself. Some traditional doctrines of socialism now seem outmoded or mistaken, but I remain absolutely convinced of the need for a democratic and radical renovation of society, through which to give a fresh embodiment to the ideals of fraternity and freedom.

Now there are people who delight in pouncing upon such remarks and pointing to the difficulties, even the disarray of contemporary radical thought. They are quite within their rights. But is there any mode of serious political thought in the mid-twentieth century which is not in a condition of similar difficulty? Or which should not be in a condition of similar difficulty? And then there are a few old and true believers who feel it scandalous to make such admissions: as if silence or a fine show of rhetoric could veil the troublesome reality. No; candor is the beginning and the end of intellectual recovery. To remain a socialist is to be convinced that the values and procedures of democracy must be spread through areas of our social life to which they have barely penetrated; it means to refuse the empiric, sometimes mean-spirited "realism" of acquiescence in the status quo, as if, somehow, the ultimate stage of human development, never to be transcended, had been reached in the garrison-welfare state; it means to insist upon the relevance of images of utopia, a vision of society that has men acting for motives finer than accumulation, values better than manipulation, an ethic beyond the appetites of self. Yet to say these things is also an admission that we cannot, so late in the day—not after all the failures and betrayals of our time—come forward as if we had not been battered by history, or as if we could bring to the world a fistful of irrefutable answers, or a monopoly of righteousness, or some secret alliance with the future of History. We radicals are men like other men, bewildered, troubled, eager, and we stay with our tradition because we believe that its true promise has yet to be realized and that this promise can make better the life of all.

Precisely because of that belief, the stress in this book is not merely upon reflection but also upon action, not merely upon rethinking the socialist idea but upon working now, within the present society, in behalf of human needs and democratic goals. If we find insufficient the empiricism of those liberals content to function merely within the limits of "the given"—since what is "given" can itself be changed by the action of men—we find intolerable the snobbism of a certain sort of academic radical, the certainty of apocalypse tucked into his pocket, who in the name of his total vision disdains the limited struggles of the moment. It is not always easy to link the idea of the future with the issues of the present, yet that is a central obligation of democratic radicals.

As I organized the material in this book, trying to see what remains valid and where some of the pieces were mistaken, the question occurred to me: Why not write a new book entirely, one that would state in rounded, coherent and up-to-date terms the outlook of democratic radicalism in America? Surely a book like that would be useful. Yet it was not, I think, mere impatience or laziness which has led me to prefer the present volume as it now stands. For my purpose has been not to present a finished rendition of a political viewpoint: it is not, by its very nature, at all finished. My purpose has been to chart an intellectual history, without the illusion of completeness, and to preserve the immediacy of responses as they were first made, even if this means to record hesitations and contradictions.

In honesty, however, I have another purpose. There has grown up during the last few years a new radicalism on and near the American campus. It is a radicalism that, from my point of view, has both immensely encouraging features—it is vital, selfless and brave—and some discouraging features—it is intellectually undeveloped, excessively self-righteous, and inclined, at times, to authoritarianism. The gap between generations is a great one, much more so than usual, and one reason for this can be located within the history of American radicalism itself. Between those radicals in their forties, like myself, and those to whom thirty seems an unimaginable fate, there is an urgent need for communication, even if only to find proper limits of disagreement. I want this book to be read by the younger radicals, not as a fixed statement of opinion which they must accept or reject completely, but as a record of intellectual struggle and political commitment. I want them to read this book so they will understand, for example, why it is that people like myself cannot accept their fashionable "agnosticism" toward Communist dictatorship, or why it is that, after costly and painful debates with ourselves, we have come to believe in the primacy of democratic values for any political reconstruction. Then, if they wish, they can disagree and if they trouble to write books I promise to read them.

Finally, a word about journalism. There is a certain kind of academic who, from motives I shall not here examine, enjoys the dismissal of "mere journalism," just as there is a certain kind of reviewer who likes to label a book of essays as a "mere collection." Such designations strike me as mere cant. Journalism, seriously undertaken, can yield pleasure and information; it is indispensable to a free political life; and it is a token of engagement with the world in which one lives. The essay has been, and in our day remains, one of the major forms of intellectual discourse: it enforces economy, discourages pedantry, and is more pitiless than the longer forms in exposing a writer's failings. Most of the intellectual figures in America about whose work one really cares, whether to accept or dispute, have done their best writing in essays.

Some of the pieces in this book are frankly journalistic, but even when such comment seems "dated" it can have its own decided interest, as part of the texture of political and intellectual life in the recent past: we should reject the tyranny of novelty quite as much as the vanity of scholasticism. Some of the pieces in this book are, I hope, more than topical, efforts to deal with or describe long-range problems. They will be criticized; they should be. They are offered as contributions to political and intellectual discourse, marked by the realities of the moment but aspiring to a vision for the age.

July 1, 1966

PART I *Turmoil in the Sixties*

✡ RADICAL CRITICISM AND THE AMERICAN INTELLECTUALS

IN the spring of 1965 there was held at Rutgers University, under the auspices of *Partisan Review*, a conference on "The Idea of the Future." Its aim was to set into motion a series of political and historical speculations as to the shape of Western society in both the immediate and long-range future. Among the papers written for this conference was the one that appears below, dealing with the possibilities of radical criticism in the society of tomorrow, and addressed largely, though not exclusively, to American intellectuals.

The topic assigned to me was disconcertingly broad, and I had to discuss both the role of radical criticism during the years immediately ahead (which means primarily within the limits of the welfare state) and its role over a longer span of time (which immediately raised the question as to the possibilities for "transcending" the welfare state, preserving freedom in a technological age, and moving toward an egalitarian and democratic socialism). The paper suffers, no doubt, from the need to cover so wide a range of topics, yet there may be some value in having a general perspective for radicalism sketched out at the beginning of this book.

SUPPOSE we were to ask ourselves, "What have been the decisive trends in American intellectual life these past few decades?" The answer, I think, would have to include some of the following:

The disintegration of Marxism as a frequently accepted mode of social analysis and subsequent efforts to patch together surrogate ideologies or, finding virtue in necessity, to dispense with ideology entirely.

Even those intellectuals who were never under the sway of Marxism have been strongly affected by its crisis and collapse, both as a system of politics and an encompassing *Weltanschauung*. At least part of what has happened among our intellectuals these past twenty-five years can be regarded as the result of the loss or abandonment of a powerful sustaining belief: one that, in its psychological dynamics, operated as a variety of religious experience. Future historians of ideas are likely to see this experience as similar in consequence—in pain, disorientation, and a series of brilliant reactive improvisations—to the experience of those mid-nineteenth-century English writers who broke away from orthodox Christianity yet could not rid themselves of a yearning for transcendence. A whole generation has been marked, often marred, by the deflation of the revolutionary mystique. Some intellectuals have, in fact, been so thoroughly captive to a nostalgia for apocalypse that they have failed to respond to the urgencies of political life today.

Others have conducted a frantic search for a substitute "proletariat," ranging from hipsters to the alienated underclass, that might provide a new motor for social energy. Still others have settled into political empiricism, content to work within the limits of "the given."

While it seems to me almost impossible for a man of critical intelligence to retain belief in such crucial aspects of political Marxism as the "revolutionary potential" of the working class, the "withering away" of the state, and the "dictatorship of the proletariat," we must acknowledge that the Marxist heritage, no doubt shaping our thought in more ways than we know, remains powerful, and that the Marxist method, especially if it becomes absorbed with a minimum of self-consciousness into a larger style of thought, can still be valuable in sharpening the issues of political debate.

A considerable change in the social status, economic condition and prestige ranking of the intellectuals as a group.

The intellectuals can no longer be said to live beyond the margin or within the crevices of society. Those who continue in Bohemian poverty must often choose to remain there. The honorific role accorded the intellectuals under the Kennedy administration was merely a symbolic climax to a process long under way—a process bringing to a virtual end that condition of psychic displacement and political estrangement which had first begun in the early or mid-nineteenth century. Today the intellectuals are, as a rule, firmly entrenched within the society: as academicians in a growing university system; as middlemen whose skills are exploited, while their tastes are violated, in the industries of cultural entertainment; as members of a slowly cohering elite within or near the government. The term "Establishment" has been used with a comic recklessness in the last few years, mostly as a "put-down" of those unfortunate enough to be over thirty, regularly employed, and addicted to suits and shaving; but for the first time we are perhaps beginning to have in the United States the kind of coherent and influential formation of intellectuals which in England is called "the Establishment."

The Cold War has shaped—I would say, mostly misshaped—intellectual life to a very large, though unmeasured, extent.

It requires an effort to remember the atmosphere in this country during the early fifties. A good many intellectuals formerly on the left were engaged in a flight to conservatism that was as ungainly as it was premature. Seriously entertained, conservatism can be a respectable point of view; but the sour hostility toward their own past, the frantic pursuit of intellectual "novelties," the barely disguised contempt for freedom which many ex-radical intellectuals showed in their devotion to the Cold War—all this was a good deal worse than conservatism. Do I exaggerate in saying that for the ex-radical intellectuals there was a steady need to depreciate the menace of Senator McCarthy's hooliganism, and that what really mattered was a kind of *union sacrée* in behalf of "anti-Communism?" Or that under the tranquilizing influence of a new affection for the American system, social problems were regarded as largely solved or, in more exalted moments, as symptoms of that impulse toward evil forever lodged in the human soul?

An increasing tendency toward and an implicit acceptance of intellectual specialization, what might be called the "privatization of work," so that the very idea of the intellectual vocation has come into question.

We are all familiar with the troubled inquiries as to whether the intellectual as a distinct type is likely to survive in an increasingly managerial and technological society. We are also familiar with privately voiced complaints—some may reflect no more than the sourness of people getting older, but some are a recognition of painful truth—that among younger writers these days there is no shortage of talent, energy or ambition, but rarely evidence of that free-wheeling and "dilettantish" concern with general ideas which we take to be characteristic of the intellectual life. No one supposes that in any future society intellectual work can possibly cease; what is at stake is whether such work can be broken down into a series of discrete and specialized functions, so that the larger animating concerns with values and ideals may gradually (or at least sooner than the state) wither away. What in some accounts is said to have happened to modern philosophy, seems a possible terminus for the life of the intellectual as an historical type.

Criticism of social institutions has in the last few decades been increasingly appropriated by journalists who combine useful exposé with a lack of fundamental theory and/or values.

Much of the muckraking—the attack upon specific deformations and failures of the welfare state which appeared during the fifties and early sixties—was composed by journalists with little grasp of what their material signified and with an inclination to transform their exposures into mere amusements for middle-brow readers. The intellectuals, having virtually ceded this area of work, largely confined themselves to criticizing the superficiality and vulgarity of such journalism, but without recognizing that their own abdication was in part responsible for its influence.

Moods and theories of political resignation, and sometimes assertions as to the inherent recalcitrance of social problems, became frequent among the older or more sophisticated intellectuals.

The welfare society throws up certain kinds of social troubles which cannot be as precisely delineated—nor can solutions be as confidently proposed—as we felt it possible to do for the economic problems of a few decades ago. These new social troubles seem so endemic and pervasive, so much a matter of tone, atmosphere, and malaise, that an impression grows up that neither revolution nor reform, and not even social engineering, can significantly affect them. And some intellectuals proclaimed during the fifties what was presumably never known before: that solutions to problems engender further problems; there is no end to the chain. All of this reflected a decrease of confidence in the powers of human reason, and a growing doubt as to the uses of human will.

One of the main avenues for intellectual activity and self-assertiveness—our common opposition to the products, the very idea of "mass culture"—has recently been little taken.

Not that intellectuals became noticeably slacker in their critical standards or less contemptuous of popular trash. The problem is rather that, almost unwittingly, they resigned themselves to the supposedly intractable evils of "mass culture," just as some have learned to resign themselves to the supposedly intractable evils of society in general—or (in a response to which I am more sympathetic) they became weary with the Sisyphean task of cultural hygiene. The once numerous and, up to a point, fruitful discussions of "mass culture," have by now almost disappeared from the serious journals. And in truth the problems connected with "mass culture" have become more slippery than they were, or seemed, a few decades ago. It is increasingly difficult, in that no man's land where the middle-brow abuts upon the serious, to draw a line between the authentic and a skillful simulation of the authentic. The theoretical analyses of "mass culture" begun in the thirties and forties have run into a dead end, and none of them seems fully applicable at the present moment. The militant zeal of the critics of "mass culture" has cooled; a few find themselves quite at home in the atmosphere and institutions they were among the first to attack. And meanwhile, perhaps in consequence, there has arisen a new school of sensibility which denies the relevance of esthetic discrimination, insisting that the Beatles are as "good" or "important" as Stravinsky, and priding itself upon a capacity to submit to every variety of cultural or pseudo-cultural experience.

*

The last few decades have been characterized by a quick, often facile, sometimes exciting shift in cultural fashions; by a quantity of stylistic and temperamental display; and by a drive toward personal distinction as an end in itself, such as must surely always be present in intellectual life but has seemed especially strong since the end of the war.

At no point in the life of American intellectuals during the twentieth century has the *idea* of an intellectual community been weaker than it is today. Yet at no point has the life of the intellectuals been more clearly or fully structured into a compact, miniature society than it is today.

The picture is bleak, but in the last few years there have been changes, though not yet changes strong enough to reverse the general drift of American intellectual life. People seem more inclined to question and speculate than they were ten years ago; radicalism, as a mood if not a movement, is beginning to revive; at the very least, we are done with the suffocating complacency of the fifties. Poverty was then mentioned nowhere but in the radical press; today it has become a theme for national discussion, if not yet sufficient national action. A decade ago merely to suggest that there was a problem of power in the United States—a concentration of resources, wealth, and "decision-making" which undercuts the formal claims of democracy—would call down scorn for clinging to "Marxist clichés"; today the matter is seriously discussed even among moderate analysts. In the fifties American foreign policy met with little sustained criticism; now a portion of the academic world is pressing its criticisms with great vigor. Why this shift in political and intellectual attitudes? A few reasons can be suggested:

The Cold War has largely run its course. That Western Europe has been stabilized on a more or less democratic basis is certainly a major achievement; otherwise, the record of the West in the Cold War is largely one of sterility. The inadequacies of Western power, especially in regard to areas like Latin America, have become clear; and it will not do simply to keep repeating the anti-Communist catchwords of a decade ago.

It seems likely that we shall not soon be plunged into a nuclear war through the deliberate choice of one or both of the major powers. At least a partial relaxation can therefore begin, as a result of which new problems, not accessible to Cold War politics, can come to the forefront.

It is increasingly hard to maintain that American society has reached a state of health so complete that little more than marginal problems remain to be solved—and those (as Arthur Schlesinger, Jr. suggested a few years ago) having less to do with gross exploitations than with psychological disturbances and esthetic needs.

While a sharp distinction between democratic and totalitarian values remains a moral imperative, the view of the world as polarized between extremes of good and evil, "we" and "they," becomes increasingly tiresome.

In the United States the civil rights movement has had a substantial liberating effect, not merely in gaining victories for the Negroes and in providing the idealistic young with opportunities for activity and sacrifice, but also in opening up the country to fresh moods and sentiments. Mostly as an aftermath of the civil rights movement, there has appeared a "new left"—about which more later.

The Kennedy administration, more through its civilized tone than actual achievements, helped clear the air of McCarthyite fumes and brought to national consciousness at least the possibility of further social advance.

The ideological, or what may come to the same thing, the anti-ideological zealousness characterizing a good part of the intellectual world in the early fifties was bound to exhaust itself. Just as after the crude Marxism of the thirties, there has followed a period of sobering second thoughts.

Nevertheless, the truth is that radical criticism remains scattered, limited in impact, uncertain as to intention, ill-developed in program, and confined to a very few writers.

Suppose, however, there were or could be such a criticism. To what order of problems would it address itself?

The Function of Criticism in the Welfare State

The welfare state preserves the essential character of capitalist economy, in that the interplay of private or corporate owners in the free market remains dominant; but it modifies the workings of that economy, in that the powers of free disposal by property owners are regulated and controlled by political organs. A more detailed description of the welfare state as a static "model" is provided by Henry Pachter:

> The welfare state is a capitalistic economy which largely depends on the free market but in which the countervailing powers have been politicized and are consciously employed to balance the economy, to develop the national resources or to pursue fixed goals of social policy. . . . The fully developed welfare state has at its disposal a wide range of economic instruments, classical as well as Keynesian and statist . . . The welfare state may achieve techniques of industry-wide planning, price-fixing and over-all control of development, but though it will nationalize the coal industry in France and England, erect a TVA in the United States and build a government steel mill for India, it stops short of expropriation. On the contrary, its proclaimed aim is to preserve the structure of property and to protect the formation of a free market. Whatever expropriating is to be done must come through the free play of the market, as is being done, e.g., in our farm economy despite price supports. The basic relationships of buyer and seller, employer and employee, owner and non-owner are no different from those prevailing under pure capitalism, but they are supplemented by state interference in two important areas: where classical capitalism is indifferent to the distribution of income, the welfare state at least tries to make income differentials less steep; also, whereas under pure capitalism the development of resources is but an accidental by-

product of the profit incentive, the welfare state sets itself definite goals of developing public and private facilities. . . .

. . . we should not be misled by its efforts to plan, regulate and control production, to redistribute income and to curb the uninhibited use of private property. At the hub of its mechanics, it is different from socialism. Though some prices and wages are determined politically, on the whole they are still determined by the market, and that is true even of the public enterprises; the regime of property prevails throughout, with the dead weight of past investments burdening the calculation of profit and the decisions on future investments, with at least a theoretical obligation to balance all budgets, and with remuneration still tightly ruled by a man's contribution to the value of the product. Public projects still need to be justified in terms of national policy rather than human needs, and expenditure for defense and similar competitive purposes still exceeds the welfare expenditure.

What this excellent description does not claim to provide is any sense of the way in which the welfare state tends to be open-ended at both sides, the way—within limits that need not be rigidly fixed in advance—the welfare state is an algebraic container that can be filled with the arithmetic of varying sociopolitical contents. Nor does it provide a sense of the welfare state as the outcome, not necessarily a "final" one, of prolonged social struggle to modulate and humanize capitalist society. It would be hard, perhaps impossible, to say to what extent the welfare state is the result of a deliberate intent to stabilize capitalist society from above, so that it will avoid breakdown and revolutionary crises; to what extent it is the outcome of relatively autonomous economic processes; and to what extent it is the partially realized triumph in the struggle of masses of men to satisfy their desires. As against those intellectuals who feel the major need for the immediate future to be a benevolent social engineering and those who see the welfare state as a device for maintaining, through diversions and concessions, the traditional forms of economic power, I would stress the idea that welfarism represents, both in achievements and potential, a conquest that has been *wrested* by the labor, socialist, and liberal movements.

For radical intellectuals the welfare state presents a set of new difficulties. The bulk of the intellectuals, to be sure, have adapted only too easily to its comforts and inducements; a society with an enormously expanded need for administrators, teachers, and cultural agents can offer position and prestige to intellectuals. But for those of us who wish to preserve a stance of criticism while avoiding the sterility of total estrangement, the welfare state has been an unsettling experience. Here are some of the characteristic responses of leftist intellectuals in the past few decades:

A feeling that the high drama (actually, the vicarious excitement) of earlier Marxist or "revolutionary" politics has been lost, and that in the relatively trivial struggles for a division of social wealth and power within a stable order there is neither much room nor need for intellectual activity. By now, this response is simply tiresome. The snobbism of nostalgia can easily decline into a snobbism of abstention; but those who care to act within history as it is, no matter in how modest a way, must accept the possibilities of today in order to transform those of tomorrow.

A belief that the welfare state will, in effect, remain stable and basically unchanged into the indefinite future; that conflict will be contained within the limits prescribed by the welfare state; and that problems of technique (e.g., how to administer a poverty program, how to retrain workers left jobless by automation) will supersede the "irresponsible" tradition of fundamental criticism. By accepting the "givenness" not merely of the welfare state but also its present forms and boundaries, this view underestimates the value of basic moral-political criticism. To cite a simple example: is the shameful failure to tear down the vast slum called Harlem due to difficulties in technique and administration or is it due to moral indifference, social timidity, and racial meanness? Another example: whether poverty can be entirely abolished within the present society is not so much a matter for analysis or speculation as for experiment and action. Such an effort might well require a radical restructuring of the welfare state to include a large program of public works, a degree of economic planning and a new allotment of social resources; and what keeps it from being enacted is not so much difficulties in execution as a failure of social will, responsibility and imagination. If I am right in saying this, the traditional responses of the intellectual—even if these are dismissed in certain quarters as utopian, impractical, etc.—remain quite as necessary as in the past. It might be maintained that even for new proposals to alleviate social troubles within the present society, a degree of utopian perspective and intellectual distance is required. For essential to such alleviation is a continued extension of the idea of the practical. One need not agree with Paul Goodman's general outlook or his schemes for social improvement in order to recognize that his recent utopian writings may have a more practical effect than the routinism and blundering of the practical men—and precisely because his writings are, in the current sense of things, less "practical."

A belief that the welfare state is characteristic of all forms of advanced industrial society; that it offers bread and television, palliatives and opiates, to disarm all potential opposition; and that it thereby perpetuates, more subtly but more insidiously than in the past, class domination. Such views have recently become popular in academic circles which in part are profiting from those struggles of yesterday that made possible the advantages of today. Despite their seeming intransigence, these views strike me as essentially conservative—they lead to passivity, not to action—and inhumane—they ignore, or minimize, the improvements in the immediate life-conditions of millions of human beings. Ignore or minimize, above all, the fact that the welfare state has meant that large numbers of working-class people are no longer ill fed, ill clothed and insecure, certainly not to the extent they once were. That automobile workers in Detroit can today earn a modest, if insufficient, income; that through union intervention they have some, if not enough, control over their work conditions; that they can expect pensions which are inadequate yet far better than anything they could have expected twenty years ago—all this is *good:* politically, socially, in the simplest human terms. To dismiss or minimize this enormous achievement on the lordly grounds that such workers remain "alienated" and show little awareness of their plight, is to allow ideology to destroy human sympathy.

Concerning these matters I want to quote some cogent remarks from the English writer Alasdair MacIntyre:

> It was only gradually that people in Britain became conscious of themselves as living in a society where a right to minimal standards of welfare was presupposed. . . . Even a modern affluent working class, even a working class with a socialist tradition . . . has to learn that the welfare state is *essentially a realm of conflict* in which the real benefits of welfare are always in danger of being undermined by defense spending, by the encroachments of private interests, or simply by inflation, and thus a realm in which it needs a good deal of running even to keep standing in the same place. So a working-class political self-consciousness about welfare as a point at which elementary rights have continually to be reclaimed seems to be one of the preconditions of the maintenance of welfare in an advanced capitalist society. . . .
>
> The problem of a politics that goes further than this is partly the problem of a working class that sixty years ago had to set itself the goals of welfare and now has to find for itself new political goals. . . .

In contrast to these three attitudes toward the welfare state, let me suggest the following position. The struggles and issues raised within the welfare state are real, not mere diversionary shadow-plays or trivial squabbles. They matter. They affect the lives of millions. Regardless of how mundane or inadequate the "level of consciousness" at which they are conducted, the struggles for social betterment within the welfare state merit our concern and involvement.

No magical solution is available for the problems faced by American radicals; if there were, someone would by now have discovered it. I am myself committed to the "coalition" approach suggested by Bayard Rustin and Michael Harrington: it proposes a loose and intermittent association of the major "progressive" forces in the country—labor, Negro, liberal, church groups, intellectuals, students—in order to work for current and intermediate goals. Socialism not being an immediate option, it is necessary for radicals, while continuing to speak for their views in full, also to try to energize those forces that are prepared to stretch the limits of the welfare state. Such a dynamic once set in motion, there may be possibilities for going still further; but any political approach that dismisses movements embodying the hard-won victories of yesterday, must doom itself to sectarian isolation today.

This strategy has many difficulties, not the least being that it isn't very dramatic. For young people who have just "made it" into radicalism, it sometimes seems insufficiently radical. But radicalism is neither a quantity nor a measure of purity and rectitude; it is a political outlook, and if a rough adaptation of Fabianism is a possibility, then we must seize upon it.

One reason for this political stress has been suggested by Meyer Schapiro: that American society is now significantly different from what it was thirty years ago, in that it formally accepts the values of social welfare, but that it repeatedly fails to realize those values. Among the consequences of this disparity between norm and reality are: the more complacent liberals feel, though they do not quite say, that there really are not many short-range goals still to be reached; the left-liberals have not succeeded, nor perhaps tried, to work out a clear program of immediate objectives such as they had a few decades ago; and the impression grows that problems are insoluble, or that those who claim to be solving them are mere hypocrites, etc.

Carey McWilliams has listed immediate problems for which the answer is *more* (welfare measures) and those for which the answer is *new* (automation, allocating national resources); his catalogue is worth noticing if only to remind ourselves of the urgency of the obvious:

> Is a "great society" one that, on an ever larger scale, continues to despoil the environment? Are present budget priorities really designed to produce a "great society" or a caricature of one? Can we continue to guide our foreign policy with compulsive slogans: "anti-communism," "containment," "the free world"? How is the scale of the military budget to be determined? How is a policy of reconversion to be brought about? How should resources be allocated? Should we plan and for what? How do we propose to cope with the consequences of the scientific-technological revolution?

Now there is in our society an occasional effort, more often a half-effort, and sometimes a mere pretense at coping with such problems; but increasingly the result is to blur the issues and discredit the very idea of rational action. What happens more often than not, has been pungently described, perhaps overstated a little, by Paul Goodman:

> "Education" means subsidizing schools to train National Science Foundation grade-getters for higher status and salaries in Research and Development, and as professional institutional personnel. "Urban Reconstruction" is the cabal of Washington, city party-bosses, real-estate promoters and automobile manufacturers to destroy neighborhoods and communities. . . . "Agriculture" is the underwriting of chain-grocers and *latifundia*, pesticides, the eradication of farmers, and the enclosure of the countryside for motels. . . . "Political Economy" is the galloping Gross National Product, stepping up TV advertising, the unchecked aggrandizing of the broadcasting networks . . . and more highways when there are already too many cars. . . .

*

In the teeth of this magnitude of bucks, one cannot seriously point to the minimum wage of $1.25 (excluding many categories) or 10,000 in the Peace Corps (after three years and $300 million) or the anti-discrimination housing order (applied to a minority of cases). Indeed a good synonym for Liberalism is Tokenism. But where are good neighborhoods, or clean rivers, or rural reconstruction, or liberating education, or an effort to improve the quality of the standard of living, to countervail regimenting and brainwashing?

Old problems fester and new ones appear, threatening the precarious equilibrium of the welfare state. For the great temptation in thinking about the welfare state is to assume *in effect* what we deny in theory: that it is stable and static. The inner motions of economic development, the heavy impact of technology, the complicating effects of international politics—all disturb, if not dissolve, the seeming fixity of the welfare state. Perhaps the most immediately threatening force is the cybernetic revolution which cuts through technique, management and economy, with some of the following possible repercussions:

We face the danger of drifting into a society in which there will appear new and fierce class divisions: not so much between owners and workers or even rich and poor, though these will persist, but between various skilled elites living in affluence and a stratum of permanent unemployables, an "underclass" consisting mainly of older workers, the young, and the Negroes.

The power and size of the trade unions seem certain to decline, even if they undertake—which they probably will not—bold steps to meet the new conditions.

The problem of government intervention in economic life will become a sharper political issue than it has been these past several years.

That such problems, inherently difficult enough, should come to the forefront simultaneously with the upsurge of the American Negroes is something of a tragedy. For automation threatens most severely the jobs that have been traditionally open to Negroes; it intensifies difficulties which, under the best of circumstances, would have been severe enough. (The recently fashionable "leftist" counterposition of "revolution" against "integration" as strategies for the Negro movement fails to take into account the context in which the movement must act: it fails to recognize that to achieve integration, even in the presumably limited terms proposed by Martin Luther King, would indeed *be* a revolution, probably greater in consequence and impact than that effected by the rise of industrial unionism in the thirties.) Bayard Rustin, one of the most perceptive Negro leaders, has remarked upon this problem:

> The civil rights movement, because of its limited success, is now confronted with the problem that major Negro demands cannot be met within the context of the civil rights struggle. The frustration in the Negro community is not merely the result of difficulties in the struggle, but also of the fact that these demands are made in a context where *the Negro alone* is in motion. So that the major problem before us is how to relieve the Negro of this isolation. If there were a democratic left in this country, the Negro movement would be in it along with labor, liberals, and intellectuals and people from the churches.
>
> But now the Negroes have to deal not only with discrimination but also the problems of the whole society. While many Negroes would not so analyze it, they know in a visceral way that this is true. They know there is really no way to get jobs for Negroes unless something else happens. And they also know, and I know, that the labor movement, affected by automation, is itself unable to provide jobs for the people already enrolled in the unions; that the only way labor can handle this problem is if it allies with the Negro in a bigger struggle in which it can then afford to be an ally because its problems are being simultaneously met. . . . Such an alliance should be programmatic-political: that is, around questions like total employment, limited planning, work training within planning and a public-works program.

There is no easy solution to the dilemma Rustin describes: that the Negro movement is, at least intermittently, more active and alive than its potential allies, but that the socio-economic situation makes it impossible for the movement to achieve its aims short of stirring those potential allies into a bolder action they may resist or refuse. Consequently, within the Negro movement there will be sharper internal strains and factionalism than during the past few years, with some following Rustin's policy, others exhausting themselves in an increasingly desperate activism, and still others straying into an apocalyptic, seminationalist radicalism. For through the very intensity of its work and the defined limits of its success, the civil rights movement dramatizes its own insufficiency. It is a movement desperately in need of political-intellectual help; yet the very situation giving rise to that need also creates intense resistance to any efforts that might satisfy it. Nor, for that matter, is the Negro movement a movement in the traditional sense. It is a loose alliance of organizations, some of them large and with nominal demands upon their members, others composed of full-time elite activists; and, as a result, there are special difficulties in working out programs and strategies. One can barely speak of a Negro political intelligentsia attached to or associated with the movement, who might provide some intellectual substance; indeed, given the kind of advice offered by certain Negro writers, it is perhaps just as well that they are detached from the movement. And it is a further difficulty that the most active, though not necessarily most representative, sectors of the Negro movement are often hostile to liberals and intellectuals, partly for reasons that can be understood if not accepted, but also for perfectly sound reasons: too many liberals and intellectuals, still sunk in the apolitical moods of the fifties, have shown little inclination toward active participation or help.

That the Negro protest movement will emerge from its present state of uncertainty—a condition at least partly the result of its notable victories these past several years—seems quite certain. The very magnitude of the tasks still facing it will be a powerful stimulus to strategic innovation and tactical ingenuity. But the hope of a few years ago that as a direct consequence of the civil rights struggle there might emerge a larger movement for social radicalism seems unlikely to be fulfilled. Though it has already had a profoundly refreshing and valuable impact upon American society, the Negro movement cannot, by itself, be expected to do what more powerful and numerous segments of the society have neither cared nor been able to.

The alignment of forces within the United States which makes possible a moderate if insufficient progress in domestic affairs simply breaks down when it has to confront foreign policy. For here the issues are ambiguous, complex, and charged with emotion, certainly more so than in regard to, say, an education bill; here the psychic smog of the Cold War still hangs across the national horizon. The loose coalition of labor, liberal, Negro, church, and minority groups which usually supports welfare measures has no consensus within itself regarding foreign policy—or, perhaps more accurately, a large part of this coalition tends unreflectively to go along with the Johnson administration. Except for a tiny fringe emotionally caught up with charismatic figures abroad, the Negro movement has little to say about Vietnam and the Dominican Republic, and its constituency cares even less. In regard to foreign policy the trade unions are quiescent, ritualistically liberal in one or two instances, and sometimes merely reactionary. Sustained dissent on foreign policy comes only from minority segments of the academic world, small groups of pacifists, and some liberals. The result is more impressive for articulateness than mass support.

Yet if one remembers how narrowly based this dissent actually is within the academic and intellectual worlds, one is struck by the moderating effect it has had upon the formation of foreign policy. Certain academics, hand-wringers of alienation, complain that no one listens; I, aware of how few people are complaining, am astonished that anyone does listen. Perhaps this is due to the fact that in a mass society, which may necessarily mean a society in which large portions of the population are politically indifferent and passive, there is always the possibility for aggressive minority groups to exert a disproportionate influence: a fact, if it is one, that should not lead to dancing in the streets, since the results could be quite as disturbing as they are momentarily pleasing. Still another reason may be that the intellectuals occupy a more important place in American politics than they did thirty or forty years ago; they shape opinion in the universities; and the universities, in turn, serve as the training school for the American political elite. From a persistent and thoughtful criticism in the universities there may follow a crisis in morale among sections of this political elite, especially if the country stumbles deeper and deeper into the Vietnam disaster while preparing for itself still greater disasters in Latin America tomorrow.

But let us not delude ourselves. On the issue of foreign policy even these modest hopes for a progressive coalition may be dashed, and on this issue the new academic dissidence may be driven—or may drive itself—into a hopeless isolation. In principle there is no reason why those who oppose the Vietnam war and at least some of those who support it should not be able to co-operate for desirable legislation and action in domestic politics. Between opponents of the war and *some* of its supporters there exists a common interest in not allowing the war to become a pretext for cutting back or refusing to initiate necessary domestic measures. Yet if the war in Vietnam drags on for months and years, with one probable consequence a growing embitterment in political and intellectual life at home, radicals will find it difficult to maintain a balance between coalition on the domestic front and criticism of foreign policy. For in the actuality of experience it is hard to keep clear the distinctions that seem persuasive in the logic of discourse. Whatever hope there is for a new political upsurge in the United States—and by this I mean something more substantial than the outbursts of student rebellion—largely depends on a quick solution to the problem of Vietnam. That is hardly the main reason for wanting to see the war end, but it is a reason.

Otherwise, the consequences could be disastrous, both for the political life of the entire nation, perhaps again infected with a low-charged version of the McCarthyite sickness, and for the still very weak and insecure radicalism that has begun to appear on the campus. There is already a tendency among academic protestors to fall back upon postures of rectitude instead of trying to engage in the far more difficult business of influencing the shape of politics, just as there is a destructive and at times nihilistic fringe in the essentially healthy student protests. But if the war in Vietnam continues, there may in conscience be nothing left for its critics except postures of rectitude and declarations of conscience—partly because of a tightening in the political atmosphere, partly because of righteous misdirection in the protest movement itself. What would then happen? Locked into isolation, academic protest would risk the danger of becoming merely shrill, righteously impotent, and foolishly "anti-American"; some would be tempted—disastrously, I think—to see themselves as shock troops of the campus waging a battle of advertisements against United States imperialism in a way parallel to the war of bullets waged by Castroite guerillas in Latin America. And one consequence of such a development could well be a wave of anti-intellectualism in this country, a new attack upon the academy as the reservoir (*the last reservoir*) of sedition. It is a frightening prospect.

There is nevertheless, a growing sentiment of moralistic radicalism, attached to visions of apocalypse and the theory of mass society, which accepts this prospect as virtually inevitable. Among sections of the student left there also flourish feelings that call into question the viability of politics in the various senses that have been traditional to the Western world. There follows a desperate search for a "substitute proletariat," located by some among the hipsters, by others among the middle-class students, by still others among the underclass of poverty. And the consequence can only be a strategy of raids, dramatic in character but dubious in impact.

Mass Society, Technology and the Specter of Contentment

The sentiments and feelings to which I have just referred are attached to a political outlook of great importance; its most distinguished spokesman is probably Herbert Marcuse. This theory seems so opposed in tone and spirit to everything I have been saying that if I now suggest that both perspectives—the politics of democratic radicalism I have outlined and the vision of "mass society" I shall now describe—need to be kept in some sort of uneasy and uneven balance, I may open myself to the charge of intellectual schizophrenia. I cheerfully (or given the subject, gloomily) accept the risk. For there are sharply opposing tendencies and potentialities in Western society; we cannot yet know which will prevail. To say that for a grasp of American society one must simultaneously employ the traditional Marxist analysis of class conflict, the approach I will label "mass society," and a study of competing power groups within a more or less balanced pluralist system—to say this is not necessarily to lapse into an easy eclecticism. It is rather to acknowledge the mixed character of the present reality, and that the various theories, none complete or satisfactory by itself, point to different elements within that reality.

The school of political-social thought associated with the idea of "mass society" singles out the potential in modern industrialism for a drift toward a bureaucratic, nonterrorist and prosperous authoritarianism. Whatever our wish to qualify this kind of theorizing, and whatever our impatience with the grisly fascination some of its proponents seem to take in envisioning a universal passivity, there can be no question but that it points to significant realities. Such theories rest upon a number of related assumptions:

The alleged automatism of technology. Jacques Ellul writes as an extreme reductionist:

> . . . because of its proliferation, the technical phenomenon has assumed an independent character quite apart from economic considerations, and . . . it develops according to its own intrinsic laws. Technique has become man's new milieu, replacing his former natural milieu. And just as man's natural environment obeys its own physical, chemical and other laws, our artificial, technical environment is now so constituted that it has also its own laws of organization, development and reproduction. . . .

> . . . this view of technique leads me to think that modifications in economic structure, a *détente* in international relations, and improved cooperation among nations will cause practically no change in the technical phenomenon.

And on a somewhat wider plane, Herbert Marcuse writes:

> The world tends to become the stuff of total administration, which absorbs even the administrators themselves.

The decay of the Western party system. Though touched upon in many studies, this theme has, to my knowledge, not yet received a definite statement. It is clear that in most of the Western countries the party system has been steadily drained of content. It survives, in some places, as mere ritual or anachronism, and sometimes as a mechanism for the efficient division of power and spoils among an elite; it no longer reflects, certainly not to the extent that it once did, basic differences of class interest, political allegiance or moral value. Even in those countries where the apparatus of representative democracy survives, it tends to become vestigial, confined to a minority of professionals, and of decreasing interest to the mass of citizens. Yet for democrats this party system, even in decline, remains precious, a concrete embodiment of freedoms for which, thus far, no substitute nearly as satisfactory has been found.

The satisfaction of material wants tends to undercut the possibility for social transcendence. Herbert Marcuse writes:

Technical progress, extended to a whole system of domination and coordination, creates forms of life (and of power) which appear to reconcile the forces opposing the system and to defeat or refute all protest in the name of the historical prospects of freedom from toil and domination.

There develops, partly in consequence of the above-listed elements, a new kind of society, what we call "mass society." It is a relatively comfortable, half-welfare and half-garrison society in which the population grows passive, indifferent, and atomized; in which "primary groups" tend to disintegrate; in which traditional loyalties, ties, and associations become lax or dissolve entirely; in which coherent publics based on definite interests and opinions gradually fall apart; and in which man becomes a consumer, himself mass-produced like the products, diversions, and values he absorbs.

When one is involved in concrete political analysis that involves firm and immediate choices, it seems to me both intellectually facile and morally disastrous to affirm an identity between the societies of East and West. Though there is a tendency for the two to move closer together in certain ways, the differences remain enormous and crucial. But if one turns from the immediate political struggle to a kind of speculation about the indefinite future, there may be some reason for anticipating a society ruled by benevolent and modernized Grand Inquisitors, an efficient political-technical elite that will avoid terror and the grosser aspects of totalitarianism, that will perhaps even go through the motions of democracy but in its essential character be thoroughly authoritarian. It would be a society in regard to which Huxley's prophecy would seem more accurate than Orwell's.

If there will not be a war within the next period and a way is found for controlling the birth rate, it becomes possible to envisage a world, at least the part of it that has been industrialized, in which material wants will be moderately satisfied. This possibility arises, not, as radicals once thought, because there is an immediate likelihood that the race will create for itself a free and humane order, but largely because of the sheer cascading growth of technology.

To advance such a speculation at a time when the majority of human beings on our planet still suffers from terrible poverty, may seem irrelevant and heartless. It is a speculation which rests on grossly simplified ideas, partly on a technological determinism that cannot be accepted by a sophisticated mind. But I offer it *not* as a prediction, only as a possibility. That this possibility will not be realized in the next several decades, seems certain. But it remains worth considering in its own right.

Suppose, then, that the goal of moderate material satisfaction is reached after the next several decades in large areas of the world and in societies that are not socialist and often not democratic. What would the intellectuals say? We may assume that large numbers of ordinary people, fed regularly and diverted by the mass media, would be satisfied. But the intellectuals? Would they still remember or care about the vision of human freedom?

In our time the Grand Inquisitor is no longer a withered Churchman: stern, ascetic, undeluded. He is now a skilled executive who knows how to manage large-scale enterprises and sustain the morale of his employees. In the West he is a corporation official, in the East he belongs to the Central Committee. He is friendly. And he feeds the hungry.

What, then, can one say about this mode of speculation? Its main value is that it counters to the ameliorative optimism (the twentieth-century version of the supposedly discredited nineteenth-century theory of "progress") held by conventional liberals. By this I mean not merely something as obvious yet basic as the fact that our welfarism is deeply tied in with a steadily burgeoning militarism and would face a severe crisis if the prop of "defense spending" were removed. I mean also the fact that a serious radical politics must seek not merely for the extension of welfarism but for controls to check the accompanying bureaucratic expansion; must concern itself not merely with what happens to or is done for people, but with their capacities toward self-assertion and autonomy.

That there have been in recent years outbursts of political activity on the campus and in the civil rights movement, does not in itself invalidate the "mass society" prognosis. The Negro demands are, after all, largely concerned with the kinds of issues that could and should have been settled before "mass society" was imagined. The student rebelliousness may prove to be no more than the futile effort of a small minority to diverge from a dominant pattern. We do not yet know.

The central difficulty with the "mass society" style of thought is that, pushed hard enough, it posits a virtual end or blockage of history. Now much modernist literature, as Georg Lukacs has shrewdly noted, does exactly the same thing: it abandons the idea of historicity, falls back upon notions of a universal *condition humaine* or a rhythm of eternal recurrence, even as it is committed within its own realm to change, turmoil, ceaseless re-creation. Powerful as this vision is in the modernist novel, it will not suffice for political analysis. In studying the novel we must explain the vision of a historical blockage in essential historical terms, and thus posit, at some point, an end to modernism. In social life itself, however, all experience points to the certainty of change. We should profit here from the fate of Hannah Arendt's brilliant theory of totalitarianism: it lacked a sense of the dynamic that might lead to disintegration from within or transformation from without. And what the experience of the postwar years strongly impresses upon one is that even institutions seemingly invulnerable crack under the pressure of internal conflict (*including conflicts we can-*

not foresee) and thereby call into question the nightmare-vision of stasis.

One of the things that today distinguishes a radical from a liberal is not merely that the radical holds to a vision of social transformation going beyond the limits of the welfare state while the liberal acts within those limits; it is also that the radical sees the possibility that from, or with, the evolution of the welfare state there may arise the kind of appalling "double" signified by the idea of the "mass society," while the liberal is not as a rule disturbed by speculations of this kind. The radical is both more optimistic and more pessimistic. Yet he has no choice but to act as if the mass society can indeed be averted; otherwise, he may doom himself to a self-confirming prophecy. And meanwhile there is surely enough evidence of continued social conflict and change to warrant the assumption that history will continue, that we have by no means reached the end of major social transformations, and that the impulse to a secular transcendence remains a living force.

The Problem of Socialism, Again

About this complex and entangled subject I want to say only one thing: the one thing that indicates the central difficulty of a radical criticism that would go beyond "the given."

Does a great historical movement ever get a second chance? Suppose Saul of Tarsus and the rest of the original "cadre" had been destroyed, or had committed some incredible blunder: could Christianity have regained its momentum after an interval of isolation and despair? For socialism, it is clear, the great historical opportunity came in the first quarter of this century, and for a variety of reasons—the Social Democrats and Leninists were keen enough in their criticism of each other—the chance was not taken.

Historical energy and idealism cannot be whipped up at demand; once a generation becomes exhausted or an idea contaminated, it takes a long time before new efforts can be made, if they can be made at all. Meanwhile history does not stand still. Socialism having failed to transform Western society in the first quarter of the century, part of what it had supposed to be its "historical mission" was now appropriated by the existing society. Where that did not happen, as in the backward countries, there arose a corrupt mockery of socialism, a total state (I quote Proudhon's uncanny anticipation)

> having the appearance of being founded on the dictatorship of the masses, but in which the masses have no more power than is necessary to ensure a general serfdom in accordance with the precepts and principles borrowed from the old absolutism; indivisibility of public power, all-consuming centralization, systematic destruction of all individual, corporative and regional thought, and inquisitorial police.

Whether socialism as a movement—I leave aside the European Social Democracy, which has mostly a formal relation to the idea of socialism—can be revived, or whether it will have served historically as a bridge toward some new radical humanism, I do not know.

Socialists remain: a few. They are people devoted to a problem, or a memory that gives rise to a problem. The socialist idea signifies, first, a commitment to the values of fraternity, libertarianism, egalitarianism, and freedom. It means, secondly, commitment to an envisioned society in which a decisive proportion of the means of production shall be commonly and democratically controlled. What, however, is the relation between these two commitments?

One great failing of the socialist movement in the past was that it did not recognize, or recognize sufficiently, the inherent tension between the values it claimed to embody and the social scheme it proposed to enact. Traditionally, it was assumed that a particular change in property forms and relations would be adequate to, or at least largely prepare for, the desired change in the quality of life. (At its most Bourbonlike level, this meant the notion that mere state ownership or nationalization of the means of production would be a sufficient criterion for bestowing the label "workers' state.") Now we know from sad experience that the transformation of economy from private to public forms of ownership is not necessarily "progressive," and that such transformations seem, in any case, to be part of a general world-wide drift.

The dominant stress of the Marxist movements has been upon political means (strategy, tactics, propaganda) concerning which it often had sophisticated theories; but in regard to the society it envisaged, the content of its hope, it had surprisingly little to say, sometimes no more than the threadbare claim that once "we" take power, "we" will work things out. Martin Buber is right in saying:

> To the questions of the elements of social re-structure, Marx and Engels never gave a positive answer, because they had no inner relation to this idea. . . . The political act remained the one thing worth striving for. . . .

By now the more reflective socialists feel differently, but as often happens in human affairs, a growth in awareness does not necessarily facilitate confidence in action. If today we are asked what we mean or envision by socialism, our first instinctive response—even if it never reaches our lips—is likely to be in negative terms: "We don't mean such and such. . . . we don't mean simply nationalization of industry. . . ." Our first response, that is, rests upon a deviation from a previously held norm, and thereby constitutes a kind of self-criticism. (That listeners may not even know the tradition from which we are deviating, is one of the perils of the passage of time and American ahistoricism.)

We now try to describe our vision of the good society in terms of qualities, sentiments of freedom and fraternity, norms of conduct and value, priorities of social allocation;

whereas, by and large, the tradition of socialism has been to speak in terms of changing institutions and power relationships. Yet in undertaking this shift of emphasis we cannot but admit the cogency of a certain kind of criticism: "A society, even one envisaged in the future, cannot be described simply by specifying desired qualities. You may hope to infuse a future society with those qualities; you may expect that a new social structure will promote or encourage those qualities. But a society must also, perhaps even primarily, be described or foreseen in structural terms."

For most of the European Social Democratic parties, this problem barely exists, since they have decided, usually in practice and sometimes in program, to abandon the idea of socialization of the economy. In doing so, they become little more than liberal welfarist parties. Arguing against Anthony Crossland's theoretical defense of such a course, George Lichtheim properly remarks:

> . . . the Conservative party could in principle accept all his reform demands and still retain control of the country. What would really undermine its hold—a major shift in the ownership of property—is precisely the thing he regards as unnecessary. The residual demand for it is, he thinks, a vestige of Marxism. In that case the Tories must be regarded as full-blooded Marxists, for the one thing they seem determined to prevent is a drastic change in the social balance which would transfer the power of decision-making from private firms to public authorities.

If, then, we do retain the perspective of a long-range socialization of economy, the problem becomes how to reconcile the traditional socialist emphasis upon property forms—an emphasis necessary but not sufficient—with a more sophisticated understanding of the relationship between social structure and humane values. In any case, we neither can nor should wish to recapture the innocence of traditional socialism. We may try to develop schemes for autonomous and pluralistic social institutions within a collectivist economy. We may wish to place a decisive stress upon the idea of democratic participation. We may argue that the trend toward economic collectivism is historically unavoidable and the only choice facing men is whether it should be allowed to drift into bureaucratic authoritarianism or brought under the sponsorship of a democratic polity. But in the end we know that "history" guarantees us nothing: everything is now a question of human will.

Perhaps another way of saying all this is to insist that the vision of utopia remains a genuine option, a profound need. (Could one imagine the survival of the intellectuals as a distinct group if that vision were extinguished?) It is the sense of a possible good society that provides a guiding norm for our day-to-day political life. Without such an assumption, radical criticism runs the danger of declining into mere complaint or veering into elitist manipulation. Perhaps, then, the accumulation of defeats suffered by socialism can yet provide a premise for new beginnings.

Finally, the Intellectuals

It is tempting to end with a call for greater political involvement. But what, in the present circumstances, would that mean? The American intellectual world, except in regard to an occasional issue or figure arousing strong emotions, is not greatly interested in politics. Things have, to be sure, improved a little since the fifties: one encounters less frequently the smugness of literary people who regard politics as a sign of vulgarity. But the idea of a sustained political involvement seems abstract or unlikely to most American intellectuals. Some of the reasons for this are not at all admirable: narcissism, lucrative busywork, exhibitionism, competitiveness, all related to an affluent but insecure culture. Other reasons deserve to be taken seriously: a genuine doubt as to what intellectuals can achieve, uncertainty as to how to act. That there is no party or movement to which radical intellectuals can attach themselves does not bother me as much as certain intellectuals claim it bothers them. I am more concerned with the development of a serious political consciousness within the arena in which intellectuals live and work. Concerning which, three concluding remarks:

The American university has recently become more alive, more concerned politically, than it had been for several decades. This, on the whole, is a cheering development, but some aspects are also disturbing. There are available on the American campus—which, as it grows at an astonishing rate, becomes one of the major centers of national life—far more spokesmen for a democratic radicalism than are now making themselves heard. To the extent that they fail to speak out and establish relations with the aroused students, to that extent will the rising campus rebelliousness be diverted and entangled. Silence, abstention, indifference may not have mattered very much in university life these past few decades; now they matter enormously. To carry the moods of the fifties into the sixties will have bitter consequences.

A major shift or shake-up of "power relations" seems in prospect for the intellectual world. For the first time in several decades, the generation of intellectuals associated with the thirties—a generation bound together by common problems, experiences, and quarrels—seems in danger of losing its dominant position in American intellectual life. That it has kept that position for so long and through such a bewildering series of political-intellectual changes, is itself extraordinary. But now there is beginning to appear in the graduate schools, and near the student and civil rights movements, a younger generation of intellectuals and semi-intellectuals, perhaps not as well-equipped dialectically as the older leftists, semileftists and ex-leftists, and certainly not as wide-ranging in interest or accomplished in style, yet endowed with a self-assurance, a lust for power, a contempt for and readiness to swallow up their elders which is at once amusing, admirable, and disturbing. Thinking of themselves as "new radicals," these young people see as one of their major tasks the dislodgment of the old ones; and they are not inclined to make precise distinctions as to differences of opinions among the old ones. A *Kulturkampf* seems in prospect, and one in which, I must confess, my own sympathies would be mixed.

For radical intellectuals one theme should stand out above all others: the articulation of democratic values. In the American academy today, as in our intellectual life, there is a considerable fallout of authoritarianism, that major blight of the twentieth century. (A significant study could be undertaken of the way American political scientists and sociologists, in their recent passion for hard-headed "realism," have provided rationales for authoritarian societies and outlooks.) It is a blight spread across the entire political spectrum: conservative, liberal, radical. It fits the age only too well. It rides the wave of the future—perhaps. To speak out in behalf of the ideal of democracy; to resist all rationalizations for authoritarian rulers and movements; to proclaim our pleasure in the appearance of the "revisionist" intellectuals in Eastern Europe who also insist that without freedom there can be no good society, no life worth living: that would be a task which could again make the calling of intellectual a reason for pride.

✡ BERKELEY AND "LEFTISM"

IN the middle sixties the young spoke, and when they did, it was with a vigor, even a violence, that sent an electrical charge through American society. After a decade of torpor, in which petty cautions and middling careerism dominated our academic life, the campus was once again what in part—though only in part—it should always be: a place of controversy and protest. Berkeley; the summer treks to Mississippi; demonstrations against the war in Vietnam; the beginnings of an amorphous "new left"—these were among the signs of new life. By and large, good signs.

Marked by stylistic bravado, intellectual aggressiveness and social conscience, the spirit of revolt spreading across the campus was entirely welcome; yet, it being an unusual wind that brings no bad news, some of the ideological notions embraced by a section of the young people in the "new left" were not at all attractive to people like myself, who believed both in basic social change and unambiguous democratic values. Once again we had to turn to the vocabulary of ambivalence and complexity, insisting upon the lessons of the last few decades to which the rebellious young were largely indifferent—for they were characterized by a moral absolutism that made it hard to persuade them of the values of shading in political thought.

Here are two essays written in 1965: "Berkeley and Beyond," first composed as a preface for a collection of pieces about the events in Berkeley, and "New Styles in 'Leftism,' " written as a description of and argument against ideological tendencies within the "new left." The article on Berkeley, essentially sympathetic to the students, received little attention. Naturally enough; it was not polemical. But among people who care about such matters, the essay on "leftism" created something of a storm; it has, in any case, been decisively refuted several times.

A question asked by friend and foe alike has been this: Don't you find some contradiction in outlook, or at least temper, between these two essays, one of them sympathetic to the student rebels and the other critical of the ideas some of them hold? My answer is, I think not. The Berkeley events were an authentic expression of student sentiment, triggered by a free-speech dispute but drawing upon energies and complaints that go far beyond that problem. By contrast, the section of the "new left" against which I argued was an ideological grouping, even if sometimes in the costume of anti-ideology, and it was open to the same kind of critical scrutiny to which any such grouping must be. That some of the "new leftists" I criticized were also involved, in a positive way, in the Berkeley events is certainly true; what we do in one of our roles, we may undo in another.

But if there is a conflict in spirit between the two essays, that should not be excessively disturbing. Life is complex, so is politics: more complex than the rebellious students are prepared, as a rule, to admit. I felt no obligation either to embrace or reject them wholly; I wished to discriminate among their activities and opinions, and simply to say about and to them what seemed to me the truth—or, as they might put it, to "level with" them.

Two kinds of issues are at stake here: first, a series of political-moral disputes, and second, an incipient disagreement as to the nature of politics in the present time. The problem of "anti-Communism" is a good example of the first. While the "new leftist" students are often justified in their revulsion against the deceits and crimes committed in the name of the Cold War, some of them lapse, by way of an extreme reaction, into a tacit denial that Communism, whether in the Moscow or Peking version, remains on a world scale a menace to human freedom. Or they write as if Communism were simply a bogey invented by McCarthyite reaction, rather than a political fact in its own right, toward which serious people must have views that go deeper than a distaste for "Red-baiting." The "new leftists"—not all of them, but a good many—tend to be careless in identifying any kind of anti-Communism with McCarthyism, so that the reasons a Norman Thomas has for opposing a one-party dictatorship get mashed up with the reasons a Barry Goldwater has for opposing the welfare state.

Apart from issues of this kind, immediately relevant as they are, something else was involved in my polemic—something not yet brought into sufficient focus but of great importance. At stake in these discussions has been the question of whether politics in the traditional senses remains a viable human activity in the Western world. Many of the "new left" people would agree with me that the Marxist-Leninist model for revolutionary activity is neither morally acceptable nor strategically plausible. What kind of politics remains possible, then, in a modern industrialized society? Obviously, the politics of power groups which tend to accept the *status quo* as a given. But can there still be a significant politics involving masses of people which follows the more or less traditional path of liberalism and/or democratic socialism? Or, as certain "new leftists" imply, have the major social classes and institutions become so thoroughly absorbed into the existing society, either through comfort or corruption, that they can no longer be expected to work toward any basic social change? Do we live in a mass society become so complacent and static that the only politics available to us is a politics of minor readjustment?

Now there is no way of proving that such assumptions are untrue, and there is even some evidence to support them. If one does accept such a view of things, the only recourse for those people who still see a need for large-scale changes in the relationships of social power, or still feel a desire to release sentiments of rebellion, is to set themselves up on the margin of society and from there to conduct an occasional raid as intellectual guerrillas or shock troops of apolitical revolt.

This kind of apolitical politics, it was a premise of my essay, is often misdirected, no matter how well we may understand its emotional sources and sympathize with some of its public manifestations; indeed, it was my further premise that ultraradical gestures had a way of playing into the hands of the dominant powers, who would soon come to look with tolerance and amusement upon the antics of an opposition that threatened neither power nor privilege and, in fact, helped to liven up the scene. This problem, of course, is by no means resolved, and during the coming years one may expect that it will be debated with a growing intensity.

When "New Styles in 'Leftism'" first appeared, I was the happy recipient of a considerable amount of advice about the inappropriateness of my tone. It is always hard to cope with such criticism, since often enough it is right. It is hard to cope with such criticism for another reason: it is often irrelevant. For what is the use in telling people who feel strongly about an intellectual matter that they should keep their voices low and sweet? In the political tradition from which I derive, it has been common to write with polemical sharpness—hopefully an impersonal sharpness—and then to expect one's opponent to reply in kind. You argue, you let some heat come through, you don't pretend that gentility is the ultimate virtue; and then, a little later, it may even be possible to come to agreement, or work together, or accept the fact of difference. This may not be the best of traditions, but after watching the style of low-keyed and tightly aggressive coolness that is cultivated these days, I feel less unhappy about my own.

A few critics felt it was hopeless at the present time to argue with the more fanatic wing of the "new left," and that before engagement was possible, time would have to teach and experience soften. Perhaps; but someone of my convictions could not allow himself the luxury of this "philosophical" attitude. Other critics felt I was too harsh with the young, alienating them, etc. Perhaps; but there are obligations to one's beliefs that take precedence over expediency. What gave me a modest amount of satisfaction was that the "new left" students with whom I debated in this essay, though often answering strongly and with fervor, did not seem particularly wounded. Perhaps they recognized that I was taking them seriously.

And that is all that need be said on the matter of tone. I wrote out of a conviction that the best of the student radicals would respond to serious criticism; that they knew an exchange of ideas, however sharp, was more useful than any amount of flattery; and that in time they would find themselves, like all the rest of us, in repeated crises from which the only possible way out would be the grim exercise of intellectual reconsideration and self-scrutiny. The single unforgivable sin in talking to the young, whether rebellious or not, is to forgo candor simply because they are young. For they will not always remain young, and later they will hate those who condescended and flattered.

✡ NEW STYLES IN "LEFTISM"

I propose to describe a political style or outlook before it has become hardened into an ideology or the property of an organization. This outlook is visible along limited portions of the political scene; for the sake of exposition I will make it seem more precise and structured than it really is.

There is a new radical mood in limited sectors of American society: on the campus, in sections of the civil rights movement. The number of people who express this mood is not very large, but that it should appear at all is cause for encouragement and satisfaction. Yet there is a segment or fringe among the newly blossoming young radicals that causes one disturbance—and not simply because they have ideas different from persons like myself, who neither expect nor desire that younger generations of radicals should repeat our thoughts or our words. For this disturbing minority I have no simple name: sometimes it looks like kamikaze radicalism, sometimes like white Malcolmism, sometimes like black Maoism. But since none of these phrases will quite do, I have had to fall back upon the loose and not very accurate term, "new leftists." Let me therefore stress as strongly as I can that I am not talking about all or the majority of the American young and not-so-young who have recently come to regard themselves as radicals.

The form I have felt obliged to use here—a composite portrait of the sort of "new leftist" who seems to me open to criticism—also creates some difficulties. It may seem to lump together problems, ideas, and moods that should be kept distinct. But my conviction is that this kind of "new leftism" is not a matter of organized political tendencies, at least not yet, and that there is no organization, certainly none of any importance, which expresses the kind of "new leftism" I am here discussing. So I would say that if some young radicals read this text and feel that much of it does not pertain to them, I will be delighted by such a response.

1. Some Background Conditions

A.

The society we live in fails to elicit the idealism of the more rebellious and generous young. Even among those who play the game and accept the social masks necessary for gaining success, there is a widespread disenchantment. Certainly there is very little ardor, very little of the joy that comes from a conviction that the values of a society are good, and that it is therefore good to live by them. The intelligent young know that if they keep out of trouble, accept academic drudgery, and preserve a respectable "image," they can hope for successful careers, even if not personal gratification. But the price they must pay for this choice is a considerable quantity of inner adaptation to the prevalent norms: there is a limit to the social duplicity that anyone can sustain.

The society not only undercuts the possibilities of constructive participation, it also makes very difficult a coherent and thought-out political opposition. The small minority that does rebel tends to adopt a stance that seems to be political, sometimes even ideological, but often turns out to be little more than an effort to assert a personal style.

Personal style: that seems to me a key. Most of whatever rebellion we have had up to—and even into—the civil rights movement takes the form of a decision on how to live individually within this society, rather than how to change it collectively. A recurrent stress among the young has been upon differentiation of speech, dress, and appearance, by means of which a small elite can signify its special status; or the stress has been upon moral self-regeneration, a kind of Emersonianism with shock treatment. All through the fifties and sixties disaffiliation was a central impulse, in the beatnik style or the more sedate Salinger way, but disaffiliation nevertheless, both as a signal of nausea and a tacit recognition of impotence.

I say, recognition of impotence, because movements that are powerful, groups that are self-confident, do not opt out of society: they live and work within society in order to transform it.

Now, to a notable extent, all this has changed since and through the civil rights movement—*but not changed as much as may seem.* Some of the people involved in that movement show an inclination to make of their radicalism not a politics of common action, which would require the inclusion of saints, sinners, and ordinary folk, but rather a gesture of moral rectitude. And the paradox is that they often sincerely regard themselves as committed to politics—but a politics that asserts so unmodulated and total a dismissal of society, while also departing from Marxist expectations of social revolution, that little is left to them but the glory or burden of maintaining a distinct personal style.

By contrast, the radicalism of an earlier generation, despite numerous faults, had at least this advantage: it did not have to start *as if* from scratch, there were available movements, parties, agencies, and patterns of thought through which one could act. The radicals of the thirties certainly had their share of Bohemianism, but their politics were not nearly so interwoven with and dependent upon tokens of style as is today's radicalism.

The great value of the present rebelliousness is that it requires a personal decision, not merely as to what one shall do but also as to what one shall be. It requires authenticity, a challenge to the self, or, as some young people like to say, an "existential" decision. And it makes more difficult the moral double-bookkeeping of the thirties, whereby in the name of a sanctified movement or unquestioned ideology, scoundrels and fools could be exalted as "leaders" and detestable conduct exonerated.

This is a real and very impressive strength, but with it there goes a significant weakness: the lack of clear-cut ideas, sometimes even a feeling that it is wrong—or worse, "middle-class"—to think systematically, and as a corollary, the absence of a social channel or agency through which to act. At first it seemed as if the civil rights movement would provide such a channel; and no person of moral awareness can fail to be profoundly moved by the outpouring of idealism and the readiness to face danger which characterizes the vanguard of this movement. Yet at a certain point it turns out that the civil rights movement, through the intensity of its work, seems to dramatize . . . its own insufficiency. Indeed, it acts as a training school for experienced, gifted, courageous people who have learned how to lead, how to sacrifice, how to work, but have no place in which to enlarge upon their gifts. There may in time appear a new kind of "dropout"—the "dropout" trained by and profoundly attached to the civil rights movement who yet feels that it does not, and by its very nature cannot, come to grips with the central problems of modern society; the "dropout" who has been trained to a fine edge of frustration and despair.

The more shapeless, the more promiscuously absorptive, the more psychologically and morally slack the society becomes, the more must candidates for rebellion seek extreme postures which will enable them to "act out" their distance from a society that seems intent upon a maliciously benevolent assimilation; extreme postures which will yield security, perhaps a sense of consecration, in loneliness; extreme postures which will safeguard them from the allure of everything they reject. Between the act of rebellion and the society against which it is directed, there remain, however, deeper ties than is commonly recognized. To which we shall return.

B.

These problems are exacerbated by an educational system that often seems inherently schizoid. It appeals to the life of the mind, yet justifies that appeal through crass utilitarianism. It invokes the traditions of freedom, yet processes students to bureaucratic cut. It speaks for the spirit, yet increasingly becomes an appendage of a spirit-squashing system.

C.

The "new leftism" appears at a moment when the intellectual and academic worlds—and not they alone—are experiencing an intense and largely justifiable revulsion against the immediate American past. Many people are sick unto death of the whole structure of feeling—that mixture of chauvinism, hysteria, and demagogy—which was created during the Cold War years. Like children subjected to forced feeding, they regurgitate almost automatically. Their response is an inevitable consequence of over-organizing the propaganda resources of a modern state; the same sort of nausea exists among the young in the Communist world.

Unfortunately, revulsion seldom encourages nuances of

thought or precise discriminations of politics. You cannot stand the deceits of official anti-Communism? Then respond with a rejection equally blatant. You have been raised to give credit to every American power move, no matter how reactionary or cynical? Then respond by castigating everything American. You are weary of Sidney Hook's messages in *The New York Times Magazine?* Then respond as if talk about Communist totalitarianism were simply irrelevant or a bogey to frighten infants.

Yet we should be clear in our minds that such a response is not at all the same as a commitment to Communism, even though it may lend itself to obvious exploitation. It is rather a spewing out of distasteful matter—in the course of which other values, such as the possibility of learning from the traumas and tragedies of recent history, may also be spewed out.

D.

Generational clashes are recurrent in our society, perhaps in any society. But the present rupture between the young and their elders seems especially deep. This is a social phenomenon that goes beyond our immediate subject, indeed, it cuts through the whole of society; what it signifies is the society's failure to transmit with sufficient force its values to the young, or perhaps more accurately, that the best of the young take the proclaimed values of their elders with a seriousness which leads them to be appalled by their violation in practice.

In rejecting the older generations, however, the young sometimes betray the conditioning mark of the very American culture they are so quick to denounce: for ours is a culture that celebrates youthfulness as if it were a moral good in its own right. Like the regular Americans they wish so hard not to be, yet, through wishing, so very much are, they believe that the past is mere dust and ashes and that they can start afresh, immaculately.

There are, in addition, a few facts to be noted concerning

the relationship between the radical young and those few older people who have remained radicals:

A generation is missing in the life of American radicalism, the generation that would now be in its mid-thirties, the generation that did not show up. The result is an inordinate difficulty in communication between the young radicals and those unfortunate enough to have reached—or, God help us, even gone beyond—the age of forty. Here, of course, our failure is very much in evidence too: a failure that should prompt us to speak with modesty, simply as people who have tried, and in their trying perhaps have learned something.

To the younger radicals it seems clear that a good many of the radicals of the thirties have grown tired, or dropped out, or in some instances, sold out. They encounter teachers who, on ceremonial occasions, like to proclaim old socialist affiliations, but who really have little or no sympathy with any kind of rebelliousness today. They are quick—and quite right—to sense that announcements of old Young People's Socialist League ties can serve as a self-protective nostalgia or even as a cloak for acquiescence in the *status quo*. But it must also be said that there is a tendency among the "new leftists" toward much too quick a dismissal of those who may disagree with them—they are a little too fast on the draw with such terms as "fink" and "establishment."

All this may describe the conditions under which the new political outlook appears, but it does not yet tell us anything about the specific culture, so to say, in which it thrives. Let me therefore indicate some of the political and intellectual influences acting upon the "new leftism," by setting up two very rough categories:

2. *Ideologues and Desperadoes*

A. IDEOLOGUES, WHITE

The disintegration of American radicalism these last few decades left a good many ideologues emotionally unemployed: people accustomed to grand theorizing who have had their theories shot out from under them; people still looking for some belated evidence that they were "right" all along; people with unexpended social energy and idealism of a sort, who desperately needed new arenas in which to function.

1) *The Remains of Stalinism.* The American Communist Party was broken first by McCarthyite and government persecution, and second by an inner crisis following Khrushchev's revelations and the Hungarian revolution. Those who left out of disillusionment were heartsick people, their convictions and sometimes their lives shattered. But those who left the party or its supporting organizations because they feared government attack were often people who kept, semi-privately, their earlier convictions. Many of them had a good deal of political experience; some remained significantly placed in the network of what might be called conscience-organizations. Naturally enough, they continued to keep in touch with one another, forming a kind of reserve apparatus based on common opinions, feelings, memories. As soon as some ferment began in the civil rights movement and the peace groups, these people were present, ready and eager; they needed no directives from the Communist Party to which, in any case, they no longer (or may never have) belonged; they were quite capable of working on their own *as if they were working together,* through a variety of groups and periodicals like the *National Guardian.* Organizational Stalinism declined, but a good part of its heritage remained: people who could offer political advice, raise money, write leaflets, sit patiently at meetings, put up in a pleasant New York apartment visitors from a distant state, who, by chance, had been recommended by an old friend.

2) *True Believers.* On the far left there remains a scatter of groups still convinced that Marxism-Leninism, in one or another version, is "correct." What has failed them, however, is the historical motor provided by Marxist theory: the proletariat, which has not shown the "revolutionary poten-

tial" or fulfilled the "historical mission" to which it was assigned. Though the veteran Marxists cannot, for fear of shattering their whole structure of belief, give up the *idea* of the proletariat, they can hardly act, day by day, as if the American working class were indeed satisfying Marxist expectations or were the actual center of revolutionary ferment. Thus, in somewhat schizoid fashion, they have clung to their traditional faith in the proletariat as the revolutionary class, while in practice searching for a new embodiment of it which might provide the social energy they desire. And in the Negro movement they sometimes think to have found it.

That this movement, with great creative flair, has worked out an indigenous strategy of its own; that it has developed nonviolent resistance into an enormously powerful weapon; that the Negro clergy, in apparent disregard of Leninist formulas, plays a leading and often militant role—all this does not sit well with the old Marxists. They must therefore develop new theories, by means of which the Negroes become the vanguard of the working class or perhaps the "true" (not yet "bought-off") working class. And, clustering around the Negro movement, they contribute a mite of wisdom here and there: scoffing at nonviolence, employing the shibboleth of "militancy" as if it were a magical device for satisfying the needs of the Negro poor, etc. They are experienced in "deepening the struggle," usually other people's struggles: which means to scorn the leadership of Dr. King without considering that the "revolutionary" course they propose for the Negro movement could, if adopted, lead it into a *cul de sac* of isolation, exhaustion, and heroic blood. Understandably, they find allies in Negro nationalists who want not so much to deepen as to divert the struggle, and among young militants who dislike the idea that Negroes might, if successful in their struggle, come to share some of the American affluence and thus become "middle-class."

3) *Authoritarian Leftists.* In figures like Isaac Deutscher

and Paul Sweezy we find the true intellectual progenitors of at least part of the "new leftism"; the influence they exert has been indirect, since they are not involved in immediate struggles, but it has nevertheless been there.

Sweezy's *Monthly Review* is the main spokesman in this country for the view that authoritarianism is inherent or necessary in the so-called socialist countries; that what makes them "socialist" is simply the nationalization of the means of production; that democracy, while perhaps desirable in some long-range calculation, is not crucial for judging the socialist character of a society; that the claim that workers must be in a position to exercise political power if the state can in any sense be called "theirs," is a utopian fallacy. At times this technological determinism, put to the service of brutal dictatorship, has been given a more subtle reading by Sweezy: namely, that when the conditions supposedly causing the Communist dictatorship—economic backwardness and international insecurity—have been overcome, the Soviet regime would in some unspecified way democratize itself. In November 1957, after the Khrushchev revelations, *Monthly Review* printed a notably frank editorial:

> The conditions which produced the [Soviet] dictatorship have been overcome. . . . Our theory is being put to the crucial test of practise. And so far—let us face it frankly—there is precious little evidence to confirm it. In all that has happened since Stalin's death we can find nothing to indicate that the Communist Party or any of its competing factions, has changed in the slightest degree its view of the proper relation between the people and their leadership . . . there is apparently no thought that the Soviet people will ever grow up enough to decide for itself who knows best and hence who should make and administer the policies which determine its fate.

And finally from Sweezy: "forty years is too long for a dictatorship to remain temporary"—surely the understatement of the Christian Era!

One might suppose that if "our theory is being put to the

crucial test" and "there is precious little evidence to confirm it," honest men would proceed to look for another theory, provided, that is, they continued to believe that freedom is desirable.

A good number of years have passed since the above passage appeared in *Monthly Review*, the "precious little evidence" remains precious little, and Sweezy, once apparently dismayed over the lack of democracy in Russia, has moved not to Titoism or "revisionism." No, he has moved toward Maoist China, where presumably one does not have to worry about "the proper relation between the people and their leadership. . . ." Writing in December 1964 the *Monthly Review* editors declared with satisfaction that "there could be no question of the moral ascendency of Peking over Moscow in the underdeveloped world." They agreed with the Chinese that Khrushchev's fall was "a good thing" and they wrote further:

> The Chinese possession of a nuclear potential does not increase the danger of nuclear war. Quite the contrary. The Chinese have solemnly pledged never to be the first to use nuclear weapons . . . and their revolutionary record of devotion to the cause of socialism and progress entitles them to full trust and confidence.

The logic is clear: begin with theoretical inquiry and concern over the perpetuation of dictatorship in Russia and end with "full trust and confidence" in China, where the dictatorship is more severe.

There is an aphorism by a recent Polish writer: "The dispensing of injustice is always in the right hands." And so is its defense.

B. IDEOLOGUES, NEGRO

1) Black Nationalism. Here is a creed that speaks or appears to speak totally against compromise, against negotiating with "the white power structure," against the falsities of white liberals, indeed, against anything but an indulgence of verbal violence. Shortly before his tragic death Malcolm X spoke at a Trotskyist-sponsored meeting and listening to him I felt, as did others, that he was in a state of internal struggle, reaching out for an ideology he did not yet have. For the Negroes in his audience he offered the relief of articulating subterranean feelings of hatred, contempt, defiance, feelings that did not have to be held in check because there was a tacit compact that the talk about violence would remain talk. For both the Negroes and whites in the audience there was an apparent feeling that Malcolm and Malcolm alone among the Negro spokesmen was authentic because . . . well, because finally he spoke for nothing but his rage, for no proposal, no plan, no program, just a sheer outpouring of anger and pain. And that they could understand. The formidable sterility of his speech, so impressive in its relation to a deep personal suffering, touched something in their hearts. For Malcolm, intransigent in words and nihilistic in reality, never invoked the possibility or temptations of immediate struggle; he never posed the problems, confusions, and risks of maneuver, compromise, retreat. Brilliantly Malcolm spoke for a rejection so complete it transformed him into an apolitical spectator, or in the language of his admirers, a "cop-out."

2) Caricature. If, nevertheless, there was something about Malcolm which commands our respect, that is because we know his life-struggle, his rise from the depths, his conquest of thought and speech. Leroi Jones, by contrast, stands as a burlesque double of whatever is significant in Malcolm.

In his success as both a New School lecturer and prophet of "guerrilla warfare" in the United States; in his badgering of white liberal audiences; in his orgies of verbal violence committed, to be sure, not in Selma, Alabama, but Sheridan Square, New York; in his fantasies of an international race war in which the whites will be slaughtered, Jones speaks for a contemporary sensibility. But he speaks for it in a special way: as a distinctively American success, the pop-art guerrilla warrior.

He speaks at that center of revolutionary upsurge, the Village Vanguard. He explains that the murder of Negroes in the South does not arouse the kind of horror and indignation that the murder of white civil rights workers does. *He is absolutely right*, the point cannot be made too often. But Jones cannot stop there: it would be too sensible, too humane, and it would not yield pages in *The Village Voice*. Instead, responding to a question, "What about Goodman and Schwerner, the two white boys killed in Mississippi, don't you care about them?" Jones continues, as quoted in the *Voice:*

"Absolutely not," rapped out Jones. "Those boys were just artifacts, artifacts, man. They weren't real. If they want to assuage their leaking consciences, that's their business. I won't mourn for them. I have my own dead to mourn for."

Is this not exactly the attitude Jones had a moment earlier condemned in regard to killings in the South, but the same attitude in reverse? And is it really impossible for the human heart to mourn for *both* Negro and white victims? *Not*, to be sure, for ordinary whites, since they, we all know, are "white devils"; but at least for those who have given their lives in the struggle?

The essential point about Jones's racist buffoonery has been made by George Dennison in a recent review of Jones's plays:

Just as he mis-labels the victims *black,* he mis-labels the authority *white*. Certainly he knows, or should know, that the authority which in fact pertains is not the authority of race . . . but an authority of property and arms; and certainly he knows, or should know, that the life-destroying evil inheres in the nature of the authority, not in the color of those who wield it. But if Jones wanted change, he would speak change. He speaks, instead, for the greatest possible rejection, a rejection so absolute, so confined to fantasy, that it amounts to nothing more than hands-off-the-status-quo. . . . Point by point his is an upside down version of the most genteel, middle-class, liberal position. And I think that the liberals see him as one of their own, albeit a Dropout. He addresses every word to them and is confined to their systems of values because he is in the business of denying no other values but those. That spurious anger, so resonant with career, can be trusted not to upset the applecart.

C. DESPERADOS, WHITE

In effect, I have already described this group, so let me here confine myself to a few remarks about one of its central battle-cries, "alienation."

The trouble with the recurrent use of alienation as a mode of social analysis is that it includes almost everything, and thereby explains almost nothing. The term has become impossibly loose (like those other handy tags, "the Establishment" and "the Power Structure"). As used by Marx, alienation had a rather precise reference: it pointed to the condition of the worker in the capitalist productive process, a condition in which "the worker's deed becomes an alien power . . . forcing him to develop some specialized dexterity at the cost of a world of productive impulses." This kind of analysis focuses upon the place of the proletarian within the social structure, and not upon the sediment of malaise among those outside it.

Since Marx wrote, the term has acquired an impossible load of signification. During most of the bourgeois era, the European intellectuals grew increasingly estranged from the social community because the very ideals that had animated the bourgeois revolution were now being violated by bourgeois society; their "alienation" was prompted not by Bohemian wilfulness but by a loyalty to Liberty, Fraternity, Equality, or to an induced vision of pre-industrial society which, by a twist of history, came pretty much to resemble Liberty, Fraternity, Equality. Just as it was the triumph of capitalism which largely caused this sense of estrangement, so it was the expansion of capitalism which allowed the intellectuals enough freedom to release it. During the greater part of the bourgeois era, intellectuals preferred alienation from the community to alienation from themselves. Precisely this choice made possible their boldness and strength, precisely this "lack of roots" gave them their speculative power.

By now the term "alienation" frequently carries with it a curious reversal of moral and emotional stress. For where intellectuals had once used it as a banner of pride and self-assertion, today it tends to become a complaint, a token of self-pity, a rationale for a degree of estrangement from the society which connotes not an active rebellion against—nor even any active relation to—it, but rather a justification for marginality and withdrawal.

Somewhere amid the current talk about "alienation" an important reality *is* being touched upon or pointed to. There *is*, in our society, a profound estrangement from the sources of selfhood, the possibilities of human growth and social cohesion. But simply to proclaim this estrangement can be a way of preserving it. Alienation is not some metaphysical equivalent of the bubonic plague which constitutes an irrevocable doom; it is the powerlessness deriving from human failure to act. It is neither a substitute for thought, nor a dissolvent of human will, nor even a roadblock in the way of useful work. To enter into the society which in part causes this estrangement and by establishing bonds with other men to transform the society, is one way of partially overcoming alienation. Each time the civil rights movement brings previously mute Negroes into active political life, each time a trade union extends its power of decision within a factory, the boundaries of alienation are shrunk.

There is much truth in Harold Rosenberg's remark that

> The sentiment of diminution of personality ["alienation"] is an historical hypothesis upon which writers have constructed a set of literary conventions by this time richly equipped with theatrical machinery and symbolic allusions. . . . By all evidence, the hollow-man tradition has completely captured our "serious" prose

[and some of our serious youth]. . . . Once vanguardist, this tradition . . . has lately come to dominate popular literature and feeling. The individual's emptiness and inability to act have become an irrefrangible cliché, untiringly supported by an immense phalanx of latecomers to modernism. In this manifestation, the notion of the void has lost its critical edge and is thoroughly reactionary.

D. DESPERADOES, NEGRO

A new kind of young Negro militant has appeared in the last few years, and he is a figure far more authentic and impressive than any of those I have thus far mentioned. He is fed up with white promises. He is proud to be estranged from white society. He has strong, if vague, "nationalist" inclinations. He is desperate—impatient with the tactics of gradualism, nonviolence and passive resistance. He sees few, if any, allies upon whom he can count; few, if any, positive forces in society that might stir people into action. In effect, he decides that he must "go it alone," scornful of the white liberal and labor groups, as well as of those Negro leaders who choose to work with them. He seeks to substitute for a stagnant history his own desire and sacrifice.

Let me suggest a very limited comparison. This kind of young Negro militant, though not of course interested in any kind of individual terrorism, acts out of social and psychological motives somewhat like those of the late-nineteenth-century Russian terrorists, who also tried to substitute their intransigent will for the sluggishness of history. And the consequences will perhaps be similar: the best cadres exhausted in isolation and defeat.

Such a response may well be the inevitable result of an abrupt and painful coming-to-awareness on the part of young Negro militants who had previously suppressed their suffering simply in order to survive but now feel somewhat freer to release it. Their devotion is beyond doubt, as their heroism is beyond praise; yet what I'm here tempted to call kamikaze radicalism, or what Bayard Rustin calls the "no win" outlook, can become self-defeating in political life.

3. The "New Leftist"—A Sketch

We can now venture a portrait of the "new leftist," not as one or another individual but as a composite type—with all the qualifications I stated at the outset.

A. CULTURAL STYLE

The "new leftist" appears, at times, as a figure embodying a style of speech, dress, work, and culture. Often, especially if white, the son of the middle class—and sometimes the son of middle-class parents nursing radical memories—he asserts his rebellion against the deceit and hollowness of American society. Very good; there is plenty to rebel against. But in the course of his rebellion he tends to reject not merely the middle-class ethos but a good many other things he too hastily associates with it: the intellectual heritage of the West, the tradition of liberalism at its most serious, the commitment to democracy as an indispensable part of civilized life. He tends to make style into the very substance of his revolt, and while he may, on one side of himself, engage in valuable activities in behalf of civil rights, student freedom, etc., he nevertheless tacitly accepts the "givenness" of American society, has little hope or expectation of changing it, and thereby, in effect, settles for a mode of personal differentiation.

Primarily that means the wish to shock, the wish to assault the sensibilities of a world he cannot overcome. If he cannot change it, then at least he can outrage it. He searches in the limited repertoire of sensation and shock: for sick comics who will say "fuck" in night clubs; for drugs that will vault him beyond the perimeters of the suburbs; for varieties, perversities, and publicities of sex so as perhaps to create an inner, private revolution that will accompany—or replace?—the outer, public revolution.

But the "new leftist" is frequently trapped in a symbiotic

relationship with the very middle class he rejects, dependent upon it for his self-definition: quite as the professional anti-Communist of a few years ago was caught up with the Communist Party which, had it not existed, he would have had to invent—as indeed at times he did invent. So that for all its humor and charm, the style of the "new leftist" tends to become a rigid anti-style, dependent for its survival on the enemy it is supposed to panic. *Épater le bourgeois*—in this case, perhaps *épater le père*—is to acquiesce in a basic assumption of at least the more sophisticated segments of the middle class: that values can be inferred from, or are resident in, the externals of dress, appearance, furnishings, and hairdos.

Shock as he will, disaffiliate as he may choose, the "new leftist" discovers after a while that nothing has greatly changed. The relations of power remain as before, the Man still hovers over the scene, the "power structure" is unshaken. A few old ladies in California may grow indignant, a DA occasionally arrest someone, a *Village Voice* reporter arrange an interview; but surely that is all small change. And soon the "new leftist" must recognize that even he has not been greatly transformed. For in his personal manner he is acting out the dilemmas of a utopian community, and just as Brook Farm had to remain subject to the laws of the market despite its internal ethic of co-operation, so must he remain subject to the impress of the dominant institutions despite his desire to be totally different.

Victimized by a lack of the historical sense, the "new leftist" does not realize that the desire to shock and create sensations has itself a long and largely disastrous history. The notion, as Meyer Schapiro has remarked, that opium is the revolution of the people has been luring powerless intellectuals and semi-intellectuals for a long time. But the damnable thing is that for an almost equally long time the more sophisticated and urban sectors of the middle class have refused to be shocked. They know the repertoire of sensationalism quite as well as the "new leftist"; and if he is to succeed in shocking them or even himself, he must keep raising the ante. The very rebel who believes himself devoted to an absolute of freedom and looks with contempt upon any mode of compromise, is thereby caught up in the compulsiveness of his escalation: a compulsiveness inherently bad enough, but rendered still more difficult, and sometimes pathetic, by the fact that, alas, each year he gets a year older.

Let me amend this somewhat. To say that the urban middle class has become jaded and can no longer be shocked, is not quite correct. No; a kind of complicity is set up between the outraged and/or amused urban middle class and the rebels of sensation. Their mutual dependency requires that each shock, to provide the pleasures of indignation, must be a little stronger (like a larger dose) than the previous one. For the point is not so much that the urban middle class can no longer be shocked as that it positively yearns for and comes to depend upon the titillating assaults of its cultural enemies. So that when a new sensation (be it literary violence, sexual fashion, intellectual outrage, high-toned pornography, or sadistic denunciation) is provided by the shock troops of culture, the sophisticated middle class responds with outrage, resistance and anger—*for upon these initial responses its pleasure depends.* But then, a little later, it rolls over like a happy puppy on its back, moaning, "Oh baby, *épatez* me again, harder this time, tell me what a sterile impotent louse I am and how you are so tough and virile, how you're planning to murder me, *épatez* me again . . ."

Thus a fire-eating character like LeRoi Jones becomes an adjunct of middle-class amusement and, to take an enormous leap upward in talent and seriousness, a writer like Norman Mailer becomes enmeshed with popular journalism and publicity.

The whole problem was anticipated many years ago by Trotsky when, writing about the Russian poet Esenin, he remarked that the poet thought to frighten the bourgeoisie by making scenes but as it turned out, the bourgeoisie was delighted, it adored scenes.

One thing alone will not delight the bourgeoisie: a decrease in income, a loss in social power, a threat to its property.

There is another sense in which cultural style dominates the behavior of the "new leftists." Some of them display a tendency to regard political—and perhaps all of—life as a Hemingwayesque contest in courage and rectitude. People are constantly being tested for endurance, bravery, resistance to temptation, and if found inadequate, are denounced for having "copped out." Personal endurance thus becomes the substance of, and perhaps even a replacement for, political ideas.

Now this can be a valid and serious way of looking at things, especially in extreme situations: which is, of course, what Hemingway had in mind. Among civil rights workers in the deep South such a vision of life reflects the ordeal they must constantly face; they *are* under extreme pressure and their courage *is* constantly being tested. Yet their situation cannot be taken as a model for the political life of the country as a whole. If one wants to do more than create a tiny group of the heroic, the tested and the martyred, their style of work will not suffice. If one wants to build a movement in which not everyone need give "the whole of their lives," then the suspicion and hostility such an outlook is bound to engender toward the somewhat less active and somewhat less committed can only be damaging. For in effect, if not intent, it is a strategy of exclusion, leaving no place for anyone but the vanguard of the scarred.

It is, at times, a strategy of exclusion in a still more troubling sense: it reduces differences of opinion to grades of moral rectitude. If, for example, you think Martin Luther King or Bayard Rustin were wrong in regard to certain tactical matters; if you disagree with what Rustin proposed at the Democratic national convention in 1964 and what King did in Selma, then you call into question their loyalty and commitment: you charge them with "copping out" or "fooling with the power structure." This approach makes it impossible to build a movement and, in the long run, even to maintain a sect.

B. DOMESTIC POLITICS

A division of opinion, still incipient and confused, has appeared among people in the radical, student, and civil rights movements. There are those who, in effect, want to "go it alone," refusing to have anything to do with "the Establishment," and those who look forward to creating a loose coalition of Negro, labor, liberal, and church groups in order to stretch the limits of the welfare state. To an inexperienced eye, this may suggest a division between the more and less radical; but it is not. Radicalism is not a quantity.

The "go it alone" tendency in the civil rights movement starts from a recognition that the obstacles to success are enormous. It sees no forces within the society that could provide a new social dynamic. It shares with the liberals the questionable assumption that everyone in our society, except perhaps the bottom-dog poor, is bound to it by ties of material satisfaction. The labor movement is mired in its own fat; the ministers are Sunday allies; the liberals are two-faced, unreliable, perhaps cowards. What remains is a strategy of lonely assault, which must necessarily lead to shock tactics and desperation.

For if the above estimate of the American situation is valid, if there is so little possibility of a new social dynamism arising from or within its major social segments, then the outlook of the Black Muslims has to be acknowledged as persuasive. For obviously an estimate which sees major reforms as unlikely makes a traditional revolutionary overthrow seem still more unlikely; and the talk among irresponsibles about "guerrilla warfare in America" is mere self-indulgence since guerrilla warfare can succeed only when a large portion or a majority of the population is profoundly disaffected, something certainly not true in the United

States. Consequently—the logic of this argument moves inexorably—there is nothing left for American Negroes but the separatism of the Muslims.

Unless, of course, one turns to the tactic of shock, inducing such misadventures as the 1964 stall-ins at the World's Fair or the Triborough Bridge fiasco. Neither of these demonstrations had a precise objective, neither had any way of measuring achievement, accumulating allies, registering victory. Such methods, born of desperation, could only cut off the dedicated minority of civil rights activists from their white allies and, more important, from the mass of Negroes.

Now it is not our business to give advice to the civil rights movement on tactical issues or to rush into taking positions about its inner disputes. It is not the business of anyone except those directly engaged. But about some larger aspects of its problem we can speak.

One issue has been posed simply but conveniently by a *Village Voice* reporter, Jack Newfield, who writes that Dr. King's "basic goal is integration, and SNCC's is a revolution." Earlier Newfield had described this revolution as being not against capitalist society but "against Brotherhood Weeks, factories called colleges, desperation called success, and sex twice a week."

(An aside: I think it is a totalitarian invasion of privacy for a political or social movement to concern itself with the frequency its adherents or anyone else engage in sexual relations. For the right to make love to whomever you wish, of whatever sex you choose, in whatever posture you prefer, I will fight . . . well, almost . . . to the death; but beyond that, the frequency of your encounters, like the quality of your orgasms, is no one's business but your own.)

What the people who talk about integration vs. revolution don't see is that to achieve integration, even in the limited terms presumably favored by Dr. King would indeed *be* a revolution, greater in consequence and impact than that effected by the rise of industrial unionism in the thirties.

Bayard Rustin puts the matter as follows:

*

While most Negroes—in their hearts—unquestionably seek only to enjoy the fruits of American society as it now exists, their quest cannot objectively be satisfied within the framework of existing political and economic relations. The young Negro who would demonstrate his way into the labor market may be motivated by a thoroughly bourgeois ambition . . . but he will end up having to favor a great expansion of the public sector of the economy. . . .

. . . the term revolutionary as I am using it, does not connote violence; it refers to the quantitative transformation of fundamental institutions, more or less rapidly, to the point where the social and economic structure . . . can no longer be said to be the same. . . . I fail to see how the [civil rights] movement can be victorious in the absence of radical programs for full employment, abolition of slums, the reconstruction of our educational system, new definitions of work and leisure. Adding up the cost of such programs, we can only conclude that we are talking about a refashioning of our political economy.

To this lucid analysis I would only add a word concerning the desire of Negroes "to enjoy the fruits of American society as it now exists." Certain intellectuals bemoan this desire because they don't want the Negro poor integrated into a "rotten middle-class society" and thereby end up with two cars, barbecue pits, and ulcers. Even more than wrong, these intellectuals seem to me snobbish. For Negroes should have just as much *right* to suburban pleasures as anyone else; they should be in a position just as much as the whites to choose the middle-class style of life. We need not approve, we can argue against that choice, but we are obliged to support their right to make it. And why not? I don't notice James Baldwin or LeRoi Jones taking vows of poverty. Nor should they. There is something a bit manipulative in the view that Negroes should be preserved from the temptations that, presumably, all the rest of us are entitled to. What's more, the Negroes themselves are far too experienced in the ways of the world to allow themselves to be cast in the role of sacrificial ascetic.

But let us return to "integration vs. revolution" and for the sake of the argument accept this formulation. Naturally enough—it's an old habit—we then opt for revolution; there remains only the little detail of who is going to make it.

Clearly, the vast majority of whites are in the grip of the Establishment. The liberals? Establishment. The churches? Establishment. The unions? Establishment. Intellectuals? Establishment.

But not only the whites, also the Negroes. Wilkins, Young, Powell, King, Farmer? The black Establishment. Rustin? He sold out to it.

Where then does that leave us? Well, some students . . . but can we be so sure of *them*? May they not in time decide to go back to graduate school, perhaps after discovering that "the people," in refusing to heed the revolutionary missions from the campus, are a rather hopeless quantity? What is left, then, is a handful . . . and where that handful must end is in despair, exhaustion, burning themselves out in the all-too-characteristic rhythm of American radicalism, which too often has tried to compensate for its powerlessness in reality by ferocity in words.

At this point I hear a voice crying out: "No, not just a vanguard of the desperate! We are going to organize the poor, the millions beneath the floor of society, those who have been mute and unrepresented for too long . . . and it is they who will form the basis of a new movement, beyond the pale of Establishment politics."

Good. The poor need to be organized, and more power to those who try. Every such effort, big or small, deserves the approval and support of socialists and liberals. But some problems remain. I leave aside the fact that twentieth-century history indicates a high rate of failure in previous efforts of this kind; that the unstructured, atomized and often demoralized "underclass" has been the most resistant to organization. History need not always repeat itself, and perhaps this time the effort will succeed. No, the questions I would raise have to do not with failure but success.

Imagine a campaign to organize the poor in a large city,

undertaken by young people who will have no truck with the Establishment. Through hard work and devotion, they build up a group of, let's say, 150 people in a slum of mixed racial composition—a notable achievement. What happens next? The municipal "power structure" begins to pay some attention and decides either to smash the group as a dangerous nuisance or to lure away some of its leading members. If the local organization of the poor must now face attack, it would seem to have no choice but quickly to find some allies—in the unions, among churchmen, perhaps even in the American Jewish Congress, "establishmentarian" as all of these may seem. Suppose, however, the "power structure" decides to offer various inducements—jobs, improved housing—to some of the Negro members, and various other organizations, like the reform wing of the Democrats and certain trade unions, also enter the picture. What will the uncompromising, anti-Establishment leaders of the poor do now? Does not the reality of the situation require them to enter negotiations, formally or informally, and thereby become involved in the socioeconomic life of the city? Can they remain exempt from it? And if so, how long do you suppose their followers will remain with them? For that matter, why should they? The goods and services that, with enough pressure, the "power structure" can be made to provide, the poor need, want and deserve. Can one seriously suppose they will be exempt from such "temptations"? There is only one way to be certain the poor will remain beyond the temptations of our society, and that is to keep them hopelessly poor.

Nor is this quite a new problem. It was faced, in somewhat different form, years ago when revolutionists led trade unions and discovered that they had to sign agreements which in practice signified acquiescence in the bargaining arrangements between capital and labor within the confines of the *status quo*. Had these revolutionists, in the name of principle, refused to sign such agreements with the employers, they would have been sabotaging the functions of the union and would soon, deservedly, cease to be leaders.

The idea of coalition or realignment politics as advanced by socialists is not a rigid formula, or a plot to deliver our souls into the hands of the Establishment. It is meant as a strategy for energizing all those forces within the society that want to move forward toward an extension of the welfare state. In some places, such a loose coalition might take the form of politics outside the established institutions, like the Freedom Democratic Party of Mississippi—though that movement, if it is to succeed, must begin to find allies within the white community. In other places, as in Texas, there is a coalition of labor, liberal, intellectual and minority groups (Negro, Mexican) within the Democratic Party—and by all accounts a pretty good coalition. Can one say, as if all wisdom were bunched into our fists, that such a development should not be supported simply because it grows up within the framework of a major party?

If we are serious in our wish to affect American political life, we must learn to see the reality as it is. We have to seek out and prod the forces that exist. And I think it is a gross error—the kind of deep-seated conservatism that often alloys ultraradicalism—to say that everything in the major sectors of American society is static, sated, "Establishment." Who, twenty-five or thirty years ago, could have foreseen that Catholic priests and nuns would be marching into Montgomery? Who could have foreseen the more thoroughgoing ferment in the American churches of which this incident is merely a symptom? Instead of scoffing at such people as civil rights "tourists," we ought to be seeking them out and trying to get them to move a little further, up North too.

And a word about the labor movement. Its failures, ills, and decline have been documented in great detail by American socialists—perhaps because we ourselves have not quite understood what its nature and possibilities are, preferring instead to nag away when it did not conform to our preconceptions. Right now, to be sure, the unions look pretty sluggish and drab. Still, two leaders named David MacDonald and James Carey have recently been toppled by membership votes (and when something like that happens to a trade union leader in Russia, China, Cuba, North Vietnam or Zanzibar, please let me know).

Bayard Rustin says: "The labor movement, despite its obvious faults, has been the largest single organized force in this country pushing for progressive social legislation." That is true, but not enough. What seems the static quality of the trade unions may be a phase of rest between the enormous achievements of the past forty years and possible achievements of the future. If the civil rights movement succeeds, may it not also enter such a phase? And do you suppose that the struggles a few decades ago to organize unions were any the less difficult, bloody, and heroic than those in the South today? And if it's a revolution in the quality of American life that you want, then have not the industrial unions come closer to achieving that for millions of people than any other force in the country?

We are speaking here partly of speculations, partly of hopes. None of us has any certain answer or magic formula by which to overcome the painful isolation of the radical movement: if there were such a thing, someone would by now have discovered it. We are all groping to find a way out of our difficulties. I don't wish to draw a hard-and-fast line between "realigners" and "go-it-aloners." There is room for both disagreement and co-operation. You want to organize the poor? Splendid. We propose certain sorts of coalitions? An essential part of such a coalition ought to be drawn from the poor you propose to organize. And in turn, if you're to keep them organized, you will have to engage in coalitions. Right now—let's be candid—you don't have very many of the poor and we don't have much of a coalition. Disagreements of this kind are fraternal, and can be tested patiently in experience.

The true line of division between democratic socialists and left authoritarians concerns not tactics, but basic commitments, values, the vision of what a good society should be. It concerns:

*

C. POLITICS AND FREEDOM

The "new leftists" feel little attachment to Russia. Precisely as it has turned away from the more extreme and terroristic version of totalitarianism, so have they begun to find it unsatisfactory as a model: too Victorian, even "bourgeois." Nor are they interested in distinguishing among kinds of anti-Communism, whether of the right or left.

When they turn to politics, they have little concern for precise or complex thought. A few years ago the "new leftists" were likely to be drawn to Communist China, which then seemed bolder than Khrushchev's Russia. But though the Mao regime has kept the loyalty of a small group of students, most of the "new leftists" seem to find it too grim and repressive. They tend to look for their new heroes and models among the leaders of underdeveloped countries. Figures like Lumumba, Nasser, Sukarno, Babu, and above all Castro attract them, suggesting the possibility of a politics not yet bureaucratized and rationalized. But meanwhile they neglect to notice, or do not care, that totalitarian and authoritarian dictatorship can set in even before a society has become fully modernized. They have been drawn to charismatic figures like Lumumba and Castro out of a distaste for the mania of industrial production which the Soviet Union shares with the United States; but they fail to see that such leaders of the underdeveloped countries, who in their eyes represent spontaneity and anarchic freedom, are themselves—perhaps unavoidably—infused with the same mania for industrial production.

Let me specify a few more of the characteristic attitudes among the "new leftists":

1) An extreme, sometimes unwarranted, hostility toward liberalism. They see liberalism only in its current version, institutional, corporate, and debased; but avoiding history, they know very little about the elements of the liberal tradition which should remain valuable for any democratic socialist. For the "new leftists," as I have here delimited them, liberalism means Clark Kerr, not John Dewey; Max Lerner, not John Stuart Mill; Pat Brown, not George Norris. And thereby they would cut off the resurgent American radicalism from what is or should be, one of its sustaining sources: the tradition that has yielded us a heritage of civil freedoms, disinterested speculation, humane tolerance.

2) *An impatience with the problems that concerned an older generation of radicals.* Here the generational conflict breaks out with strong feelings on both sides, the older people feeling threatened in whatever they have been able to salvage from past experiences, the younger people feeling the need to shake off dogma and create their own terms of action.

Perhaps if we all try to restrain—not deny—our emotions, we can agree upon certain essentials. There are traditional radical topics which no one, except the historically minded, need trouble with. To be unconcerned with the dispute in the late twenties over the Anglo-Russian Trade Union Committee or the differences between Lenin and Luxembourg on the "national question"—well and good. These are not quite burning problems of the moment. But *some* of the issues hotly debated in the thirties do remain burning problems: in fact, it should be said for the anti-Stalinist left of the past several decades that it anticipated, in its own somewhat constricted way, a number of the problems (especially, the nature of Stalinism) which have since been widely debated by political scientists, sociologists, indeed, by all people concerned with politics. The nature of Stalinism and of post-Stalinist Communism is not an abstract or esoteric matter; the views one holds concerning these questions determine a large part of one's political conduct: and what is still more important, *they reflect one's fundamental moral values.*

No sensible radical over the age of thirty (something of a cut-off point, I'm told) wants young people merely to rehearse his ideas, or mimic his vocabulary, or look back upon his dusty old articles. On the contrary, what we find disturbing in some of the "new leftists" is that, while barely knowing it, they tend to repeat somewhat too casually the tags of the very past they believe themselves to be transcending. But we do insist that in regard to a few crucial issues, above all, those regarding totalitarian movements and societies, there should be no ambiguity, no evasiveness.

So that if some "new leftists" say that all the older radicals are equally acceptable or equally distasteful or equally inconsequential in their eyes; if they see no significant difference between, say, Norman Thomas and Paul Sweezy such as would require them to regard Thomas as a comrade and Sweezy as an opponent—then the sad truth is that they have not at all left behind them the old disputes, but on the contrary, are still completely in their grip, though perhaps without being quite aware of what is happening to them. The issue of totalitarianism is neither academic nor merely historical; no one can seriously engage in politics without clearly and publicly defining his attitude toward it. I deliberately say "attitude" rather than "analysis," for while there can be a great many legitimate differences of analytic stress and nuance in discussing totalitarian society, morally there should be only a candid and sustained opposition to it.

3) *A vicarious indulgence in violence, often merely theoretic and thereby all the more irresponsible.* Not being a pacifist, I believe there may be times when violence is unavoidable; being a man of the twentieth century, I believe that a recognition of its necessity must come only after the most prolonged consideration, as an utterly last resort. To "advise" the Negro movement to adopt a policy encouraging or sanctioning violence, to sneer at Martin Luther King for his principled refusal of violence, is to take upon oneself a heavy responsibility—and if, as usually happens, taken lightly, it becomes sheer irresponsibility.

It is to be insensitive to the fact that the nonviolent

strategy has arisen from Negro experience. It is to ignore the notable achievements that strategy has already brought. It is to evade the hard truth expressed by the Rev. Abernathy: "The whites have the guns." And it is to dismiss the striking moral advantage that nonviolence has yielded the Negro movement, as well as the turmoil, anxiety, and pain—perhaps even fundamental reconsideration—it has caused among whites in the North and the South.

There are situations in which Negroes will choose to defend themselves by arms against terrorist assault, as in the Louisiana towns where they have formed a club of "Elders" which patrols the streets peaceably but with the clear intent of retaliation in case of attack. The Negroes there seem to know what they are doing, and I would not fault them. Yet as a matter of general policy and upon a nationwide level, the Negro movement has chosen nonviolence: rightly, wisely and heroically.

There are "revolutionaries" who deride this choice. They show a greater interest in ideological preconceptions than in the experience and needs of a living movement; and sometimes they are profoundly irresponsible, in that their true interest is not in helping to reach the goals chosen by the American Negroes, but is rather a social conflagration which would satisfy their apocalyptic yearnings even if meanwhile the Negroes were drowned in blood. The immediate consequence of such talk is a withdrawal from the ongoing struggles. And another consequence is to manufacture a cult out of figures like Malcolm X, who neither led nor won nor taught, and Robert Williams, the Negro leader who declared for violence and ended not with the Negroes in Selma, or at their strike in the hospitals of Westchester County, or on the picket line before the Atlanta Scripto plant (places where the kind of coalition we desire between Negro and labor was being foreshadowed), but by delivering short-wave broadcasts from Cuba.

4) An unconsidered enmity toward something vaguely called the Establishment. As the term "Establishment" was first used in England, it had the value of describing—which is to say, delimiting—a precise social group; as it has come to be used in the United States, it tends to be an all-purpose put-down. In England it refers to a caste of intellectuals with an Oxbridge education, closely related in values to the ruling class, and setting the cultural standards which largely dominate both the London literary world and the two leading universities.

Is there an Establishment in this, or any cognate, sense in the United States? Perhaps. There may now be in the process of formation, for the first time, such an intellectual caste; but if so, precise discriminations of analysis and clear boundaries of specification would be required as to what it signifies and how it operates. As the term is currently employed, however, it is difficult to know who, besides those merrily using it as a thunderbolt of opprobrium, is *not* in the Establishment. And a reference that includes almost everyone tells us almost nothing.

5) *An equally unreflective belief in "the decline of the West"*—apparently without the knowledge that, more seriously held, this belief has itself been deeply ingrained in Western thought, frequently in the thought of reactionaries opposed to modern rationality, democracy and sensibility.

The notion is so loose and baggy, it means little. Can it, however, be broken down? If war is a symptom of this decline, then it holds for the East as well. If totalitarianism is a sign, then it is not confined to the West. If economics is a criterion, then we must acknowledge, Marxist predictions aside, that there has been an astonishing recovery in Western Europe. If we turn to culture, then we must recognize that in the West there has just come to an end one of the greatest periods in human culture—that period of "modernism" represented by figures like Joyce, Stravinsky, Picasso. If improving the life of the workers is to count, then the West can say something in its own behalf. And if personal freedom matters, then, for all its grave imperfections, the West remains virtually alone as a place of hope. There remains, not least of all, the matter of racial prejudice, and here no judgment of the West can be too harsh—so long as we remember that even this blight is by no means confined to the West, and that the very judgments we make draw upon values nurtured by the West.

But is it not really childish to talk about "the West" as if it were some indivisible whole we must either accept or reject without amendment? There are innumerable strands in the Western tradition, and our task is to nourish those which encourage dignity and freedom. But to envisage some global apocalypse that will end in the destruction of the West, is a sad fantasy, a token of surrender before the struggles of the moment.

6) A crude, unqualified anti-Americanism, drawing from every possible source, even if one contradicts another: the aristocratic bias of Eliot and Ortega, Communist propaganda, the speculations of Tocqueville, the ressentiment *of postwar Europe, etc.*

7) An increasing identification with that sector of the "third world" in which "radical" nationalism and Communist authoritarianism merge. Consider this remarkable fact: In the past decade there have occurred major changes in the Communist world, and many of the intellectuals in Russia and eastern Europe have re-examined their assumptions, often coming to the conclusion, masked only by the need for caution, that democratic values are primary in any serious effort at socialist reconstruction. Yet at the very same time most of the "new leftists" have identified not with the "revisionists" in Poland or Djilas in Yugoslavia—or even Tito. They identify with the harder, more violent, more dictatorial segments of the Communist world. And they carry this authoritarian bias into their consideration of the "third world," where they praise those rulers who choke off whatever weak impulses there may be toward democratic life.

About the problems of the underdeveloped countries, among the most thorny of our time, it is impossible even to begin to speak with any fullness here. Nor do I mean to suggest that an attack upon authoritarianism and a defense of democracy exhausts consideration of those problems; on the contrary, it is the merest beginning. But what matters in this context is not so much the problems themselves as the attitudes, reflecting a deeper political-moral bias, which the "new leftists" take toward such countries. A few remarks:

a) Between the suppression of democratic rights and the justification or excuse the "new leftists" offer for such suppression there is often a very large distance, sometimes a complete lack of connection. Consider Cuba. It may well be true that United States policy became unjustifiably hostile toward the Castro regime at an early point in its history; but how is this supposed to have occasioned, or how is it supposed to justify, the suppression of democratic rights (including, and especially, those of all other left-wing tendencies) in Cuba? The apologists for Castro have an obligation to show what I think cannot be shown: the alleged close causal relation between United States pressure and the destruction of freedom in Cuba. Frequently, behind such rationales there is a tacit assumption that in times of national stress a people can be rallied more effectively by a dictatorship than by a democratic regime. But this notion—it was used to justify the suppression of political freedoms during the early Bolshevik years—is at the very least called into question by the experience of England and the United States during the Second World War. Furthermore, if Castro does indeed have the degree of mass support that his friends claim, one would think that the preservation of democratic liberties in Cuba would have been an enormously powerful symbol of self-confidence; would have won him greater support at home and certainly in other Latin American countries; and would have significantly disarmed his opponents in the United States.

b) We are all familiar with the "social context" argument: that for democracy to flourish there has first to be a certain level of economic development, a quantity of infrastructure, and a coherent national culture. As usually put forward in academic and certain authoritarian-left circles, it is a crudely deterministic notion which I do not believe to be valid: for one thing, it fails to show how the suppression of even very limited political-social rights contributes, or is *in fact* caused by a wish, to solve these problems. (Who is prepared to maintain that Sukarno's suppression of the Indonesian Socialists and other dissident parties helped solve that country's economic or growth problems?) But for the sake of argument let us accept a version of this theory: let us grant what is certainly a bit more plausible, that a full or stable democratic society cannot be established in a country ridden by economic primitivism, illiteracy, disease, cultural disunion, etc. The crucial question then becomes: can at least some measure of democratic rights be won or granted? —say, the right of workers to form unions or the right of dissidents within a single-party state to form factions and express their views? For if a richer socioeconomic development is a prerequisite of democracy, it must also be remembered that such democratic rights, as they enable the emergence of autonomous social groups, are also needed for socioeconomic development.

c) Let us go even further and grant, again for the sake of argument, that in some underdeveloped countries authoritarian regimes may be necessary for a time. But even if this is true, which I do not believe it is, then it must be acknowledged as an unpleasant necessity, a price we are paying for historical crimes and mistakes of the past. In that case, radicals can hardly find their models in, and should certainly not become an uncritical cheering squad for, authoritarian dictators whose presence is a supposed unavoidability.

The "new leftists," searching for an ideology by which to rationalize their sentiments, can now find exactly what they need in a remarkable book recently translated from the French, *The Wretched of the Earth.* Its author, Frantz Fanon is a Negro from Martinique who became active in the Algerian revolution. He articulates with notable power the views of those nationalist-revolutionaries in the underdeveloped countries who are contemptuous of their native bourgeois leadership, who see their revolution being pushed beyond national limits and into their own social structure, who do not wish to merge with or become subservient to the Communists yet have no strong objection in principle to Communist methods and values.

Fanon tries to locate a new source of revolutionary energy: the peasants who, he says, "have nothing to lose and everything to gain." He deprecates the working class: in the Western countries it has been bought off, and in the underdeveloped nations it constitutes a tiny "aristocracy." What emerges is a curious version of Trotsky's theory of permanent revolution, concerning national revolts in the backward countries which, to fulfill themselves, must become social revolutions. But with one major difference: Fanon assigns to the peasants and the urban declassed poor the vanguard role Trotsky had assigned to the workers.

What, however, has really happened in countries like Algeria? The peasantry contributes men and blood for an anticolonial war. Once the war is won, it tends to disperse, relapsing into local interests and seeking individual small-scale ownership of the land. It is too poor, too weak, too diffuse to remain or become the leading social force in a newly liberated country. The bourgeoisie, what there was of it, having been shattered and the working class pushed aside, what remains? Primarily the party of nationalism, led by men who are dedicated, uprooted, semieducated and ruthless. The party rules, increasingly an independent force perched upon and above the weakened classes.

But Fanon is not taken in by his own propaganda. He recognizes the dangers of a preening dictator and has harsh things to say against the Nkrumah type. He proposes, instead, that "the party should be the direct expression of the masses," and adds, "Only those underdeveloped countries led by revolutionary elites who have come up from the people can today *allow* the entry of the masses upon the scene of history." (Emphasis added.)

Fanon wants the masses to participate, yet throughout his book the single-party state remains an unquestioned assumption. But what if the masses do not wish to "participate"? And what if they are hostile to "the"—always "the"—party? Participation without choice is a burlesque of democracy; indeed, it is an essential element of a totalitarian or authoritarian society, for it means that the masses of people act out a charade of involvement but are denied the reality of decision.

The authoritarians find political tendencies and representative men with whom to identify in the Communist world; so do we. We identify with the people who have died for freedom, like Imre Nagy, or who rot in prison, like Djilas. We identify with the "revisionists," those political *marranos* who, forced to employ Communist jargon, yet spoke out for a socialism democratic in character and distinct from both Communism and capitalism. As it happens, our friends in the Communist world are not in power; but since when has that mattered to socialists?

In 1957, at the height of the Polish ferment, the young philosopher Leszek Kolakowski wrote a brief article entitled "What Is Socialism?" It consisted of a series of epigrammatic sentences describing what socialism is not (at the moment perhaps the more immediate concern), but tacitly indicating as well what socialism should be. The article was banned by the Gomulka regime but copies reached Western periodicals. Here are a few sentences.

Socialism is not

A society in which a person who has committed no crime sits at home waiting for the police.

A society in which one person is unhappy because he says what he thinks, and another happy because he does not say what is in his mind.

A society in which a person lives better because he does not think at all.

A state whose neighbors curse geography.

A state which wants all its citizens to have the same opinions in philosophy, foreign policy, economics, literature and ethics.

A state whose government defines its citizens' rights, but whose citizens do not define the government's rights.

A state in which there is private ownership of the means of production.

A state which considers itself solidly socialist because it has liquidated private ownership of the means of production.

A state which always knows the will of the people before it asks them.

A state in which the philosophers and writers always say the same as the generals and ministers, but always after them.

A state in which the returns of parliamentary elections are always predictable.

A state which does not like to see its citizens read back numbers of newspapers.

These negatives imply a positive, and that positive is a central lesson of contemporary history: the unity of socialism and democracy. To preserve democracy as a political mode without extending it into every crevice of social and economic life is to allow it to become increasingly sterile, formal, ceremonial. To nationalize an economy without enlarging democratic freedoms is to create a new kind of social exploitation. Radicals and liberals may properly and fraternally disagree about many other things; but upon this single axiom concerning the value of democracy, this conviction wrung from the tragedy of our age, politics must rest.

✡ BERKELEY AND BEYOND

LET'S start with a happening—or, more precisely, an imagining. Somewhere in Berkeley a group of students (veterans of "the action") is beginning to discuss the December uprising; perhaps one or two young professors, of the kind the students trust and admire, are there too, joining in the reminiscence. As if by common need, they find themselves moving toward the one question that for them requires notable courage to ask—for it must be painful even to admit that it is a question. *Did it really matter?* At first it might have struck them as outrageous, a kind of self-betrayal, even to hint at such a question, but now, as the months slip away, it becomes a question hard to avoid. After all the excitement, after the thrill of victory, after the speeches and negotiations and policy-making: *did it really matter?*

In one obvious sense, yes. There were student grievances concerning freedom of speech; these grievances were fought to a climax dramatic beyond anyone's anticipation; the immediate results look good. Such actions, though smaller in scope, have been fought through before, and they will have to be fought through again. Academic freedom, never a permanent conquest, must frequently be regained.

So far, so good. But when my imaginary students ask themselves *did it really matter?* they are obviously thinking about more than immediate reforms on the campus; they are worrying about long-range repercussions and possibilities. To ask whether the Berkeley uprising marked a mere colorful incident in their lives or was a milestone toward some encompassing commitment; to wonder whether it was a flareup of youthful energy and rebelliousness or the beginning of a sustained inquiry by American students into the nature and purpose of the education they receive—these are the more enduring, difficult, and important questions. And they do not yet permit of any certain answer.

I think (perhaps it would be more accurate to say I hope) that out of the Berkeley struggle and the turmoil that has since occurred at such schools as St. John's, Brooklyn, and Fairleigh Dickinson there will come a persistent series of questionings, by students and teachers alike, directed to problems such as these: (1) Can the idea of the university as a center of learning and free intellect survive in the age of bureaucratic structure, the age of the "multiversity"? (2) At a time when young people spend more and more of their lives in universities, is there not a need for new definitions of their rights, freedoms, and responsibilities as students? (3) Will the rebellious students be able to provide a new social energy for this country, will they come to be a new source of ideas and commitment for a revitalized democratic radicalism? Only if they, and we, now turn our attention to questions such as these, will the Berkeley events really have mattered.

*

The Idea of the University

At the risk of seeming naïve or utopian, I want to posit the idea that almost every student who comes to an American university has somewhere in the back of his mind a true vision of what a university is supposed to be. He may be hostile or confused, he may already be cynical about it, but somewhere, however dimly, he knows—for it is an idea that has been with us for a long time—what a university should be.

The language I use is not his, but some glimpse of the following he does have: that the university should serve as a center for disinterested learning; that it should be quick with the passions of controversy yet dedicated to those studies which the outer world may dismiss as esoteric; that it should be a sanctuary for opinion; and that in its precincts he should be able to encounter men who will serve as models of intellectual discipline and enthusiasm.

Now there are some American universities in which the student can find all of these, though it takes a bit of looking; but only rarely can he find them as the dominant voice of a university or find them uncontaminated by the grossness of utilitarian measurement and the calculations of the business ethic. What has been happening to the American university is a gradual and all-too-cheerful adaptation to the surrounding social landscape: It has become too absorbed with weapon-producing research, too subject to the creed of material growth and power, too caught up in the mystique of quantification.

Yet all of these problems thrown up by the sudden turn to "mass education" might be manageable if only there were present in our universities a firm and self-assured intellectual leadership which understood and was prepared to fight for the values of an "active cloister," a leadership which knew what Cardinal Newman meant when he wrote that the university is "the high protecting power of all knowledge . . . it maps out the territory of the intellect, and sees that . . . there is neither encroachment nor surrender on any side." Of how many university administrations in America, indeed, of how many faculties, could one say that they live or try to live by this standard?

Neither encroachment nor surrender . . . The reality is closer to the opposite. There are steady encroachments by the spirit of hucksterdom, the blight of weaponry, the disease of tainted research. There is a steady surrender to educational gimmickry which short-changes the students and educational big-enterprise which seduces the professors. (Students sometimes complain about professors who lack social awareness and continue to do their own abstruse research. In the present circumstances, this complaint seems to me misdirected. The old-fashioned traditional scholar sticking by his narrow specialty no matter who gets bombed or what freedom march occurs, may not be an intellectual hero or an inspiring model for the young; but at least he sustains the values of disinterested scholarship which are essential for the survival of a true university. Much more menacing, as it seems to me, is the professor-entrepreneur busy with a mess of grants, textbooks, institutes, conferences, consultations, indeed, with everything but serious teaching and intellectual work.)

Lest all this seem exaggerated, I quote at some length from two quite moderate professors at the University of California at Berkeley, Sheldin Wolin and John Schaar:

> For some time now, the students, especially the undergraduates, have felt themselves to be an alien presence within the multiversity, an "Other Academia" analogous to the "Other America," ill fed, ill housed and ill clothed not in the material sense, but in the intellectual and spiritual senses. As the multiversity has climbed to higher and higher peaks of research productivity, material riches, and bureaucratic complexity, the students have fallen into deeper and deeper abysses of hostility and estrangement. The students' own favorite word for their condition is

"alienation," by which they mean . . . a sense of not being valued members of a genuine intellectual and moral community. Their feeling is grounded in reality.

The architects of the multiversity simply have not solved the problem of how to build an institution which not only produces knowledge and knowledgeable people with useful skills, but which also enriches and enlightens the lives of its students—informing them with the values of the intellect, preparing them to serve as the guardians of the society's intellectual honesty and political health, arming them with the vision by which society seeks its own better future. It is the performance of these latter tasks that distinguishes a genuine educational community from a mere research factory and training institution. . . .

By any reasonable standard, the multiversity has not taken its students seriously. At Berkeley, the educational environment of the undergraduate is bleak. He is confronted throughout his entire first two years with indifferent advising, endless bureaucratic routines, gigantic lecture courses, and a deadening succession of textbook assignments, and bluebook examinations testing his grasp of bits and pieces of knowledge. . . . It is possible to take a B.A. at Berkeley and never talk with a professor. To many of the students, the whole system seems a perversion of an educational community into a factory designed for the mass processing of men into machines.

This indictment is severe, but not, I am prepared to testify, excessive. Nor is it complete. A diagnosis of the malaise afflicting the American university would have to say a good deal about the increase in the size and power of administrative bureaucracies which regard the university as essentially "their" institution to be spared the troubles of restlessness and innovation. Something would have to be said about that prime vulgarity known as "publish or perish," a travesty of scholarship and common sense. And something more would have to be said, as I am glad the Berkeley students did, about the pressures faced by state universities from boards of regents heavily weighted toward conservative and business ideologies and almost always without faculty or student representation.

In short: the future of the American university, insofar as it will remain a university, is severely problematic; the ideal of the "active cloister" put forward by Mumford remains to be clarified and defended; and no one can do this as well as teachers and students together, for their interests, while not identical, are at least congruent.

The Place of the Student

Partly because the university has come to play a larger role in the socioeconomic life of the country than ever before, hundreds of thousands of young people now spend larger portions of their lives in the universities than ever before. And not merely their lives as minors subject to institutional control, but also as young adults usually able to vote, expected to pay taxes, and liable to military service.

One consequence ought to be a serious effort to reconsider the relationship between university and student, the terms of which were originally set under radically different conditions. In regard to public discussion and the rights of political minorities, the American university remains, by and large, a stronghold of democratic freedom; but its inner life as an institution is usually far from democratic. The system of authority governing the American university ranges from the outright dictatorship of the "strong" president to academic control by a faculty conscious of its traditional privileges; in most cases there is an uneasy compromise between top administration and faculty, with an intervening bureaucracy slowly accumulating more and more power.

But as far as students are concerned, they are supposed to remain in and be content with a state of almost complete dependence. University administrators, brimming with rectitude, presume to supervise the private lives of students. Decisions concerning academic standards and procedures are generally made without so much as consulting students. This is not, I think, a healthy situation, and without indulging in any mystique about the spontaneous wisdom or virtue of the young, we ought to recognize the appropriateness of student participation in academic affairs.

The doctrine by which administrators justify their supervision of student life is called *in loco parentis*, the institution acting in place of parents. Concerning this dubious rationale Dean Kathryn Hopwood of Hunter College has written that it is "quite at variance with the genesis of the European universities, such as the ones at Bologna and Paris, where the students employed visiting scholars to teach them." And here is the testimony of a young man recently self-removed from graduate school, Thomas Hayden, who writes with understandable bitterness about *in loco parentis:*

> To go to college involves a partial surrender of the freedoms of speech, press, and assembly, and often the freedom of privacy. It means arbitrary hours for women students and compulsory functions for both sexes. It means the "double jeopardy" of receiving punishments from the university for crimes committed in and adjudicated by the city. It means tolerating personal dossiers and students who spy for the dean of men or congressional investigating committees. It means the supervision and regulation of privacy. It means living under threat of punishment for "conduct unbecoming a student" or "inability to adjust to the university pattern." Margaret Mead has commented forcefully on the distinction between the work force and student force in the same age range:
>
>> A handful of tugboat employees or flight engineers, because of their admitted rights in a complex system in which they are working members, can hold up a city or a country until their demands are met, but in some states students are not even allowed to vote.
>
> And, unlike parents of students not in college,
>
>> parents of studying children must both support them and, correlatively, retain control of their conduct or delegate comparable control to some quasi-parental educational institution. In either case the student is treated like a dependent child.
>
> Needless to say, student extracurricular activities are organized

with this dependent status clearly in mind. The philosophy of student activities is articulated by most universities as either the "preparation" theory or the "privilege" theory. The first and most important of these goes like this: college is a "preparatory" period when the student, through incubation, is equipped with the skills he will need later in life. "Preparation" means involving the students in a make-believe laboratory world of student activities where they can safely practise being a citizen.

Is this, asks the writer, a serious educational philosophy? Surely the answer must be that it is not. All that can be said in behalf of *in loco parentis* is that it is a convenience for deans.

The usual attitude toward students in the American university is that they constitute a mixture of necessary consumer and irksome dependent. They pay their money (or receive their fellowships) and must then submit to whatever disciplines and routines the university proposes. Now there is a sense in which this seems quite proper: the student, being a novice, has come to learn from his superiors, and before the latter admit him to their ranks they have the obligation to test his competence. Yet this hardly justifies the present systematic refusal to consider seriously student opinion concerning such matters as teaching procedures, curriculum, course requirements, etc. (Actually, student opinion *is* taken into account, even about such sacrosanct matters as faculty tenure; but this happens in the worst possible way, through gossip, hearsay, comparison of class sizes, etc.)

At the graduate level the situation becomes still more galling. The graduate student, though presumed to be a serious person and often one who makes notable sacrifices to pursue his studies, is placed in a condition of dependency far more severe than that of the undergraduate. The whole career of the graduate student can be at the mercy or whim of a few professors, sometimes only one professor. Anyone who has taught in an American university knows how often the bright and lively undergraduate undergoes a depressing change in style soon after entering graduate school: he becomes professionally cautious, intellectually timid, concerned to please and adapt to professors. This is hardly a system calculated to encourage manliness and independence of spirit. Surely, without challenging the authority of the faculty or creating that state of "anarchy" which is said to haunt the dreams of educational administrators, it should be possible to consult systematically with our graduate students concerning a wide range of educational policies.

Even to raise such a possibility is to provoke outcries from certain professors about the danger of reducing our universities to "banana republics" where overpoliticized students would establish a terrorist reign of laxness. How far-fetched a fantasy this seems in the actual context of American university life! And besides, such fears would seem a bit more worthy if American professors had shown themselves proudly resistant against the real danger to their authority, which comes from the steady encroachments of academic bureaucracies.

What our more thoughtful and restless students are requesting is not that academic decisions be turned over to "student mobs" but that they be allowed, through democratic channels, to express their views about matters of the greatest concern to them. Often enough students are wrong in their opinions about academic life and educational policy, but then so too are the rest of us; and a supply of fresh mistakes might be invigorating. We professors ought to appreciate the value of constructive—even not-so-constructive—restlessness: for while it might make our lives less comfortable, it would surely make them more interesting.

Students and Politics

In one crucial sense, what happened at Berkeley must be considered apart from the political views, real or alleged, of the student leaders. For the grievances of the Free Speech

Movement had an intrinsic weight and meaning; they required satisfaction and settlement, no matter what anyone might have felt about the political opinions of this or the other FSM leader; and at the height of the struggle, the students were right to insist that questions about the leaders' politics could only distract attention from the urgencies of their campaign.

Yet, in any larger perspective, it is obviously important to consider the motivating ideas of the student leaders; and while these do range, as they insist, across the entire political spectrum, it would be disingenuous to deny that a number of them think of themselves as radicals. Their radicalism is vague and nonideological; it places a heavy stress upon individual integrity, perhaps more than upon collective action; it seldom follows from any coherent theory of modern society. The campus radicals respond most strongly to immediate and morally unambiguous issues, such as Negro rights, free speech, etc., yet they also feel strongly that they are "alienated" from the prevalent norms and values of the society. Suspicious of older radicals, tending to dismiss (a little too casually, I think) the experience of the last forty years, properly hostile to what Orwell once called "smelly little orthodoxies," and sometimes a bit impatient with systematic thought, they cast about for a mode of sociocultural criticism which will express their strong ethical revulsion from the outrages, deceits, and vulgarities of our society. They react violently against the hypocrisies of "success" and worry about finding kinds of work and ways of life that seem to them authentic.

It is an encouraging development. One reason for the dullness of American political and intellectual life these past fifteen years has been the absence of a new generation of campus radicals who could stir things up a little. We have badly needed such young people—devoted, passionate, educated—who will not be content with "the given," but will set to work patiently to reconstruct American society along democratic lines. Now it appears that such a generation is beginning to make itself heard.

But the question must always arise in regard to student politics: how long, how deeply will this new generation persist? We are all familiar with the rhythm of a certain kind of campus radicalism. A sudden flare of political interest; a fury of activism, sometimes accompanied by premature ideological hardening and an impatience with those outside the campus who are regarded as insufficiently "revolutionary"; and then, often because the original commitment was not well thought out, a slide into disillusionment, leading to the frenetic weariness of careerism, or the cautions of official liberalism, or literary reflections on the tragic limitations of mankind. Now this is, of course, a caricature, but it is a caricature based on more than a little reality. And the question must inevitably arise whether the radicalism of the students at Berkeley and elsewhere rests upon serious thought or is the kind of one-shot affair which in the past has often paved the way for a later adjustment to the *status quo*.

The question cannot yet be answered, but it seems to me of great importance. For it leads us to a larger problem concerning the possibilities of new social and intellectual energy in our country. Previous social movements, like the CIO in the thirties, and even the Negro liberation movement of our own day, can largely be seen as drawing their strength from the justified grievances of particular classes and groups. Radical intellectuals hoped that expressions of working-class discontent would lead to a larger effort toward social change; those under the influence of Marxism spoke of the proletariat's "historical mission" and its "inherent revolutionary potential." Right now, it is hard to think in these terms. We find ourselves, instead, wondering whether some new impulse toward democratic radicalism might emerge in the United States which would rest not merely on the demands of oppressed classes and mistreated groups but also on a commonly apprehended need for a better society. That is, we wonder whether intelligent people, on various levels of the economic scale, can be drawn into a new politics based on their sense of responsibility, a vision of idealism, a wish to remake the world. If anything of the sort is ever to happen in the United States, it may well begin on the campus.

We can end only with questions. Will the energy of student rebellion be frittered away or will it grow into something stable, enduring, and reflective? It is so hard for young people to wrench themselves away from our sticky world of "success" that when now and again they do become radicals, they tend to think of their commitment mainly as an extreme posture—a rebellion against the middle class, a nose-thumbing at the world of their fathers—rather than an effort to initiate a serious politics. And sometimes this difficulty leads to an unearned impatience, or even contempt, for the procedures of democracy and an accompanying submission to the allure of charismatic leaders and authoritarian ideologies.

The student rebels will have to work their ideas out for themselves, and there is little reason why they should repeat the experience of an older generation, even that segment of an older generation which may have learned something from its experience. Yet it may be useful to stress what it is we believe we have learned: that for a radical (or any other) politics ever to make a deep and lasting impact upon American society, it must be rooted in democratic values and be committed to democratic procedures. Anything else would serve merely to illustrate Santayana's remark that those who refuse to learn from the mistakes of the past are doomed to repeat them.

Meanwhile, as at least a minority of American students begins to stir to a new consciousness and activity, we look on with hope and interest.

☼ THE VIETNAM PROTEST MOVEMENT

THIS statement was composed toward the very end of 1965, when the American involvement in Vietnam was being bitterly debated and the protest movement, while narrow in scope, had taken on a certain intensity, at least within the intellectual and academic worlds. I wrote as someone who supported the protest movement but was uneasy about some of its methods and allies.

A few of the topics discussed here (e.g., the draft-card burnings) have proven to be of momentary concern, but the larger political and intellectual issues seem to be of continuing relevance. For what was really at stake was the problem of the role and limits of social protest within a democratic society.

In its original appearance in *The New York Review of Books* and *New America*, the statement was also signed by several friends and political colleagues: Michael Harrington, Bayard Rustin, Lewis Coser, and Penn Kimble.

AS critics of the current United States policy in Vietnam, we wish to make some proposals and comments about the protest movement that is beginning to appear in this country. We believe that the debate concerning Vietnam is far from over, in fact, that it has just begun; and we think that the protest movement has an important role to play.

1.

Uneasiness about the war in Vietnam seems more widespread among the American people than the size of the recent protest demonstrations might suggest. That we have drifted into a full-scale Asian war which is likely to grow in magnitude; that this war requires for its prosecution bombings in South Vietnam that could devastate the entire country; that the Vietnamese government we are helping lacks both popular support and the moral legitimacy that might come from a commitment to democracy; that no matter what military "victories" are won here and there, the probable outcome of the fighting will be a stalemate, with the United States holding the coastal areas and cities and the Vietcong the rural interior—all this, and more, seems slowly to be filtering into the consciousness of a growing segment, though still a minority, of the population. If this supposition has any truth at all there is now a genuine opportunity for the movement that wishes to change United States policy in Vietnam—provided it resolves upon a set of proposals and a program of action which can gain the approval of more than the small band already committed to protest.

2.

The response of the Johnson administration to the recent protests has been disgraceful, a mixture of hysteria and foolishness. One might suppose from the cries of anguish coming out of Washington that the burning of a draft card by a young Catholic pacifist threatened the very foundations of the Republic. A nation tracing its origins to the Boston Tea Party ought not to become so jittery over the possibility of a few burned cards.

Nor should there be any question as to the legitimacy of protest against a policy that has never been seriously debated in Congress or candidly presented to the country. The Johnson administration seems incapable of distinguishing between consensus and unanimity; so eager is it for total support, it begins to approach the psychology of benevolent authoritarianism; and in regard to foreign policy it tends to replace public debate with invisible decree.

As for the argument that the recent demonstrations may persuade the Chinese and Vietnamese Communists to prolong the war because they might be misled into supposing the American people do not support the government's policy, this does not even merit serious discussion. It is the kind of demagogic appeal characteristically advanced by governments embarked upon adventures in which they do not have full confidence. We believe the Communists can count as well as anyone else and know precisely (quite apart from what they may write in their press) the strength or weakness of the Vietnam protest movement.

The price—but also, let it be stressed, the glory—of democracy is that minorities may use their freedom to dissent. If the war in Vietnam drags on month after month, inconclusive in outcome but devastating in consequence, there will continue to be dismay, doubt, and opposition among serious persons in this country. At the very least, the Johnson administration must accept this prospect as a fact of life; the only alternative is to unleash or tolerate a renewal of the poisonous atmosphere associated with the name of McCarthy. (And something of that atmosphere has already reappeared, in the proposals made, for example, by some draft boards that student critics of the Vietnam war be immediately drafted as a punitive or "educational" measure.) The Johnson administration might also remember something else: that if and when the moment comes to negotiate with the Communists in Southeast Asia—and unless we are to lapse into a state of permanent war that moment must come—the administration is certain to face a barrage of attacks from the far right. No matter what the terms of agreement might then be with the Asian Communists, whether favorable or harsh, the administration will be charged with "appeasement" and worse, by Republicans ready to make political capital out of national difficulties and rightists determined to talk this country beyond the brink. In such an eventuality, the administration will very much need the support of precisely those intellectual and academic critics under whose attack it now chafes. It would be useful here to recall that the student peace movement, at one point, picketed the White House in behalf of a ban on nuclear testing; not very long afterward, this proposal, which had been dismissed as "unrealistic," was realized in official government policy.

3.

Meanwhile the Vietnam protest movement—inchoate and without structure, but drawing upon deep sentiments of moral idealism—faces some serious decisions. There is a tendency, composed mainly of students but also drawing upon a few professors and nonacademic ideological advisors, to transform the protest into an apocalypse, a "final conflict," in which extreme gestures of opposition will bring forth punitive retaliation from the authorities. Such a policy, appealing to sectarian ultimatism and impatience, is certain to produce a great deal of publicity but not much public support or political impact. It would "prove," in the eyes of its supporters, various theses about the irrevocability of the reactionary course the United States has taken in foreign policy, the fascistic mentality of the "power elite," etc., etc. Such questionable theoretical satisfactions would not, however, compensate for a failure to affect the actual course of events.

We believe there is a possibility of building a significant protest movement against the current policy in Vietnam. Such a movement would require agreement upon a reasonable program of "demands" appropriate to the present situation; it would require an appeal to large numbers of people not yet involved in any protest actions, including some in labor, Negro, church, and academic communities who lend formal assent to the Johnson policy but might be persuaded to support *specific* proposals leading to a peaceful settlement in Vietnam. One prerequisite for such a movement is that it clearly indicate that its purpose is to end a cruel and futile war, not to give explicit or covert political support to the Vietcong. This is both a tactical necessity and a moral obligation, since any ambiguity on this score makes impossible, as well as undeserved, the support of large numbers of the American people.

The protest movement cannot be organized around a full-scale analysis of the Vietnam situation; its task is not to assign historical responsibility for the present disaster to one or another side, nor to undertake a study in depth of the Asian crisis. Such an analysis, bound to evoke many disagreements, cannot be the basis for common action; each participant, each group or individual who joins to protest the current policy of the Johnson administration can provide such analyses independently, apart from the immediate joint action. At the same time, it seems to us somewhat sterile and perhaps a little disingenuous to demonstrate under a slogan so vague and unfocused—e.g., the one employed in a recent New York parade, "Stop the War in Vietnam"—that it provides no guidelines for action and could even, for that matter, be formally accepted by those who approve of the current administration policy.

We would therefore suggest the following proposals as a basis for common action:

a) We urge the United States immediately to cease bombing North Vietnam.

b) We urge the United States to declare its readiness to negotiate with the National Liberation Front, the political arm of the Vietcong.

c) We urge the United States to propose to Hanoi and the Vietcong an immediate cease-fire as a preliminary to negotiations.

d) We urge that the United States recognize the right of the South Vietnamese freely to determine their own future, whatever it may be, without interference from foreign troops, and possibly under United Nations supervision.

e) We urge Hanoi and the Vietcong to accept a proposal for a cease-fire and to declare themselves ready for immediate and unconditional negotiations.

The advantage of this program, we believe, is that it points toward a line of action, somewhat like that advocated by Senator Fulbright, which could satisfy the central need of the moment: an end to the bloodletting. It allows people of widely varying opinions to work together for a common objective, even while maintaining the separate valuations of what has been happening in Asia. And it may enable the protest movement to win support for these objectives from people who have given reluctant or partial or merely token support to the Johnson policy.

4.

While we believe that civil disobedience is a legitimate, if ultimate, means of registering dissent and statements of conscience in a democratic society, we would urge that it be employed only after intense reflection and a full resort to other, more "normal" methods. Civil disobedience by its very nature, must in a democratic society be an exceptional measure; if employed as a routine tactic, it becomes self-defeating and destructive.

Analogies sometimes advanced with the civil rights struggle in the South are largely misleading. Civil rights demonstrators violated on occasion local ordinances which denied them their constitutional privileges, or deprived them of their right to public protest. In behalf of their legal rights as American citizens, they took what the local authorities declared to be "extralegal" measures but which were frequently upheld by the higher federal courts. And they acted in behalf of the legal norms and moral values to which the nation as a whole had given its approval.

The situation of the Vietnam protest movement is somewhat different. Thus far, it has by and large been able to express its dissent openly and publicly, through the usual channels open to members of a democratic society—and this fact would seriously call into question any effort to employ civil disobedience as a political tactic by an organized movement. We question the rightness, for example, of recent efforts to stop troop trains in California: they involve an action by a small minority to revoke through its own decision the policy of a democratically elected government—which is something very different indeed from public protest against that government's decision or efforts to pressure it into changes of policy. Tactically, it might be added, such attempts at "symbolic" interference with the war effort are self-defeating, since they merely result in a display of impotence and alienate people who might be persuaded to join in political protest against the Johnson policy. A "revolutionary" tactic in a decidedly nonrevolutionary situation is likely to do little more than increase the isolation of those who undertake it.

5.

Similar considerations apply to the recent flurry of publicity and proposals concerning the draft.

Those young people who say they intend to claim a refusal to serve in a war of which they disapprove must recognize their responsibilities to authentic conscientious objectors, that is, pacifists who refuse on principle to employ violence under any circumstances. Not many of the students said to be contemplating a refusal to serve in Vietnam fall in this category, and there is consequently a possibility that, especially if public hysteria arises on this matter, the present status of conscientious objectors, achieved only after long and hard struggles, will be endangered.

We respect the scruples of anyone who feels morally obliged to refuse to fight in Vietnam and therefore requests that he be accorded a special status as a noncombatant under the provisions of the draft. But we also believe that it is the responsibility of any organization urging such a course of action upon young people to inform them of the possible consequences. It is not quite clear whether such claims would be honored under the present provisions of the law concerning conscientious objection, and it is possible that young people making these claims—or refusing to submit to the draft entirely—would face the prospect of severe jail sentences. Nor is it clear to us that the groups said to be advocating such a course have seriously considered its possible effects on the Vietnam protest movement as a whole.

At the same time, we wish to say that the insinuations of cowardice made by certain Congressmen and newspapers against the student protesters are almost entirely without basis in fact. Some of these students have proved their courage under fire in Mississippi and Alabama, as volunteers in the civil rights struggle. They now declare themselves ready to undertake hazardous service abroad, provided it does not involve active participation in a war they regard as morally insupportable. A mature and imaginative government would, we think, proceed to take them at their word.

Most important, however, is the fact that there is a crucial difference, which should not be blurred, between individual moral objection and a political protest movement. It is one thing to say, "I cannot in conscience fight this war." It is quite another thing to advocate resistance to the draft or attempt to use its provisions for conscientious objection as a tactic of the protest movement. The latter course, we believe, could lead only to disaster, the reduction of what is potentially an expression of popular outrage to an heroic martyrdom by a tiny band of intellectual guerrillas. To allow the question of the draft to become the central focus of the Vietnam protest—something that both the right wing and sections of the press would relish, for all too obvious reasons—is to forgo in advance any possibility of affecting United States policy in the immediate future.

We believe that the present United States policy in Vietnam is morally and politically disastrous. We wish to see a movement of increasing scope appear in the United States which will press for a change in this policy. And we are convinced that toward this end it is necessary to employ every channel of democratic pressure and persuasion.

☼ UNIVERSITIES AND INTELLECTUALS

HOW could it happen that a radical writing about the role of the university in modern society should find himself expressing somewhat—or what might appear to be—"conservative" views? This was the question that, to my surprise and amusement, I had to ask myself while writing the following essay for a special issue of *Dissent* on the American academy.

The question itself is answered, as well as I can answer it, in the essay: a part of our hope for the good, or at least a better, society lies in conserving what the university stands for, and the society in which we live tends to diminish and degrade the idea of the university.

In the twelve or so years since becoming a college teacher, I have come to regard the profession of teaching with seriousness and, now and again, affection. In the style customary among professors, I complain about teaching loads, academic bureaucracy, drab colleagues, and uninspired students. But I know that in a mass society all too ready to exploit the skills of intellectuals, teaching is one of the few ways we can earn a living while preserving a reasonable portion of our integrity and doing significant work.

Teaching can be enervating, disheartening, spiritually deadening; but inherently, or at least potentially, it is *good* work. It is work that needs to be done; it is work that would need still more to be done if the world we lived in were better than it is. Teaching allows one intellectual freedom—not once during my years as a professor at Brandeis, Stanford, and The City University of New York have I encountered the slightest effort to restrict my freedom in or out of the classroom. Teaching involves one with materials of beauty, ideas of importance, the masterpieces of literature, the scientific tradition, the passions of history. And sometimes teaching even yields the pleasure of stirring a young mind to knowledge and thought.

So it was that when I came to write about the role of the university in modern society, I was caught in a tension between my activist and contemplative selves, between my belief that serious men must be involved in the political struggles of their day and my belief that the university—even while allowing the widest range of opinions the freedom to be heard and its students the right to act upon their political convictions—should serve as a center of intellectual detachment, a place devoted to scholarship and disinterested thought. Both the managers of our multiversities and some of the students who rebel against them hold to other views: the managers would like the university to serve as a smooth adjunct to a bureaucratic society, the rebellious students would like to turn the university upside down and make it into a kind of training school for insurgency.

Is it possible, however, for an American university to be a place where the life of the mind can flourish without any need for "practical" justifications and to accept as part of its milieu the turmoil of protest, the anger of the idealistic young? Why not? This is not an easy goal to achieve, and there are many institutional pressures that militate against it; but then nothing worth striving for is easy to achieve.

And for the radical who wishes to see a new and better world: of what can that world be made if not—together with the work of the future—the conserved heritage of the past?

Schools reflect a culture; they do not transform it.
—Unsigned review, *The New Yorker,* November 16, 1963.

A university should not be a weather vane, responsive to every variation of popular whim. Universities must at times give society, not what society wants, but what it needs.
—Abraham Flexner, *Universities: American, British, German.*

THERE could not be a sharper contrast. The American consensus is echoed by *The New Yorker,* which even if it does not wholly approve of the society that exists, speaks nevertheless with the spirit of those who "maintain themselves by the common routine, learn to avoid expectation." And the voice of intellect comes from Abraham Flexner, historian of American education.

To suppose that many American educators strongly disagree with *The New Yorker* would be an indulgence of optimism. What the magazine says can be found, spread more thinly, in *The Uses of the University,* a recent book by Clark Kerr, president of the University of California, the largest in the country. Mr. Kerr is a decent man, and one would rather serve under him than many another college president. But in his plea for the "multiversity" (which Flexner had years ago described as a mere "service station"), Mr. Kerr makes it clear that, whatever he may know about its uses, the *idea* of a university has faded from his mind, as it has faded from all too many academic minds. He speaks now as the agent of a prevailing drift:

> The university has become a prime instrument of national purpose. . . . This is the essence of the transformation now engulfing our universities. Basic to this transformation is the growth of the "knowledge industry," which is coming to permeate government and business. . . . What the railroads did for the second half of the 19th century and the automobile for the first half of this century, the knowledge industry may do for the second half of this century: that is, to serve as the focal point for national growth. And the university is at the center of the knowledge process.

There is the voice of dominant America: knowledge as industry. And its style too: "The knowledge process." How old-fashioned, by contrast, is the opinion of Cardinal Newman that "knowledge is capable of being its own end," and how characteristically utopian of Lewis Mumford to write:

> As the cloister of the monastery might be termed a passive university, so the university might be called an active cloister: [its function is] the critical reappraisal and renewal of the cultural heritage.

2.

A few decades ago it all seemed very different. Not many writers, certainly not many liberal or leftist writers, would have presented the problem of education through the contrast I have made here. We were unhappy over the refusal of most American professors to become passionately involved with the trials of American life; we mocked the sterility, the illusion of protective distance, that characterized the work and thought of many academics.

And we had our reasons. The failure of many German

professors to resist Hitlerism had left a taste of bitterness. Mencken's academic-baiting, often vulgar yet now and again justified, remained a strong memory. In the distraught society of the thirties and forties, it seemed unworthy of a thinking man to content himself with the pose of academic detachment. And for some years now the progressive educators had been teaching us that school and society were interdependent; that the young should learn, in part, through an immersion in common experience; that the scholar who cares about the life of the mind must also take responsibility for the democratic renovation of society. I remember the pleasure with which I came upon a study of school and society by George S. Counts, a disciple of John Dewey: here, it seemed, was an educator who spoke to the urgencies of our time. Reading him once again, I think he still does:

> . . . the purpose of public education in the present epoch of American history . . . is to prepare the younger generation for labor and sacrifice in building a democratic civilization and culture on the foundations of a collective economy. This means in very considerable measure the abandonment of ideals that have dominated the schools for generations. . . . Education is still regarded primarily as a road to special privilege and personal aggrandizement. . . .
>
> The aim of public education now should be, not to elevate A above B or to lift gifted individuals out of the class into which they were born . . . but rather to abolish all artificial social distinctions and to organize the energies of the nation for improving the condition of all. (*The Social Foundations of Education,* 1934)

A little naïve? Professor Counts had not yet been taught by *The New Yorker* that "schools reflect a culture; they do not transform it." A bit one-sided? Professor Counts was not yet worried—at that time no one was—about the "knowledge industry" and its capacity for mangling human thought.

But if we take such writings to be insufficient, it would be sheer impudence to claim that they no longer matter. Inertia is fundamental to social and intellectual life: the majority of professors in the sixties, though somewhat better paid, are not very different in outlook from what they were in the thirties. Parochialism, timidity, snobbishness, indifference to human suffering, a feeble-spirited "professionalism," thin-blooded gentility—these persist in the academic world, and you need only wander away from the handful of universities that are true centers of learning in order to find all the symptoms that once led intellectuals to use "academic" as a term of derision. Sluggishness of mind and spirit remain: and if for no other reason, the prescriptive writings of men like Dewey and Counts are as vital today as they were thirty years ago.

Yet it would be disingenuous to deny that their call for social involvement, stirring as it may still be, seems far from adequate in the sixties. Today there are new troubles, new problems. When Dewey and Counts began to write, they were responding to America primarily as a class society; now we need, in addition, a sense of America as a mass society. Neither category, "class" or "mass," is wholly adequate for understanding the world in which we live; both must be used, alternatively and together, often in conflict and sometimes in contradiction.

3.

Language is deceptive, and most of all when it points toward new phenomena that cannot yet be described with precision. The word "mass" is used in sharply different ways, so that it becomes quite possible to say, as I would, that one believes in "mass education" and is hostile to "mass culture," for in the first case "mass" serves as a more-or-less neutral descriptive while in the second it tends to be a term of deprecation.

By "mass education" we have in mind an historically new

situation in which it is commonly assumed that all members of society have a right to receive as much education as they wish to or can absorb; we may also be pointing to what follows from this assumption, namely, the problems inherent in the effort to give a growing segment of the population at least some kind of college education. The term "mass culture," as usually employed, signifies not merely a description but also an implicit judgment of the mass-manufacture of synthetic pseudo-cultural products in journalism, books, television, movies, etc. This difference in usage is awkward, but it exists and must be acknowledged.

"Mass education" is here to stay, historically irreversible. Only a small number of reactionaries oppose it on principled grounds, though an alarming number of liberals, their liberalism increasingly diluted, begin to conclude that "mass education" must fatally corrupt educational standards. (There are also the harrumphing Old Humanists in the universities who wring their hands over the invasion of plebeian hordes; such people are mainly tiresome.)

Whether more American boys and girls will go to college each year is no longer a question. The question is, what will happen to them once they arrive. For "mass education" is one of the more significant democratic experiments of our time: an experiment barely begun, and under circumstances that work heavily against its realization. Our society has stumbled into the possibilities of "mass education"—perhaps more accurately, it has been forced to confront these possibilities because of military and technological pressures. But it has not yet appropriated a small fraction of the talent, energy and resources needed to make "mass education" a success. Whether *this* society can do that, is an open question; perhaps here, as in other areas of social life, we shall have to suffer the results of an uncompleted revolution.

Suppose, however, that the circumstances for introducing "mass education" were to be very favorable. Suppose the country were to throw itself heart and soul into the work of serious education. In the short run, this would lead to severe social difficulties: for work begun at the college or precollege level could not take hold with sufficient depth and urgency unless there were corresponding changes in the immediate environment. (It is all very well, for example, to propose special tutoring for Negro children in order to prepare them for academic advancement, but such measures cannot remove the handicaps of these children as long as they live in rat-infested Harlem tenements, their fathers work at substandard wages, and the fumes of discrimination poison their very being.)

Still: let us agree to imagine favorable circumstances for "mass education." Even then we would soon have to confront new kinds of difficulties, perhaps resisting immediate solution. For we would be trying to cope with the heritage of centuries of neglect, we would have to break through those thick deposits of inertia and resistance which have settled onto the consciousness of millions of people. Even to begin to do this would be highly meaningful work, for we would be facing authentic problems, not the pseudo problems thrown up by weaponry and advertising. We would be trying to fulfill the democratic revolution of the past 150 years, which for the first time in history stirred the masses into the possibility of consciousness.

The difficulties, I repeat, would be staggering. Consider, for example, the recent expansion of our colleges and the consequent appointment as professors of men who lack the necessary training and more important, the spirit of austerity and devotion which, at least occasionally, ought to characterize the scholar and the intellectual. I do not wish to be misunderstood: I would quite agree that thousands of college teachers are decent human beings trying to do a decent job. But perhaps that is just the trouble. Fifty or sixty years ago, when the American university had a relatively well-defined role as the cultural training ground for the country's upper strata, a decently mediocre professor was not likely to do much damage. As a carrier of the received culture, he might even do some good. Today, in an atmosphere of fevered expansion, lucrative busywork and harsh uncertainty as to what a university should be, the decently mediocre professor tends all too often to be a disaster. In the past, tradition could carry him; now he must float, or sink, on his own. He is a disaster because he cannot cope with the staggering task of convincing thousands of ill-prepared and poorly motivated students that, quite apart from utilitarian or national ends, there is a value to the life of the mind. And he cannot persuade his students that there is such a value because, more often than not, he does not know what the life of the mind is.

Inevitably, then, "mass education" brings with it severe and unprecedented problems. But the truth is that the turn to "mass education" has not occurred under favorable circumstances, has not been planned or thought through, and is frequently the result of drift, panic, and national egotism. Coming in a society characterized by misshapen values and economic injustice, racial prejudice and political evasiveness, "mass education" is contaminated from the very moment of its birth. To make high claims for the life of the mind in a world devoted to accumulating money and bombs is either to indulge in a pious hypocrisy or to indicate to one's students that if they are to become serious intellectuals they must be ready to accept a measure of estrangement, perhaps even deprivation.

But more. Just as the tragedy of the Negro freedom movement is that it reaches its climax at the moment automation is undercutting the Negroes' economic possibilities, so the tragedy of "mass education" is that it appears at the very moment "mass culture" is seeping into the American universities. Ideally, the university ought to be a bastion of resistance against "mass culture." Some universities are. The dominant trend, however, is toward allowing the university to become, among other things, a depository of "mass culture"—and less through deliberate intent than mild slothfulness. For if a certain lowering of standards *is* unavoidable when the number of students entering college is sharply increased, this is not nearly so great a threat to our intellectual health as is the lax acceptance by all too many administrations and faculties of the happy spirit of American hucksterdom.

That I am describing a reality I shall not stop to document: the readers of this book may be supposed to know something about such matters. I would only say, and without aspiration toward paradox, that a crucial piece of evidence is that many American professors show but the faintest awareness that "mass culture" represents a deep and insidious threat to the life they have chosen to live. All too many of them would fear that an intransigent opposition to "mass culture" marks them as "undemocratic," or snobbishly "intellectual."

The university, wrote Cardinal Newman, is "the high protecting power of all knowledge . . . it maps out the territory of the intellect, and sees that . . . there is *neither encroachment nor surrender on any side*" (emphasis added). Yet it is in the very nature of "mass culture" that it cheerfully and insidiously encroach upon the territory of intellect. The vocabulary of academic statesmanship—the university should be "pluralist" in outlook, "moderate" in tone, "responsible" to the community, "alert" to the national interest—helps to blend the university into the surrounding social landscape and thereby to rob it of its reason for existence. Fortunately there are also strong counterpressures, but insofar as this drift prevails the university becomes a place of mediocre efficiency, a busy middleman of culture, a training school for the professions, a center of usable research: indeed, almost anything but the *active cloister* of which Mumford speaks. For how can you expect people to defend the territory of intellect when they see no threat from beyond its borders?

*

4.

Enter now the intellectuals, perhaps through the back door.

A growing number of intellectuals have found shelter in the universities. Whether this is good or bad for them, the universities and society, I shall not here discuss. What matters is that more and more intellectuals spend their lives as professors and in the coming decades will surely continue to do so. Apart from a reasonably conscientious performance of duties, what are they to do with themselves in the universities?

Primarily, they are to remain what they were. Camus has described the intellectual as "someone whose mind watches itself." The value such a person has for the university depends largely on his insistence that he remain the ill-adjusted creature he previously was—quite as the value the university has for society depends upon the degree to which it resists a cozy adjustment to the prevalent norms. At evident cost and probable gain, the intellectual must continue to "watch his mind" even as his students watch it with him. And this is hard, for somehow the intellectual must maintain his spontaneity of work while in part allowing it to become a visible public act.

Intellectuals begin to cluster in the universities at the very time that students experience a profound sense of doubt as to the relevance of intellectual concerns. Every agency of our society keeps hammering at the students to tell them what in fact they already know: that there is practical advantage in getting a college education. But the more our students become convinced of the utility of a college education, the more problematic does the value of its intellectual content seem to them.

Why this should be so is an enormously complex problem, and here I shall confine myself to a single speculation:

The society we live in, especially to the extent that it really conforms to the model of a "mass society," tacitly persuades its young that the past no longer matters. It has always been true, but is now far more true than ever, that for Americans the past is not very real, the past is caught up with the blood and ideology of Europe in a way that they feel they no longer need be. Yet the past, as it happens, is that which we know, the substance of knowledge, the matter upon which the life of the mind subsists.

Now it is possible that these new assumptions about the past will prove to be correct and the United States will become a country that can indeed discard the pain and tragedy, the sheer historical accumulation, of the past. If so, people like ourselves, I who write and you who read, will become obsolete. But until that happens, we must struggle with all our wit and might against these assumptions about the past.

(I lecture to a class at Stanford, a class of bright-cheeked, goodhearted innocents: "Tell me now, apart from grades, politeness, and caution: do the questions raised by Ivan Karamazov in his talks with Alyosha seem to you deeply, burningly relevant to the life you expect to lead when you get back to your offices and suburbs in California?" Not many can honestly say Yes. The dull students say No with ease; the bright ones No with disturbance. "But then," I continue, "it means that the past exists for you as something confined to the classroom, an exercise (at best) in piety. I, your odd professor from the east, nevertheless have the impudence to say: I will try to persuade, bludgeon, excite, and coax you into believing that Ivan Karamazov's words are burningly important to your life. That is an assumption, you reply, which threatens the whole way of life you have chosen for yourselves . . . My dears, you are right.")

The central task of the intellectual in the American university is to validate the past, to insist upon its organic relationship with the present, to deny that America is exempt from history.

A piece of arrogance? Are not the universities full of scholars who live in the past and know far more about it than most intellectuals? Yes; but the struggle for the *idea* of the past can be conducted with some hope of success only by those intimately related to the crises of the present: which by definition, so to say, the intellectual is and the scholar, insofar as he remains simply a scholar, is not. For the scholar there can be no question as to the reality of the past, since that is the substance of his being and it is good that it should be. But unless (to have, improbably, the best of all possible worlds) the scholar is also an intellectual, he does not often or sufficiently grasp why in our day there should be so much difficulty in validating the reality of the past. So, without meaning either praise or disrespect to either party, I would assert that while scholarship remains the property and honor of the scholars, it is the intellectual who is particularly obligated and in the best position to teach the young the beauty of scholarship. The teacher unaware at every moment (he need not talk about it at every moment) of those forces of antihistorical dispersion and anti-intellectual technicism besetting the minds of his students, is a teacher who has lost the battle of the classroom before it has begun.*

In American society, which has lost a good part of whatever historical sense it had, the intellectual must take upon himself a conserving task. It is an unfamiliar role for the intellectual who has usually been a liberal or radical concerned primarily with the idea of the future. Well, perhaps it is a paradox; but being a radical in politics enforces a certain conservatism in regard to education. And this conservatism is now necessary not merely for the reasons I have suggested, but because in our rigidly "moderate" society the

* A friend, reading this essay, makes the observation that it is not only the sense of history which can serve to challenge the constricting "presentness" of American students: it may also be a timeless philosophical system or set of problems. True; except that with the kind of students we are here discussing such an interest is likely to manifest itself in historical terms.

idea of the future to which we radicals are pledged cannot survive unless there also survives a living sense of the past. I quote a passage from H. Stuart Hughes discussing the work of Karl Mannheim:

It is impossible to read today Mannheim's strictures on the "barrenness" of a society "absorbed by its interest in concrete and isolated details" . . . without applying them to the present situation in the United States. For his own generation, Mannheim implied, so "prosaic" an attitude was impossible. "It would require," he wrote, "either a callousness which our generation could probably no longer acquire or the unsuspecting naïveté of a generation newly born into the world to be able to live in absolute congruence with the realities of that world, utterly without any transcendent element."

That "transcendent element," one of the great privileges and conquests of the life of the mind, can in our day survive only through a living sense of the past.

5.

Such elevated sentiments, such noble rhetoric! Hadn't we better return to reality, the reality of the classroom and a girl named Clotilda Adams?

Clotilda Adams was a student a few years ago at Wayne State University, the city college in Detroit, when the writer Herbert Gold taught a course there in the Humanities ("The History of Everything in Culture"). He found it something of a trauma: "The encounter with classroom reality has caused many teachers, like Abelard meeting the relatives of Eloise, to lose their bearings." As Gold tried to introduce a few notions about the moral problems that have plagued humanity since Socrates—Humanities 610 was not, you might say, an *intensive* course—Clotilda Adams sat there, impervious and recalcitrant, the classics bouncing off her mind like rubber balls off a fence. "The Humanities," wrote Clotilda in her final exam, "are a necessary additive to any teacher's development worth her 'salt' in the perilous times of today. The West and the 'Free World' must stand up to the war of ideas against the 'Iron Curtain.' " This was in answer to a question about Beethoven, Goethe, and German romanticism. Clotilda did not pass the course but, adds Gold, she was "admitted on probation to the student teacher program because of the teacher shortage and the great need to educate our children in these perilous times."

A sobering, a disheartening reality. Still, I believe that if Abelard really loves Eloise he will marry her, relatives or no relatives.

PART II *On the Other Side*

☼ LEON TROTSKY: THE COSTS OF HISTORY

IN 1963 I edited a volume of Leon Trotsky's selected writings, for which the following essay served as an introduction. My intention was to provide an encompassing view of Trotsky's political and literary career, rather than a close argument about any of his opinions or actions.

All that need be added by way of background is that there was a brief time, during the late thirties and early forties, when Trotsky, both as a political theorist and historical personality, made a very strong impression upon left-wing intellectuals and socialists in America. He seemed an embodiment of past grandeur, a voice of corrosive honesty attacking the terror and corruption of Stalinism, a thinker in the great Marxist tradition, a revolutionist of exemplary fearlessness. The political atmosphere changed, during and after the war, and few American intellectuals could continue to think of themselves as Trotskyists, even when they wished to remain radicals. Still, the earlier admiration for his courage and style remained, and though my essay was written from the political perspective I had reached in the sixties, something of that earlier feeling must surely have found its way into what I wrote.

HAS any major figure of the twentieth century left so complete a record of his thought and experience as Leon Trotsky? Perhaps Churchill, perhaps De Gaulle; but neither of these men combined so fully or remarkably as did Trotsky the roles of historical actor and historian, political leader and theorist, charismatic orator and isolated critic. Trotsky made history, and kept an eye on history. He was a man of heroic mold, entirely committed to the life of action, but he was also an intellectual who believed in the power and purity of the word. At no point in his career, whether as a revolutionary émigré or commander of revolutionary armies, did Trotsky allow his public activities or personal condition to keep him long from his desk. "In my eyes," he once wrote, "authors, journalists and artists always stood for a world that was more attractive than any other, a world open only to the elect."

An exile in Siberia, he wrote about the 1905 Russian Revolution, the great Russian novelists of the nineteenth century, the rise of the Freemasons. An exile in Europe, he wrote about the controversies of European Marxism, the special problems of Russian society, and his own theory of "permanent revolution." A leader of the Bolshevik regime, he wrote about military affairs, literary disputes, the economics of statification, manners and morals in a proletarian state, the rise of the Stalinist bureaucracy. An exile in Turkey, France, Norway, and finally Mexico, he wrote his monumental history of the Russian Revolution, his political autobiography, studies of Lenin and Stalin, and a stream of books, pamphlets, articles on the Chinese revolution of the late twenties, the tactics of the German left confronting Hitler, the anatomy of the new despotism in Russia, the failure of the Popular Front in Europe, problems of political morality, the need for Marxist reconstruction. And in 1940, when an agent of the Russian GPU drove an ax into Trotsky's skull, the murderer gained access to his victim's study on the pretext of discussing an article.

With full, almost naïve conviction Trotsky believed in the creative possibilities of the word. But he believed not as most Western intellectuals have: not in some ironic or contemplative or symbolic way. The common distinction between word and deed Trotsky scorned as a sign of philistinism, worthy—he might have added—of liberal professors and literary dilettantes. He regarded his outpouring of brilliant composition as the natural privilege of a thinking man, but more urgently, as the necessary work of a Marxist leader who had pledged his life to socialism. The heritage of the Russian writers of the nineteenth century is stamped upon his books, for he took from them the assumption that to write is to engage in a serious political act, a gesture toward the redemption or re-creation of man.

Lev Davidovich Bronstein—only as a young revolutionist did he adopt the name of Trotsky—was born in 1879, the son of Jewish farmers living near the Black Sea. The life of the Bronsteins was somewhat unusual for Russian Jews: they worked a large farm instead of trading in cramped ghetto villages, they became well-to-do kulaks who could mistreat peasants as readily as gentile landowners did, and they showed little feeling for the religious pieties that still gripped most Jews in eastern Europe.

Growing up in the Bronstein household, young Lev Davidovich could observe something of that endless misery which had been the traditional lot of the Russian peasant; it disturbed the boy, and by the time he was sent off to school in Odessa he was already a rebel of sorts. He participated in a demonstration against an unpopular teacher and was suspended from the school for a year: the kind of incident which in a free society need not have serious repercussions but which in Czarist Russia would contribute heavily to the formation of character. For in a closed authoritarian society all behavior has political implications, and even the most innocent gesture can take on a rebellious cast. Whatever the case, young Bronstein returned to school with a heightened sense of his powers. Years later, in his autobiography, he would write:

> Such was my first political test, as it were. The class was henceforth divided into two distinct groups: the talebearers and envious on one side, the frank and courageous boys on the other, and the neutral and vacillating mass in the middle. These three groups never quite disappeared even in later years.

The passage is typical of the mature Trotsky. In his conscious thought he insisted, as a Marxist, that moral criteria were determined by social relations, or at least were crucially dependent upon them; but in part of himself he held fast to traditional valuations of character and responded strongly to such "supraclass" sentiments as honor, courage, and frankness.

A gifted student, especially in mathematics, young Bronstein was sent in 1896 to the town of Nikolayev to complete his education. It was here, in a provincial city first acquiring both modern industry and a proletariat, that he encountered the socialist ideas which had begun to filter into Czarist Russia. In the hut of a poor gardener, a group of students and workers met to discuss radical theories, and soon Bronstein's was a leading voice among them, first as a sentimental partisan of Russian populism who declared himself an enemy of "Marxist dryness," and then as a spokesman for the more rigorous concepts of Marxism, to which he was converted by a lively young woman who would soon become his first wife and always remain a political colleague. At the age of eighteen, in the tradition of sacrifice that had been established by the Russian radicals of the nineteenth century, Lev Davidovich Bronstein chose the life of a professional revolutionary. What such a life could mean has been eloquently described by Edmund Wilson in his book *To the Finland Station:*

> Whoever has known the Russian revolutionaries of these pre-war generations at their best has been impressed by the effectiveness of the Czarist regime as a training school for intellect and character in those who were engaged in opposing it. Forced to pledge for their conviction their careers and their lives, brought by the movement into contact with all classes of people, driven to settle in foreign countries whose languages they readily mastered . . . —these men and women combine an unusual range of culture with an unusual range of social experience and, stripped of so many of the trimmings with which human beings have swathed themselves, have, in surviving, kept the sense of those things that are vital to the honor of human life.

In the spring of 1897 Bronstein and his friends organized a clandestine group, the South Russian Workers' Union, which held political discussions and issued leaflets about conditions in local factories; the writing and hectographing, at the rate of two hours a page, were done by Bronstein himself. Inevitably the police closed in, and early the next year most of the members of this embryonic radical movement were arrested; some were subjected to flogging and Bronstein was kept for several months in lice-ridden solitary confinement. Next he was transferred to an Odessa prison, where he remained a year and a half, and then sentenced to four years in Siberia. The young revolutionist now found himself settled along the Lena River, above the Arctic Circle, where, as he later wrote, life was "dark and repressed, utterly remote from the world." But meanwhile he had been studying the Marxist classics, and in Siberia he saw copies of the Social Democratic paper *Iskra* and Lenin's pamphlet *What Is to Be Done?* in which the future leader of Bolshevism argued that only by creating a highly disciplined party staffed by full-time revolutionists could the Russian Social Democracy survive the persecution of the Czarist police.

In exile Bronstein felt himself sufficiently self-assured as a publicist to write essays on a range of literary figures— Ibsen, Zola, Gogol among them— and to enter the discussion as to future politics and organizational structure that was occupying the Russian Social Democrats. Most of the important Russian Marxists were then living as exiles in western Europe, debating their political course in relation to the seemingly invincible monolith of Czarism and preparing to establish an organization that might ensure tighter relations between themselves and the scattered illegal groups in Russia. Eager to meet and learn from such Marxist leaders as Plekhanov, Martov, and Lenin, young Bronstein escaped from Siberia in the fall of 1902, made his way secretly across Russia and, taking the pseudonym by which the world would come to know him, managed to smuggle himself across the frontier.

Once in Europe, Trotsky immediately threw himself into the political life of the Russian émigrés. In London he met Lenin for the first time, and the two men took long walks through the streets of the alien city, exchanging political ideas and impressions as to the underground in Russia. Trotsky began to write articles for *Iskra* distinguished by revolutionary enthusiasm, but florid and immature in style; the hard aphoristic brilliance of his later prose would come only from an accumulation of experience and a conscious self-discipline.

By all accounts he made a powerful impression on the leaders of Russian Marxism. Marvelously young, alive with eagerness and zeal, bristling with unformed talents, intellectually quick and receptive, somewhat imperious in manner and abrupt in personal relations but still reverent toward the men and women he regarded as the great names of the Russian revolutionary movement, Trotsky seemed to his new friends an incarnation of that political *élan* they hoped would spark and revive their movement. Vera Zasulich, veteran of the underground, felt him to be "undoubtedly a genius." Julius Martov, future leader of Menshevism and himself a gifted man, wrote that Trotsky's literary works "reveal indubitable talent . . . and already he wields great influence here thanks to his uncommon oratorical gifts. He speaks magnificently. Of this both I and Vladimir Ilyich [Lenin] have had sufficient proof. He possesses knowledge and works hard to increase it."

By the time the Russian Social Democratic Party held its Second Congress in 1903, Trotsky, though still in his early twenties, was a figure of some importance. He refused to align himself completely with either of the factions that were hardening into shape, the Bolsheviks led by Lenin and the Mensheviks led by Martov. This division can now be seen as a partial anticipation of the great split that would come during the First World War between revolutionists and reformists within the socialist movement, but at the time the issues were still murky, and Trotsky, disinclined in his earlier years to tie himself to a party apparatus, sided now with one group and now with the other. At stake, apparently, was a bit of phrasing as to who could be considered a member of the party: someone who "personally participates in one of its organizations" (Lenin), or someone prepared to "co-operate personally and regularly under the guidance of one of the organizations" (Martov). Scholastic as this difference might seem—two years later the Mensheviks virtually took over Lenin's phrasing—it was nevertheless a sign of divergences in political outlook that went deeper than the participants could yet grasp.

Immediately after the Congress, Trotsky sided with the Mensheviks, composing vitriolic attacks on what he regarded as Lenin's dictatorial and "Jacobin" views concerning party organization. In a pamphlet he wrote denouncing Lenin there appeared a sentence that has since been quoted many times as a prophetic anticipation, ignored by the later Trotsky himself, of the decline of the Russian Revolution:

*

Lenin's methods lead to this: the party organization at first substitutes itself for the party as a whole; then the Central Committee substitutes itself for the organization; and finally a single "dictator" substitutes himself for the Central Committee.

The remark is striking for its anticipation of the ways in which the highly centralized structure of the Bolshevik party would encourage an authoritarian psychology among the leaders and intellectual dependence among the followers. As a sociological insight, it remains valuable for the study of modern politics and political organization. Yet it is hardly as prescient as some historians have supposed, and it certainly is not sufficient evidence for the claim that in his youth Trotsky grasped the causes of the degeneration of the Russian Revolution in a way that the older Trotsky, even after his downfall, refused to acknowledge. Though anticipating the debacle of the Bolshevik party in the era of Stalinist totalitarianism, Trotsky's remark does not—nor could it—touch upon the complex of causes behind that degeneration. Any effort to explain a major historical phenomenon (like the rise of Stalinism) by the workings of an exclusive cause (like Bolshevik centralization) is doomed to be superficial, and the later Trotsky was right in rejecting such a mode of explanation.

Though siding with the Mensheviks on party organization, Trotsky began, in the early years of the century, to express views on another fundamental problem—the relationship in the coming Russian Revolution between the socialists and the liberal bourgeois parties—which brought him closer to Lenin. Since, as all Russian Marxists agreed, the first task was to overthrow the Czar and establish democratic rights, the Mensheviks argued that the liberal bourgeoisie would have to take the lead and the working class serve as a loyal opposition. Trotsky, by contrast, insisted that the socialists should keep a clear distance from the bourgeois parties and not compromise with liberalism.

These discussions, apparently so academic, soon involved the destinies of millions. For a moment, however, they were happily put aside when the Russian people, long voiceless and dormant, began in 1905 to stir against the Czarist regime. In St. Petersburg a demonstration led by an Orthodox priest called for democratic rights; the Czar ordered his troops to fire into the crowd. From Geneva, Trotsky wrote in a state of high excitement:

> One day of revolution was enough, one magnificent contact between the Czar and the people was enough for the idea of constitutional monarchy to become fantastic, doctrinaire, and disgusting. The priest Gapon rose with his idea of the monarch against the real monarch. But, as behind him there stood not monarchist liberals but revolutionary proletarians, this limited "insurrection" immediately manifested its rebellious content in barricade fighting and in the outcry: Down with the Czar. The real monarch has destroyed the idea of the monarch. . . . The revolution has come and she has put an end to our political childhood.

Throughout the year 1905 Russia was in a turmoil of rebellion. Strikes closed the factories, street demonstrations broke out in the cities, the crew of the warship *Potemkin* revolted. One of the first exiles to return to St. Petersburg, Trotsky for a time lived a political life that was half-public, half-clandestine. Belonging to neither the Menshevik nor Bolshevik faction, but contributing frequently to the press of both and acting with a boldness neither could match, Trotsky became the popular tribune of the revolutionary left. In October there met in the capital the Soviet of Workers' Delegates, a kind of rump parliament of representatives from the unions, left parties, and popular organizations, in which Trotsky rose to the post of chairman. Unlike the Bolsheviks, who until Lenin's arrival in November were skeptical about the Soviet because of fear it would threaten their political identity, Trotsky grasped the enormous revolutionary potential of this new and spontaneous organ of political action. His personal fearlessness, his combination of firm political ends with tactical ingenuity, and his incomparable gifts as an orator helped transform him, at twenty-six, into a leader of the first rank: he had entered upon the stage of modern history and only the ax of a murderer would remove him. Here is a passage from one of his speeches before the Soviet, a characteristic flare of virtuosity, in which he tells about a conversation with a liberal who had urged him to moderation:

I recalled to him an incident from the French Revolution, when the Convention voted that "the French people will not parley with the enemy on their own territory." One of the members of the Convention interrupted: "Have you signed a pact with victory?" They answered him: "No, we have signed a pact with death." Comrades, when the liberal bourgeoisie, as if boasting of its treachery, tells us: "You are alone. Do you think you can go on fighting without us? Have you signed a pact with victory?" we throw our answer in their face: "No, we have signed a pact with death."

In the fifty days of its existence the Soviet experienced the dilemma so frequently faced by revolutionary institutions: it was strong enough to frighten the government but not strong enough to overthrow it. Czarism regained the initiative, for it was not yet as fully discredited as it would be in 1917 and the revolutionary movements were still unripe and inexperienced. In the repressions that followed, thousands were killed and imprisoned; reaction once again held Russia. Together with the other leaders of the Soviet, Trotsky faced public trial, at the climax of which—for now he stood firm in the sense of his powers, secure in the knowledge that he had established himself in the line of the great European rebels—he made a brilliant, openly defiant speech:

A rising of the masses is not made, gentlemen the judges. It makes itself of its own accord. It is the result of social relations and conditions and not of a scheme drawn up on paper. A popular insurrection cannot be staged. It can only be foreseen. For reasons that were as little dependent on us as on Czardom, an open conflict has become inevitable. . . .

*

. . . no matter how important weapons may be, it is not in them, gentlemen the judges, that great power resides. No! Not the ability of the masses to kill others, but their great readiness themselves to die, this secures in the last instance the victory of the popular uprising. . . .

Again Siberia: this time deportation "for life." But it was a saving feature of pretotalitarian despotisms that they were often inefficient, so that even before reaching his Arctic destination Trotsky could make a superbly bold escape, being driven by a vodka-besotted peasant for a whole week across the frozen tundra and through ferocious blizzards. For the young Marxist who only a few months earlier had been sentenced to Siberia "for life," the escape was a personal triumph: in retrospect one might say, a personal triumph with historic portents. But now that he was safe again in Europe, Trotsky turned back to his pen, composing his first major work, *1905*, an historical study that in scope and vigor anticipates the *History of the Russian Revolution.*

These were hard times for the Russian revolutionists. The Czar took a merciless revenge as he cut away almost every vestige of popular rights. In Russia the socialist movements came close to collapse from police harassment and inner demoralization, while in exile they kept fragmenting into embittered factions. Trotsky continued vainly to urge that the Bolsheviks and Mensheviks reunite: perhaps he did not fully grasp the extent of their disagreements, perhaps he feared what the consequence of grasping it might be. Wandering from country to country, often after being expelled by the police, and earning a bare living through political journalism, he found himself in New York during the war years, and there he wrote for a radical Russian paper, until word of the March 1917 Revolution brought him rushing back to his homeland. During the years between the two Russian revolutions Trotsky's main intellectual work was the development—and defense against critics within the movement—of his theory of permanent revolution, a bold set of speculations concerning Marxist strategy in backward countries. Let me attempt here a schematic and condensed summary:

1) Czarist Russia is a backward country in which the immediate task is the bourgeois-democratic revolution that will confront those problems which, historically, have been solved by the great bourgeois revolutions of the past: such problems as the overthrow of the autocracy, the abolition of semi-feudal relations in the countryside, the right to self-determination for oppressed national minorities, the convocation of a constituent assembly to establish a republic, the proclamation of democratic liberties, etc.

2) These tasks, however, must be faced in Russia long after the bourgeoisie as a class has lost the revolutionary *élan* of its youth. Because of the special backwardness and isolation of Russian society, the Russian bourgeoisie is characterized by timidity and indecision. It has many social and economic reasons for opposing the Czarist autocracy, yet is bound to it by links of petty interest, prestige, and cowardice. Above all, it shares with the autocracy a growing fear of the two main classes at the base of Russian society: the peasantry and the workers. Because of these congenital weaknesses, the Russian bourgeoisie is incapable of a revolutionary initiative even in behalf of its own interests; it cannot make "its own" revolution. Consequently the task of the bourgeois revolution in a backward country like Russia must now be fulfilled by the plebeian classes. Or to put forward a seeming paradox, the bourgeois revolution has to be made *against* the bourgeoisie.

3) While it rests with the working class and the peasantry to carry through the bourgeois revolution, these classes are not socially or historically of equal weight. The peasantry —because of its geographical dispersion, centuries-long passivity, tradition of petty ownership, and lack of common outlook—has shown itself incapable of taking the historical lead. Its role has always been to serve as a crucial but subordinate ally of an urban class.

4) The sole urban ally now available to the peasantry—unless it remain the collective serf of Czarism—is the proletariat. For Trotsky, then, the inevitable conclusion is that the bourgeois-democratic revolution could be completed in a backward country only under the leadership of the working class, small and inexperienced though it may be—which means, more particularly, only under the leadership of the revolutionary party speaking for the working class. But the workers, having gained power, will not be able to stop short before the problems of the bourgeois revolution. The very effort to cope with these will inevitably force them to go beyond the limits of bourgeois property, so that, as Trotsky would write later, "the democratic revolution grows over immediately into the socialist, and thereby becomes a *permanent* revolution."

5) The socialist revolution thus begun in a backward country cannot be completed within national limits. For that, there would be neither a sufficiently secure economic base nor a working class sufficiently strong and conscious. Power could be held and steps toward socialism taken only if there speedily followed victorious revolutions in the advanced European countries. Russia's very backwardness would thrust her forward in the revolutionary scale and bring her under the rule of the working class, perhaps before any of those countries which, because of their economic maturity, were commonly regarded as most ripe for socialism. But this same backwardness, after having forced the working class to power, would overtake it and drag it down unless it received aid from abroad. Or as Trotsky later put it: "In a country where the proletariat has power . . . as the result of the democratic revolution, the subsequent fate of the dictatorship and socialism is not only and not so much dependent in the final analysis upon the national productive forces, as it is upon the development of the international socialist revolution."

Unquestionably this was the boldest theory, the most extreme prognosis, advanced by any Russian Marxist in the years before the First World War. The full measure of its audacity can be grasped even today by anyone who troubles to break past the special barriers of the Marxist vocabulary and examine the theory in terms of the tensions between "underdeveloped" and advanced countries in the twentieth century. The vexing problem of the relation between backwardness and industrialization, which today preoccupies all serious political thinkers, was to be solved, as Trotsky saw it, by the historical audacity of the barely developed proletariat in the colonial countries. For the Mensheviks, who believed that the bourgeoisie would have to lead the forthcoming bourgeois revolution, Trotsky's theory was an absurdity. Lenin, though agreeing with Trotsky as to the historical impotence of the Russian bourgeoisie, felt that the Russian working class was still too weak and inexperienced to play the grandiose role assigned to it by Trotsky and that the revolution would have to be carried through by an alliance between proletariat and peasantry, the exact relationship between whom he refused to specify or predict. Later, after the Russian Revolution, Lenin acknowledged the prescience of Trotsky's theory, and in retrospect it seems no exaggeration to add that of all the Marxists it was Trotsky who best foresaw the course of events in Russia.

But not entirely. There were at least two crucial respects in which history would cross his expectations. Like most Marxists, Trotsky did not foresee the extent to which the working class in western Europe, increasingly absorbed into national life and having won for itself major economic and political benefits, would choose parliamentarianism, rather than revolution, as the way to realize its aims. The help from a victorious European proletariat which Trotsky hoped would salvage the Russian Revolution was not to be forthcoming. Secondly, he failed to anticipate certain consequences of an isolated revolution in a backward country. He knew it might collapse or be overthrown, but he did not imagine that a consolidation of power from within its ranks might undo its original values. That the working class in a backward country, or a party acting in its name, could in moments of crisis approach and even take power, but that it would then reveal a fundamental incapacity to reconstruct economic and cultural life on a level high enough for achieving socialism—all this he foresaw brilliantly. But what he did not count on was that in such a debacle the revolutionary party, or a Bonapartist sector of it, would concentrate power in its upper ranks and establish itself as a bureaucratic elite above all classes—above exhausted proletariat, supine peasantry, dispersed bourgeoisie. The result would be a new, collectivist mode of authoritarianism, neither capitalist nor socialist in character. The first of these miscalculations did not necessarily call into question the validity of Marxism, but the second involved historical possibilities with which traditional Marxism was not well prepared to cope.

With the outbreak of the Russian Revolution in 1917, Trotsky moves into the center of modern history. His achievements as revolutionary leader are sufficiently known not to require a full account in these pages, but a few details may help us in tracing the curve of his political career.

Returning to St. Petersburg after the overthrow of the Czar, Trotsky thrust himself into the excitements of Russian politics, a politics that was chaotic and ultimatistic but, for the first time in history, free. Parties sprang up, debate rang passionately, the long-silent masses began to find their voice. The provisional governments that had replaced the Czar—first under the liberal monarchist Prince Lvov, then the Constitutional Democrat Miliukov, and finally the populist Kerensky—were inherently unstable. Their incapacity or unwillingness to permit a division of landed estates among the peasants and their failure to end Russia's participation in a fruitless and exhausting war made them increasingly unpopular. Since Trotsky opposed in principle any political collaboration with these regimes, even when they included some Menshevik ministers under Kerensky, he found himself at odds with both the Mensheviks and the "conciliationist" wing of the Bolsheviks. By the same token he was now closer to Lenin, whose entire political strategy beginning with the spring of 1917, to the astonishment even of many of his own comrades, was directed toward preparing the Bolshevik party for a seizure of power. In July, Trotsky formally joined the Bolsheviks, though for some months he had already been collaborating with them.

Supported by Lenin and for the first time in his political career working closely with a disciplined party organization, Trotsky became the popular spokesman for Bolshevism. Sukhanov, the gifted Menshevik whose eyewitness chronicle of the revolution is a major historical source, has recalled that Trotsky "spoke everywhere simultaneously. Every worker and soldier at Petrograd knew him and listened to him. His influence on the masses and the leaders alike was overwhelming." His biographer, Isaac Deutscher, offers a vivid picture of Trotsky as a mass orator:

> . . . he established his platform in the Cirque Moderne, where almost every night he addressed enormous crowds. The amphitheatre was so densely packed that Trotsky was usually shuffled towards the platform over the heads of the audience, and from his elevation he would catch the excited eyes of the daughters of his first marriage. . . . He spoke on the topics of the day and the aims of the revolution with his usual piercing logic; but he also absorbed the spirit of the crowd, its harsh sense of justice, its desire to see things in sharp and clear outline. . . . Later he recollected how at the mere sight of the multitude words and arguments he had prepared well in advance receded and dispersed in his mind and other words and arguments, unexpected by himself but meeting a need in his listeners, rushed up as if from his subconscious. He then listened to his own voice as to that of a stranger, trying to keep pace with the tumultuous rush

of his own ideas and phrases and afraid lest like a sleepwalker he might suddenly wake and break down. Here his politics ceased to be the distillation of individual reflection or of debates in small circles of professional politicians. He merged emotionally with the dark warm human mass in front of him . . .

Trotsky was more than a superb orator, more than a remarkably sensitive medium between the aroused masses and the straining Bolshevik leadership. In the Soviets, those improvised institutions of popular sovereignty where the left-wing parties struggled for domination, he became the main political spokesman for the Bolshevik point of view. And as preparations for the October Revolution proceeded, "all the work of practical organization of the insurrection" —even Joseph Stalin had to admit shortly afterward—"was conducted under the immediate leadership of the President of the Petrograd Soviet, Comrade Trotsky. It is possible to declare with certainty that the swift passing of the garrison to the side of the Soviet, and the bold execution of the work of the Military Revolutionary Committee [the body directing the October insurrection], the party owes principally and first of all to Comrade Trotsky."

In the government now formed under Lenin, Trotsky became foreign minister, intending, as he joked, to issue "a few revolutionary proclamations and then close shop," but in reality having to conduct the difficult Brest-Litovsk negotiations with imperial Germany, which at a heavy price brought peace to Russia. In 1918, when the civil war broke out across the whole of Russia, Trotsky became minister of war. Without military experience, he applied himself to creating a revolutionary army from almost nothing. He began with a few thousand Bolsheviks, Red Guards who had fought in the revolution; a considerable group of Russian army officers willing to serve the new regime in a nonpolitical capacity; and masses of untrained recruits who lacked discipline and often enough arms. For almost two years Trotsky lived in an armored train which served as the political-military headquarters of the new army. Moving from front to front, working with ferocious energy, exposing himself in crucial battles to rally frightened men, insisting upon the military authority of the old officers while checking their power through a network of political commissars, holding fast to standards of efficiency and discipline among soldiers who had long been demoralized, but above all else, stirring his followers to fight and die through the exaltation of his speeches and manifestoes, Trotsky created an effective army which finally defeated the Whites. He understood that in a revolutionary army it is the will to struggle which is often decisive; victory would come to his troops only as they believed themselves to be crusaders in behalf of a better world, only as they were ready to face death out of a conviction that they were—to quote from one of Trotsky's speeches to his soldiers—"participants in an unprecedented historic attempt . . . to create a new society, in which all human relations will be based on . . . co-operation and man will be man's brother, not his enemy."

Once the Red Army had ended the threat of counterrevolution, the young Bolshevik regime had for the first time to face the problems of social reconstruction. In these difficult years, when Russian economic life was reduced to chaos and hunger swept across the land, Trotsky argued in behalf of compulsory work and labor armies based on military discipline—draconian measures, he admitted, but necessary for lifting the economy to that minimal level of production where ordinary incentives might begin operating. (It is but fair to add that Trotsky advocated these measures only after his proposal for modifying "War Communism" had been rejected and that he was among the first Bolshevik leaders to urge the economic relaxation that went under the name of the New Economic Policy.)

In the public debates that followed—for a certain measure of political opposition could still be expressed in Russia—the Menshevik leader Raphael Abramovich opposed such forced labor battalions with the query: "Wherein does your socialism differ from Egyptian slavery? It was just by similar methods that the Pharaohs built the pyramids forcing the masses to labor." Trotsky replied: "Abramovich sees no difference between the Egyptian regime and our own. He has forgotten the class nature of government. . . . It was not the Egyptian peasants who decided through their Soviets to build the pyramids . . . our compulsion is applied by a workers' and peasants' government. . . ."

It was an unfortunate argument, Trotsky at his weakest. In advancing it he failed to acknowledge that by 1920 the Russian workers were not deciding very much on their own; it was the Bolshevik government that made the decisions. A great deal of the support the Bolsheviks had enjoyed among the workers since the October Revolution had by now been lost or badly weakened. The policies of this government could not be justified simply because it was, or called itself, a workers' government; its right to that title might better be justified by the nature of the policies it put forward. But most unfortunate of all, Trotsky's argument provided the formula that could later be used all too easily for rationalizing the Stalinist plunge into totalitarianism.

In arguing for labor armies and also in justifying the suppression of dissident socialist groups, Trotsky invoked the harsh necessities of fighting a desperate civil war and salvaging a collapsed economy. As he began, upon the completion of the civil war, to work at the revival of industrial production, all his enormous talents came into play; but his political role took on a harsh and authoritarian cast which cannot be justified even to the extent that certain of his measures during the civil war might be. Driven by the force of intolerable circumstances, but also trapped in the vise of a Bolshevik exclusivism which led to greater concentrations of power at the summit of the ruling party just when an opening of political and economic life might alone have saved the situation, Trotsky now condoned acts of repression which undercut the remnants of "Soviet democracy." A few years earlier the left-Menshevik leader, Julius Martov, had warned against the tendency of the Bolsheviks to equate the power of their party with the interests of the proletariat. Trotsky, flushed with the conquest of power, had replied: "You are bankrupt; your role is played out. Go where you belong from now on—into the rubbish can of history!" Sad words, from the man who in a few years would himself be harried into exile; sad words, as they reflect a failure to see that it is not always the least intelligent or good or even politically "correct" who are cast into that rubbish can.

In the years after the revolution, Lenin was more flexible, less doctrinaire than Trotsky. He opposed Trotsky's scheme for labor battalions and argued against a facile identification of the Bolshevik state with the proletariat; he described the regime as a "*deformed* workers' state" in which the workers' organization had to defend not only the state against its enemies but themselves against the state. But while this led him to propose an easing of economic life, he did not urge a parallel easing of political life. On the contrary, the turn toward the NEP in 1921, with its attendant threat to the Communist political monopoly, became for Lenin an argument against the reintroduction of even limited political freedoms.

In a speech before the Third Congress of the Comintern (1921), Lenin repeated the assumption that had been common to all the Bolshevik leaders:

> It was clear to us that without aid from the international world revolution, a victory of the proletarian revolution [in Russia] is impossible. Even prior to the Bolshevik revolution, as well as after it, we thought that the revolution would also occur either immediately or at least very soon in other backward countries and in the more highly developed capitalist countries. Otherwise we would perish.

Russia, Lenin kept insisting, was a backward peasant land that lacked technology, industry, and the accumulated culture required for surpassing the achievements of the Western capitalist countries. Consequently the fate of the Russian Revolution depended on the ability of the Communist movement to achieve power in at least one major advanced country so that assistance could come for besieged Russia. With the defeat of the 1919–1921 revolutions in western Europe, however, there were already signs that Lenin's prophecy—"otherwise we perish"—would be realized. But realized in ways that neither Lenin nor Trotsky had foreseen.

The Bolshevik party could preserve itself as master of a beleaguered state within the limits of a shrunken Russia, but in doing so it underwent large transformations in political ideology, social character and moral quality. In a country where all the means of production are owned by the state, and the state is totally in the grip of the only legal party, major changes in the nature of the party are equivalent to a social revolution creating new relationships between rulers and ruled.

Both the Russian economy and the Russian people were exhausted. To prevent economic collapse or social explosion, Lenin proposed as part of the NEP major concessions to an already hostile peasantry; but this in turn helped bring into existence a whole new conservative stratum of "rich" and middle peasants. When the mass of soldiers, demobilized after the civil war, came back drained of their revolutionary or patriotic fervor, the conservative tendencies within the villages were further reinforced.

So too in the cities. The workers were sapped of their social energy, some having fallen into demoralization and others turning against the regime. Many of the most devoted Bolsheviks had died during the civil war; others had been worn out; and still others, lacking the iron will of a Lenin or a Trotsky, displayed the characteristics of officials everywhere, with vested interests of their own which set them in increasing opposition to the workers in whose name they ruled. Apart from large amounts of economic help, what the country needed most was the ventilation of ideas, a gust of freedom to bring new life and strength; but after 1921 the Bolsheviks refused to allow any party but their own to function legally and thus contributed heavily to their own degeneration. Ruling as a minority dictatorship, though at times with mass support, the Bolshevik regime had planted the seeds of counterrevolution at the very moment the revolution triumphed. Each repressive measure taken by the dictatorship, even when truly the consequence of an emergency created by civil war or economic collapse, further undermined the ideological claims to which many of its supporters were devoted and helped create within the regime a cancerous social growth flourishing upon deprivation, cynicism, and brutality.

A new social stratum—it had sprung up the very morning after the revolution—began to consolidate itself: the party-state bureaucracy which found its roots in the technical intelligentsia, the factory managers, the military officials, and above all the Communist functionaries. It was narrow in outlook, provincial and boorish in tone, primitive in culture. It was committed to a nationalist perspective, and instinctively authoritarian in method. It looked upon the workers as material to be shaped, upon intellectuals as propagandists to be employed, upon the international Communist movement as an auxiliary to be exploited, and upon Marxist thought as a crude process for rationalizing its new ambitions.

To speak of party-state bureaucracy in a country where industry has been nationalized means to speak of a new ruling group or class which parasitically fastened upon every institution of Russian life. That many members of this new party-state bureaucracy were unaware of the significance of this process seems obvious; it was, in many respects, an historical novelty for which little provision had been made in the Marxist scheme of things. Years later, in 1928, the Bolshevik leader Bukharin, who had joined with Stalin to defeat Trotsky and was then himself shattered by Stalin, remarked that the disasters of the postrevolutionary period were all due to a "single mistake": the identification of the party with the state. There were people in the "rubbish can of history" who had been saying that for some time.

At precisely which point the revolutionary dictatorship of Leninism gave way to the totalitarianism of Stalin is hard and perhaps profitless to say. This transformation—a gradual counterrevolution—began during or shortly after the revolution itself, in the inner structure of the Leninist regime; came to its decisive moment in the mid-twenties; and reached full expression in the thirties, with the mass deportation of peasants, the Moscow trials, and the blood purges. Having consolidated its power, the new bureaucratic class proceeded to exploit the opportunities for centralized economic planning that are peculiar to a nationalized economy; it undertook a "primitive accumulation of capital" so cruel and bloody as to make the earlier accumulation of bourgeois society seem a model of humaneness.

Of this whole process Trotsky was a powerful critic, from the publication in 1923 of his brochure *The New Course*, in which he first explored the social physiognomy of bureaucratism, to his final writings in 1940, in which he showed signs of uncertainty as to some of his earlier sociological analyses of Stalinism. But especially in the earlier critiques, Trotsky made the error of supposing that in alliance with the new conservative elements in the countryside (whose interests he saw reflected in the "Right Communist" group led by Bukharin), the bureaucracy might constitute a nucleus for the restoration of private capitalism. Actually, as it slowly gathered into its hands control of the entire state, which meant control over the socioeconomic life of the nation, this new ruling stratum had every interest in preventing a return to private capitalism, for it neither owned nor could own property but instead controlled the state in whose legal custody property resided. Private capitalism would have meant the end of its power and privilege. It turned instead against every real or potential source of opposition both within and outside the party, destroying the bulk of the Bolshevik "old guard" in the purges of the next decades, reducing the intellectuals to a traumatized obedience, terrorizing the workers into passivity, and establishing itself as the sole center of power.

Until the late twenties, criticism of this bureaucratic trend could still be voiced in Russia, though in the later years not with impunity. Various opposition groups struggled to change the Bolshevik course between 1920 and 1923, that is, before Trotsky became the major critic of Stalinism and indeed, without his badly needed help. One respected Bolshevik oppositionist, G. Myasnikov, wrote: "The Soviet power must maintain at its own expense a body of detractors as did once the Roman Emperors." These words went unheeded, and their author suffered rebuke from the Central Committee. The questions Trotsky would raise in his struggle against Stalinism—questions concerning revolutionary strategy abroad, economic development at home, democracy within the ruling party—were surely important; but now it seems clear that the main significance of all the opposition groups, both Trotskyist and non-Trotskyist, was as a series of ill-connected efforts to stop or slow the trend toward totalitarianism.

For some years, roughly between 1923 and 1928, Trotsky was both political leader and intellectual guide of the left opposition groups in Russia which attacked the growing despotism of the Stalin regime. Far more skillful as the spokesman of a revolutionary upsurge than as a factional maneuverer, painfully aware that he was caught in a moment of social retreat which must prove inhospitable to his austere demands and standards, Trotsky fought doggedly, with intellectual flair and personal pride. But he fought on the terrain of the enemy, accepting the destructive assumption of a Bolshevik monopoly of power, and there were times when he suddenly withdrew into silence and illness, as if in disgust at having to cope with the hooliganism and intellectual vulgarity of his opponents. The very aspects of postrevolutionary Russia which Trotsky saw as conducive to the rise of Stalinism—social weariness, pervasive poverty, lack of culture, asphyxiation of independent thought, loss of spirit among Bolshevik cadres learning to prefer the comforts of administration to the heroism of revolution, the decline in strength and numbers of a proletariat bled white by civil war and industrial collapse—all this made it almost inevitable that Trotsky, no matter what his tactics, would fail. Years earlier, in 1909, he had provided a vivid description of parallel circumstances:

> When the curve of historical development rises, public thinking becomes more penetrating, braver and more ingenious. . . . But when the political curve indicates a drop, public thinking succumbs to stupidity. The priceless gift of political generalization vanishes somewhere without leaving a trace. Stupidity grows in insolence and, baring its teeth, heaps insulting mockery on every attempt at a serious generalization. Feeling that it is in command of the field, it begins to resort to its own means.

Many centuries earlier Thucydides had put the matter in his own words:

> Those who enjoyed the greatest advantages were the men of limited intelligence. The consciousness of their inability and of the talent of their adversaries made them fear that they would be duped by the fine speeches or the subtlety of spirit of their enemies and therefore they advanced straight toward their aim; while the others, scorning even to foresee the schemes of their adversaries and believing that action was superfluous when talk seemed to suffice, found themselves disarmed and defeated.

In only one way could Trotsky possibly have wrested power, and this was through a military coup taking advantage of his popularity in the army. But such a coup would have contributed to the acceleration of the very authoritarian decline he was now opposing; and in any case, he was too much a man of ideological rigor, too much a man devoted to his own sense of historical place and honor, to succumb to the smallness of a Bonapartist adventure. In a bitterly ironic turn of events, he was suffering from the vindication of his own theory of permanent revolution, by means of which he had predicted that a proletarian revolution in a backward country would, if it continued to suffer isolation, find itself in an historical limbo. Only, as it happened, neither he nor anyone else could predict how terrible that limbo would be.

The programs advanced by Trotsky during these years are far too complex, and far too deeply imbedded in the historical context of the time, to allow for easy summary. In general, however, at least three major themes can be noted. To cope with the economic crisis in which Soviet Russia found itself during the early and middle twenties—what Trotsky described as the problem of "the scissors," the two blades of which, moving farther apart from one another, were the rising prices of industrial goods and the declining prices of agricultural products—the Trotskyist opposition put forward an elaborate plan for the reorganization of the economy. The goals of this plan included strengthening the "socialist" industrial sector, raising the productivity of labor, supporting the poorer peasants against the new kulaks who had sprung up in the countryside since the NEP, improving the living standards of the workers and drawing them into a more active role in economic life. What was needed, wrote Trotsky, was "a *socialist* accumulation of capital," an harmonious development of the various departments of industrial production, and toward this end "Soviet democracy has become an *economic* necessity." Together with his economic program, Trotsky concentrated on the problems of democracy within the Bolshevik party and the state-dominated institutions of social life:

> Free discussion within the party has in fact disappeared; the party's social mind has been choked off. In these times the broad masses of the party do not nominate and elect the provincial committees and the Central Committee. . . . On the contrary, the secretarial hierarchy of the party to an ever greater degree selects the membership of conferences and congresses, which to

an ever greater degree are becoming executive consultations of the hierarchy.

Trotsky did not propose the restoration of freedom for the outlawed socialist parties, but confined himself to urging democracy within the Bolshevik party so that its intellectual life could be refreshed. And finally, he urged a reassertion of the principles of "socialist internationalism" in the work of the Communist parties abroad, charging that under Stalin's domination the Communist movement was being reduced to an appendage of Russian nationalism. As Trotsky saw it, the struggle between Stalin and himself was not primarily a personal dispute or a competition for power; it involved profound differences of principle between a bureaucracy that had become encrusted on the workers' state and the oppositionist forces that spoke for the socialist tradition.

Some years later, when the triumph of Stalinism had become complete in Russia and a good number of Western liberals had succumbed to an uncritical acceptance of its pretensions, it became fashionable to say that Stalin, having embarked upon a frenzied program of industrialization through his successive Five Year Plans, had "stolen Trotsky's thunder." Such remarks ignored the fact that what mattered for Trotsky was not industrialization as an end in itself, but industrialization in behalf of what he took to be socialist ends. Industrialization might be effected in any backward country prepared to employ centralized power with sufficient ruthlessness in order to sweat capital accumulation out of the people, but that was not what Trotsky believed to be the issue. For him, as he kept insisting, industrialization mattered as a means for "raising the specific gravity of the proletariat in society," and thereby moving toward the harmonious world of socialism. The industrialization of Stalin, by contrast, was achieved through the social exploitation of the working class, the imposition of totalitarian controls upon the entire country, and the destruction of political life and consciousness; it brought with it grave economic imbalances, profound social disruption, and extreme political barbarism, the effects of which will be felt for decades to come. No, this was not the "thunder" that Trotsky or any other Bolshevik leader of the twenties had proposed or even imagined. An observation by one of Trotsky's former collaborators, Max Shachtman, is worth quoting here:

> The workers' power in Russia, even in the already attenuated form of a dictatorship of the Bolshevik party, stood as an obstacle in the path of [capital] accumulation precisely because, on the one hand, genuine socialist accumulation was impossible under conditions of an isolated and backward country and, on the other hand, workers' power was incompatible with any other kind of accumulation. This power, then, had to be shattered.

It had, that is, to be shattered by Stalin's totalitarian dictatorship, which did indeed manage to impose a layer of industrialization on Russia's backward economy but in doing so created a sociopolitical structure profoundly in conflict with socialist values.

A more cogent criticism of Trotsky's course in the twenties concerns his failure to speak out in behalf of a multiparty democracy within the limits of "Soviet legality." In 1917, a few weeks before the October Revolution, when Trotsky was elected President of the Petrograd Soviet, he had promised: "we shall conduct the work of the Petrograd Soviet in a spirit of lawfulness and of full freedom for all parties." Toward the end of his life Trotsky would write that "Only when the Civil War began, when the most decisive elements of the Mensheviks and Social Revolutionaries took part in the Civil War on the other side of the barricades, we prohibited them. It was a military measure, not a permanent step." All recent political experience inclines us to suspect such arguments from necessity, so badly abused have they been; and even if one grants some force to Trotsky's claim, one must also heed the careful documentation in Leonard

Schapiro's *The Origin of the Communist Autocracy*, an account of the repeated violations of democratic procedures by the Bolshevik regime in the years between 1917 and 1922, a good many of which could not be attributed to the pressures of the civil war. In any case, Trotsky's decision to limit himself during the factional struggles of the twenties to a demand for democracy within the Bolshevik party placed him in a severe contradiction. Democracy within a ruling party, especially if it dominates a society in which property has become the possession of the state, is finally impossible unless it is extended beyond the limits of that party. Trotsky was demanding both a monopoly of power and a monopoly of freedom for the Bolsheviks: something just barely possible for a brief interval, but surely not for longer. There is no reason to suppose that if he had raised the demand for multiparty democracy it would have strengthened his cause or re-established his popularity. Such a demand would probably have isolated him still further within the Bolshevik hierarchy, and very likely not have sparked any great enthusiasm among the weary and impoverished masses. But what it would have done was to make his political and moral position more secure in the eyes of that historical posterity upon whose verdict he seemed so heavily to bank.

By 1928 Stalin had consolidated his power. The Left Opposition of Trotsky was crushed and the Right Opposition of Bukharin rendered powerless; the members of both groups were driven into exile, silenced in prison, or broken to recant. Trotsky himself was sent to a distant region of Asian Russia and early in 1929 deported from the country. A pall of obedience fell over Russia, and then: terror.

It was now, in his years as a powerless and harassed exile, that Trotsky achieved his greatest moral stature. No longer were there masses of cheering listeners to inflame with his eloquence; no longer armies to spur into heroism; no longer parties to guide to power. The most brilliant figure of the revolution was cast by the usurping dictatorship as a heretic, then a traitor, and finally, in the macabre frame-ups of the Moscow Trials, an agent of Fascism.

Driven from country to country, partly because of the pressures brought to bear by the Stalin regime and partly because the presence of the famous revolutionist, helpless and isolated though he might be, made governments feel uncomfortable, Trotsky found his final exile in Mexico. He lived in constant danger of assassination, and at least one effort involving the Mexican Communist painter David Siqueiros was made upon his life before the actual murder. A number of Trotsky's political associates were killed by agents of the Russian secret police, and his children, including a son who had never shown any interest in politics, were systematically hounded in Russia.

But Trotsky continued to cry out his defiance, unbent and unyielding, caustic and proud, a solitary Promethean figure; he continued to write his trenchant analyses of the totalitarian regime in Russia, its terrorism directed against defenseless millions, its Byzantine deification of the dictator, its blundering ventures into European politics. One need not accept the ideas of Trotsky in order to recognize that during his last decade he rose to an intellectual eminence and personal strength surpassing anything he had shown during the years of power. His productivity as a writer was amazing. Unburdened of office, he was once again the independent political analyst, historian, and literary man; it was the role in life, as he had once said, that he most enjoyed; and he wrote now with an authority of statement, an incisiveness of structure, a cutting sharpness of phrase, a brilliant freedom of metaphor which require that he be placed among the great writers of our time.

Trotsky's writings on Germany in the immediate pre-Hitler years are a model of Marxist polemic and analysis, but also of polemic and analysis that can be valuable to the non-Marxist as well. With blazing sarcasm and urgency—he was never patient toward fools—he attacked the insane policy of the German Communists, which declared the Social Democrats to be "social Fascists" representing a greater danger than the Nazis, and thereby prevented the formation of that united front of the left which he kept insisting was the one way to stop Hitler. Had his advice been followed (the Stalinists attacked him for "capitulating" to Social Democracy!), the world might have been spared some of the horrors of our century; at the very least, the German working class would have gone down in battle rather than allow the Nazi thugs to take power without resistance. Only a little less important are Trotsky's writings on Spain during the thirties, writings in which he analyzed the difficulties of modernizing a stagnant country, the way the Spanish bourgeoisie, out of social greed and cowardice, would block measures toward reform or even a dynamic economy, thereby opening the way to Fascism—in short, that complex of problems which in a few years would lead to the Spanish Civil War. Equally incisive, though—as it now seems to me—marred by dogmatic rigidity, are the writings Trotsky devoted to the social crisis of France during the late thirties, in which he analyzed the Popular Front as an unstable, inherently pusillanimous amalgam of bourgeois, socialist, and Stalinist parties lacking coherent purpose or will. With an excess of revolutionary hopefulness, he saw the French working class as an historical agent striving toward revolutionary action but restrained by its corrupted leaders.

Trotsky's most important political commentary of the thirties—a commentary which has influenced and been used even by those writers who sharply disagree with him—was devoted to the problem of Stalinism. Step by step he followed the transformation of the Stalin dictatorship into a full-scale totalitarian state, denouncing the economic policies by which the regime aggravated the exploitation of the masses in behalf of its mania for superindustrialization, enriching (though sometimes also confusing) his description of Stalinism with historical analogies drawn from the decline of the French Revolution, and riddling the claims of those

Western liberals who had begun to praise the Soviet Union only after it had sunk into totalitarianism. Again and again Trotsky was accused of exaggeration and spite in his attacks on the Stalin regime; the American liberal weeklies printed recondite discussions of the "psychological causes" behind his attacks; but almost everything he wrote would later be confirmed by the revelations that started coming out of the Soviet Union after Stalin's death. In the mid-thirties Trotsky was also forced to devote his time to refuting the lies of the Moscow Trials; he did not live long enough to hear Khrushchev admit they had been frame-ups contrived by the state, though he did live long enough to hear some American liberals accept them as truth and praise them as therapy.

All the while Trotsky kept working to create a new movement of the revolutionary left, the Fourth International, which would be loyal to the original principles of Marxism-Leninism. This effort failed. The masses of radical workers in Europe remained attached, however passively, to the traditional parties of the left and showed no interest in the tiny Trotskyist groups, while those intellectuals who broke away from Stalinism often found themselves reconsidering and then abandoning the whole Leninist outlook. As a political leader in these years Trotsky tended to be fractious and inflexible, perhaps because his imagination was still caught up with the myth of the Russian Revolution and could not easily adapt itself to the reduced scale of political action to which he was now confined. Among the scattered groups of the non-Communist left he won more admiration than adherence.

The most enduring portion of Trotsky's writings during the years of exile was not, however, directly polemical or narrowly political. It was directed to the world at large, rather than the constricted circles of radicalism, and today it is surely the most immediately accessible to readers untrained in radical ideology. Trotsky's autobiography, his unfinished book on Lenin, his severely controlled study of Stalin, that masterly compression of his basic views on Stalinism called *The Revolution Betrayed,* but above all, *The History of the Russian Revolution*—these are among the major works of his eleven years of exile. The *History* is Trotsky's masterpiece, the single greatest work of historical composition in the Marxist vein. It is a book on the grand scale, epic in proportion and tone, brilliant in color, vibrant with the passions of strongly remembered events. Throughout the book there is a rising tension, so characteristic of modern writing, between the subjective perceptions of a highly self-conscious author and the unfolding of a sequence of history taken to be determined by objective law. The book develops into great complexity—the complexity of revolutionary craft and assurance—from a simple but commanding image: the meeting of Russian worker and Russian peasant, often in his guise as soldier or Cossack, their first hesitant gropings toward each other, the subsequent drama of retreat and reconciliation, and finally, a clasp of unity. Apart from its claim to being a faithful record and true interpretation, the *History* is a major work of twentieth-century literature, deserving to be placed beside the masterpieces of modernism.

During the last years of his life Trotsky not merely wrote with great vigor in reply to the calumnies of the Moscow trials, not merely composed a number of major works, not merely produced a steady barrage of topical pieces on political and literary themes; he also engaged in sharp debates with intellectual opponents ranging from independent Marxists who disagreed with him on the "class nature" of the Russian state to liberals and socialists who challenged his assumption that between Bolshevism and Stalinism there was a fundamental conflict rather than a deep continuity. To support this assumption he wrote an ambitious essay, "Their Morals and Ours," in which he argued for the historical relativity of moral standards, tried to show the social causes of the moral distance between Bolshevism and Stalinism, reiterated his defense of the methods employed by the early Bolshevik regime, and had little difficulty in demonstrating that his liberal critics were necessarily quite as committed to the belief that "the end justifies the means" as they charged he was. In the less polemical sections of this essay Trotsky struggled with the problem of the relation between historically conditioned moral values, reflecting the interests of social classes and therefore in constant flux, and those moral "absolutes" he was inclined to depreciate as excessively abstract, but which he nevertheless found it impossible to avoid using himself.

In the last year or two of his life Trotsky plunged into a discussion concerning the political role and sociological nature of Stalinist Russia, which had been provoked by some of his American followers who found increasingly unsatisfactory his view that Russia merited "critical support" in the war because it remained a "degenerated workers' state." Trotsky clung hard to this position. When the Russian armies marched into Finland, he denounced the invasion as another instance of Stalinist reaction, yet because he saw the Russo-Finnish war as part of a larger conflict between the bourgeois West and the Soviet Union, he continued in his writings to give the latter "critical support."

This discussion might seem, at first glance, another of those exercises in ideological hair-splitting which occupy radical sects; but it had a genuine value, since the issues that were being discussed would have to be faced by anyone trying to provide a theoretical framework for the study of Stalinism. Trotsky held that Stalinist Russia should still be designated as a "degenerated workers' state" because it preserved the nationalized property forms that were a "conquest" of the Russian Revolution; in his view it was a society without an independent historical perspective, one that would soon have to give way either to capitalist restoration or workers' democracy. His critics insisted that the loss of political power by the Russian working class meant that it no longer ruled in any social sense, for as a propertyless class it could rule only through political means and not in those indirect ways that the bourgeoisie had employed in its youthful phase. Stalinism, they continued, showed no signs of producing from within itself a bourgeois restoration; quite the contrary, for the bureaucracy had become a new ruling class, with interests of its own in opposition to both capitalism and socialism. Trotsky did not live long enough to follow this dispute into the postwar years.

The last years of his life were difficult. Neither poverty nor powerlessness seemed to trouble him as much as the constrictedness of his daily existence; he worked under the constant protection of the guard his friends provided him, and he chafed at being unable to move about freely. For many years he had been living with his second wife, Natalia Sedova, in a marriage that was a model of mutual considerateness and devotion; together they now suffered blow after blow, as the news came of the death or disappearance of sons and friends. In his public conduct Trotsky remained firm and vigorous; privately, he suffered from intervals of depression. Once he apparently contemplated suicide. The indignity of needing to defend himself against the slanders pouring out of Moscow, the frustrations he suffered trying to rebuild a political movement ("I give advice because I have no other way to act," he wrote to a friend in France), the annoyance of having to write certain articles and books for merely financial reasons, the pain he felt at seeing so many people close to him persecuted by the Russian regime, the anxiety that he might not live long enough to fulfill the tasks he had set himself—all these left their mark. Trotsky was a man of enormous self-discipline, with an unshakable conviction as to his place in history and his responsibility to the idea of socialism; but he was also a complex and sensitive human being, impatient with the turn of history which had left him helpless—but only for the moment, he believed—to influence events. In the mid-thirties he kept a diary which reveals sudden flashes of unhappiness and irritation, as if he were rebelling against the disproportion between his intellectual powers and his political opportunities. But the diary also reveals capacities for human warmth and intensity of feeling, above all toward his admirable wife. And there are sentences which open a more intimate view: "Old age," he wrote, "is the most unexpected of all the things that happen to a man."

Only sixty when he was murdered, Trotsky was still a vigorous man who might otherwise have lived on for a number of years and continued to write and work. It would have been profoundly interesting to see how he would have responded to the intellectual crises of the postwar years, when as it seemed to many observers, all political systems, including both Marxism and classical liberalism, proved insufficient. Trotsky's mind was a mixture of the rigid and the flexible: he held unquestioningly to the basic tenets of Marxism, but within those limits was capable of innovation and risk. The problems he was forced to grapple with were qualitatively different from those which the greatest minds in his tradition had had to confront; for Trotsky was living in the time of the debacle of socialism and the triumph of totalitarianism, events that none of his intellectual ancestors had foreseen.

In one of his last articles, "The USSR in War," he showed a readiness at least to consider the possibility that the proletariat might not fulfill the revolutionary role that he and other Marxists had so long expected. He knew quite well that in such an event he would have to initiate a fundamental shift in political thought:

> If this war provokes, as we firmly believe, a proletarian revolution, it must inevitably lead to the overthrow of the bureaucracy in the USSR and regeneration of Soviet democracy on a far higher economic and cultural basis than in 1918. . . . If, however, it is conceded that the present war will provoke not revolution but a decline of the proletariat, then there remains another alternative: the further decay of monopoly capitalism, its further fusion with the state and the replacement of democracy whereever it still remained by a totalitarian regime. The inability of the proletariat to take into its hands the leadership of society

could actually lead under these conditions to the growth of a new exploiting class. . . .

There were other problems—already present during the last years of Trotsky's life but visible in their full significance only during the decades since his death—which call into question at least parts of his political outlook. Can, for instance, the modern phenomenon of totalitarianism, with its profound irrationality, its systematized terrorism, and its tendency to suppress traditional class dynamics, be understood adequately in terms of Trotsky's Marxism? Trotsky, it is true, had kept writing that in the absence of socialism, there would be a relapse into a kind of modern barbarism, and the Europe of the thirties and forties certainly sustained this prediction. But to predict a phenomenon is not necessarily to describe it fully or understand it adequately; and for those purposes his intellectual outlook did not, in the era of totalitarianism, suffice. Similarly, with his treatment of the problem of democracy. He was extremely sensitive to the numerous signs of the decay of European democracy during the years between the two world wars, and his writings on Germany, France, and Spain often brilliantly register the ways in which the crisis of capitalism endangered the survival of democracy. But the "class analysis" of democracy, to which Trotsky was committed, seems not at all sufficient for an era in which it has become so painfully clear that freedom and liberty—far from being mere guises of class domination—are the most precious values of human life and that without them little remains but servitude.

Staying within the limits of Trotsky's ideology, it would be difficult to account for the considerable stability and the marked rise in living standards that have characterized the life of Western capitalism and that now call into question the whole revolutionary perspective. This does not approximate what he called "the death agony of capitalism," though there does of course remain the possibility that the crises he predicted have merely been delayed. Nor have his prognoses concerning Russia been realized: the post-Stalin society has achieved a relative stability; it is neither threatened by bourgeois restoration nor within measurable distance of socialist democracy, but maintains itself as an authoritarian dictatorship, keeping terror in reserve but not employing it with the maniacal consistency of Stalin.

These apparent failures in historical prediction are not as disturbing as Trotsky's refusal or inability to reconsider some of his intellectual premises. In his last book, the biography of Stalin, there are perhaps one or two signs that he had begun to feel some uneasiness about the Bolshevik heritage, but for the most part he continued to defend it to the last. His powers of mind operated within the boundaries of a fixed political tradition, but not toward scrutinizing his own assumptions. One could hardly have expected him to repudiate his lifework, and much of the anti-Bolshevism directed against him in the late thirties must be acknowledged to have been crude in method and purpose. Yet for a Marxist theoretician who so fiercely and effectively criticized every move of the Stalinist regime and who so contemptuously swept aside all of its pretexts for the suppression of freedom, there should have been a stronger impetus to turn back to the early years of Bolshevism and submit them to the kind of objective critical study that historical distance alone makes possible.

It is very hard to imagine that Trotsky's influence in the future will be of the kind he anticipated: a renewal of orthodox Marxism in theory and proletarian revolution in practice, along the lines that have come to be known as "Trotskyism." We are living in times that disintegrate all fixed ideologies, and the idea of socialism, if it is to survive as more than an historical memory or a label incongruously attached to authoritarian states, will surely go through a good many transmutations and critical revisions in the coming years. But the writings of this extraordinary man are likely to survive, and the example of his energy and heroism likely to grip the imagination of generations to come. In the eastern European countries heretics turn instinctively to his forbidden books. In the West political thinkers must confront his formidable presence, parrying his sharp polemics and learning from his significant mistakes. Trotsky embodied the modern historical crisis with an intensity of consciousness and a gift for dramatic response which few of his contemporaries could match: he tried, on his own terms, to be equal to his time.

☼ PASTERNAK

WHEN Boris Pasternak's *Doctor Zhivago* first appeared in 1958, it proved to be not only a significant event in its own right but also a test by which intellectuals, though not they alone, revealed their deepest biases of value and opinion. From the outset I was an enthusiastic partisan of the novel, both as a work of art and a cultural-political expression. The first of the two pieces that follow was composed as a lengthy review of the novel shortly after its appearance; nor has my feeling for *Zhivago* changed over the years.

Some of the criticism to which Pasternak was subjected clearly had its origin in political hostility: the myth of Communist revolution dies hard. Some of it came from people who, by the late fifties, could no longer deny the bitter realities about the Russian dictatorship which form a historical premise of *Zhivago*, yet who felt that the book vaguely assaulted their "progressive" sensibilities. Another kind of criticism seemed merely esthetic: it declared *Zhivago* to be an old-fashioned nineteenth-century novel which failed to take into account the innovations of modernist European literature. What this kind of criticism—so deaf to the historical pathos of Pasternak's work, so locked into the provincialism of the absolutely up-to-date—failed to recognize was that in the context of contemporary Russia Pasternak's deliberate turning back to the Tolstoyan novel had a *revolutionary* significance.

The second of these pieces on Pasternak appeared as a polemic against Isaac Deutscher who printed in the spring 1959 issue of *Partisan Review* a long attack on *Zhivago* entitled "Pasternak and the Calendar of the Revolution." Deutscher had for some time occupied an influential but ambiguous position in the left-wing intellectual world: he was a critic of Stalinism, appalled by its brutality and mendacity, yet he was committed to a crude version of historical determinism which enabled him to provide a quasi-justification for Stalinism as a necessary stage in the tortuous course of the Russian Revolution. Though disagreeing sharply with Deutscher, I regarded him as a formidable opponent and felt that our differences involved not merely an estimate of Pasternak's novel but a whole range of moral and political issues.

I wish there were space in this book to reprint Deutscher's essay, but since there is not, I would urge the interested reader to look it up for himself. Meanwhile, here are a few traces of his main argument, which can also be made out in the course of my reply to him. "The most striking characteristic of Pasternak's novel," wrote Deutscher, "is its archaism, the archaism of the idea and the artistic style alike." The book "is utterly unrelated to the Russia of the 1950s and to the experiences, troubles and heart-searchings of the present Soviet generation." (A judgment, by the way, that neither the Communist rulers of Russia nor its harassed intellectuals seem to share.)

Pasternak, continued Deutscher, looks upon the Russian Revolution from the perspective of Christian humanism, and this perspective does not allow him to understand the rise of Leninism or the triumph of the Stalinist dictatorship. Like "a voice from the grave," Pasternak was still tied to the liberal hopes of the 1912–1914 years, wrote Deutscher, and therefore was unable to make out "the calendar of the revolution." The prerevolutionary liberalism to which Pasternak remained attached could not, said Deutscher, speak to the needs of post-Stalin Russia; hence the archaism of the novel's content and style.

✡ BORIS PASTERNAK:

OF FREEDOM AND CONTEMPLATION

DOCTOR ZHIVAGO, the novel which climaxes the career of the Russian poet Boris Pasternak, is a major work of fiction; but it is also—and for the moment, perhaps more important—an historic utterance. The book comes to us in extraordinary circumstances. A great Russian poet who maintains silence through years of terror and somehow, for reasons no one quite understands, survives the purges that destroy his most gifted colleagues; a manuscript sent by him to an Italian Communist publisher who decides to issue it despite strong pressures from his comrades; the dictatorship meanwhile refusing to permit this book, surely the most distinguished Russian novel of our time, to appear in print—all this comprises the very stuff of history, a re-enactment of those rhythms of brutality and resistance which form the substance of the novel itself.

Doctor Zhivago opens in the first years of the century, spans the revolution, civil war, and terror of the thirties, and ends with an epilogue in the mid-1940s. On a level far deeper than politics and with a strength and purity that must remove all doubts, it persuades us, at least for the time we read the book, that the yearning for freedom remains indestructible. Quietly and resolutely Pasternak speaks for the sanctity of human life, turning to those "eternal questions" which made the nineteenth-century Russian novel so magnificent and besides which the formulas of Russia's current rulers seem so trivial.

The European novel has traditionally depended on some implicit norm of "the human." In our time this norm has become so imperiled that the novel has had to assume the burdens of prophecy and jeremiad, raising an apocalyptic voice against the false apocalypse of total politics. Some of the most serious Western writers, turning impatiently from the task of representing familiar experience, have tried to make the novel carry an unprecedented amount of speculative and philosophical weight. Sacrificing part of the traditional richness of the European novel, they have kept searching for new, synoptic structures that would permit them to dramatize the modern split between historical event and personal existence. As a result, their work has occasionally thinned out into parables concerning the nature and possibility of freedom. Metaphysical desperation can end, surprisingly, in didacticism.

But where Western novelists have wrenched their narrative structures in order to reach some "essence" of modern terror, Pasternak has adopted a quite different strategy. With apparent awareness of the symbolic meaning of his choice, he has turned back to the "old-fashioned" leisurely Tolstoyan novel. His aim is not to mimic its external amplitude and plenitude of characters, as do many Soviet writers, but to recapture its spirit of freedom and then bring this spirit to bear upon contemporary Russian life. Given the atmosphere in which Pasternak must live and work, this kind of a return to the Tolstoyan novel comes to seem a profoundly liberating act.

Pasternak refuses to accept any claim for the primacy of ideological systems. Avoiding any quest for the "essence" of modern terror, he prefers to observe its impact upon the lives of modest and decent people. Again and again he returns to what might be called the "organic" nature of experience, those autonomous human rhythms which, in his view, can alone provide a true basis for man's freedom. The Tolstoyan narrative structure thereby takes on a new and dynamic character, embodying his belief that everything fundamental in life remains inviolate, beyond the grasp of ideology or the state.

I do not mean to suggest that Pasternak permits a facile spirituality to blind him to the power of circumstances. He knows how easy it is to debase and kill a man, how often and needlessly it has been done; some of his most poignant chapters register the sufferings of the Russian people during the past forty years. Yet he is driven by an almost instinctive need to cling to other possibilities, and he writes about ordinary experience with such affection and steadfastness that, even under the blows of accumulating historical crises, it takes on a halo of sanctity. Not the fanaticism of the will, but existence as rooted in the natural world seems to him the crux of things.

Yurii Zhivago, the central figure of the novel and in some ways Pasternak's alter ego, comes to this realization while still a young man. As he is driven from the battlefields of the First World War to revolutionary Moscow to partisan fighting in Siberia, and then back again to Moscow, Zhivago tries to keep hold of a few realities: nature, art, the life of contemplation. No matter how desperate the moment may be, he feels that the preservation of his identity is still possible if he can watch a cow grazing in the fields, read Pushkin's poems, and speak freely to himself in the journal he intermittently keeps.

It is this effort to preserve the personal basis of reality

which forms the main stress of Zhivago's experience—an effort always secured in a radiantly intense feeling for nature. One of the loveliest episodes in the novel occurs when Zhivago and his family, to avoid starvation during the civil war, decide to leave Moscow. They take a long journey eastward, and at one point their train becomes stalled in drifts of snow. For three days the passengers work in the open, helping to clear the tracks. A light of joy comes over them, a feeling of gratification for this gift: "The days were clear and frosty, and the shifts were short because there were not enough shovels. It was sheer pleasure."

Somewhat earlier in the book Zhivago reflects upon his life while traveling homeward from the First World War:

> Three years of changes, moves, uncertainties, upheavals; the war, the revolution; scenes of destruction, scenes of death, shelling, blown-up bridges, fires, ruins—all this turned suddenly into a huge, empty, meaningless space. The first real event since the long interruption was this trip . . . the fact that he was approaching his home, which was intact, which still existed, and in which every stone was dear to him. This was real life, meaningful experience, the actual goal of all quests, this was what art aimed at—homecoming, return to one's family, to oneself, to true existence.

The novel begins with a series of clipped vignettes of prerevolutionary Russia, apparently meant to suggest a Tolstoyan breadth and luxuriousness of treatment. A few of these vignettes seem hurried and schematic in effect, but many of them are brilliantly evocative, quick and sharp glimpses of another Russia.

But which Russia: the Russia of the Czars or of *War and Peace,* the country Pasternak remembers from his youth, or the marvelous landscape of Tolstoy's imagination? The alternative, of course, is a false one, for in the mind of a writer like Pasternak historical reality and literary heritage must by now be inseparable: the old Russia is the Russia of *both* the Czars and Tolstoy.

He is, in any case, rigorously objective in his treatment

of prerevolutionary Russia. He portrays both a vibrant Christmas party among liberal intelligentsia and a bitter strike among railroad workers; he focuses upon moments of free discussion and spontaneous talk such as would make some contemporary Russian readers feel envious and then upon moments of gross inhumanity that would make them think it pointless even to consider turning back the wheel of history. Pasternak accepts the unavoidability, perhaps even the legitimacy, of the revolution, and he evokes the past not to indulge in nostalgia but to insist upon the continuity of human life.

Once, however, the narrative reaches the Bolshevik revolution, the Tolstoyan richness and complexity promised at the beginning are not fully realized. Partly this is due to Pasternak's inexperience as a novelist: he burdens himself with more preparations than he needs and throughout the book one is aware of occasional brave efforts to tie loose ends together. But mainly the trouble is due to a crucial difference between Tolstoy's and Pasternak's situations. Soaring to an incomparable zest and vitality, Tolstoy could break past the social limits of his world—a world neither wholly free nor, like Pasternak's, wholly unfree—and communicate the sheer delight of consciousness. Pasternak also desires joy as a token of man's gratitude for existence; his characters reach for it eagerly and pathetically; but the Russia of his novel is too gray, too grim for a prolonged release of the Tolstoyan ethos. As a writer of the highest intelligence, Pasternak must have known this, and it is at least possible he also realized that the very difficulties he would encounter in adapting the Tolstoyan novel to contemporary Russia would help reveal both the direction of his yearning and the constrictions of his reality.

It is Pasternak's capacity for holding in balance these two elements—the direction of yearning and the constrictions of reality—that accounts for the poise and strength of the novel. Like most great Russian writers, he has the gift for making ideas seem a natural part of human experience, though what matters in this novel is not a Dostoevskian clash of ideology and dialectic but Zhivago's sustained effort, amounting to a kind of heroism, to preserve his capacity for the life of contemplation.

Zhivago's ideas, it seems fair to assume, are in large measure Pasternak's, and as they emerge in the book, subtly modulated by the movement of portrayed events, it becomes clear that the central point of view can be described as a kind of primitive Christianity, profoundly heterodox and utterly alien to all dogmas and institutions. I would agree with the remark of Max Hayward, Pasternak's English translator, that Zhivago's Christianity "would be acceptable to many agnostics." Acceptable not merely because of its ethical purity but because it demands to be understood as an historically determined response to the airless world of Soviet conformity. In such a world the idea of Christ—even more so, the image of Christ facing his death alone—must take on implications quite different from those it usually has in the West. Zhivago's uncle, his intellectual guide, suggests these in an early passage:

> What you don't understand is that it is possible to be an atheist, it is possible not to know whether God exists, or why, and yet believe . . . that history as we know it began with Christ. . . . Now what is history? It is the centuries of the systematic exploration of the riddle of death, with a view to overcoming death. That's why people discover mathematical infinity and electromagnetic waves, that's why they write symphonies. Now, you can't advance in this direction without a certain faith. You can't make such discoveries without spiritual equipment. And the basic elements of this equipment are in the Gospels. What are they? To begin with, love of one's neighbor, which is the supreme form of vital energy. . . . And then the two basic ideas of modern man—without them he is unthinkable—the idea of free personality and the idea of life as sacrifice.

Together with this version of Christianity, Zhivago soon develops a personal attitude toward Marxism—an attitude, I should say, much more complex than is likely to be noted by American reviewers seeking points for the Cold War. Zhivago cannot help but honor the early Bolsheviks, if only because they did give themselves to "the idea of life as sacrifice." His enthusiasm for the revolution dies quickly, but even he does not condemn it. He is more severe: he judges it.

Unavoidably Zhivago also absorbs some elements of the Marxist political outlook, though he never accepts its claims for the primacy of politics. Indeed, his rejection of Marxism is not essentially a political one. He rejects it because he comes to despise the arrogance of the totalitarian "vanguard," its manipulative view of man, in short, its contempt for the second "basic ideal of modern man . . . the ideal of free personality":

> Marxism is a science? [says Zhivago during a discussion on a train in Siberia.] Well, it's taking a risk, to say the least, to argue about that with a man one hardly knows. However—Marxism is too uncertain of its ground to be a science. Sciences are more balanced, more objective. I don't know a movement more self-centered and further removed from the facts than Marxism. Everyone is worried only about proving himself in practical matters, and as for the men in power, they are so anxious to establish the myth of their infallibility that they do their utmost to ignore the truth.

Still more withering is Zhivago's judgment of the Soviet intelligentsia:

> Men who are not free . . . always idealize their bondage. So it was in the Middle Ages, and later the Jesuits always exploited this human trait. Zhivago could not bear the political mysticism of the Soviet intelligentsia, though it was the very thing they regarded as their highest achievement. . . .

Such statements are plain enough, and their significance can hardly be lost upon the powers in Moscow; but it must quickly be added that in the context of the novel they are much less abrupt and declamatory than they seem in isolation. Pasternak is so sensitive toward his own characters, so free from any intention to flourish ideologies, that the novel is never in danger of becoming a tract. *The spectacle of Zhivago trying to reflect upon the catastrophe of his time is always more interesting than the substance of his reflections.* His ideas are neither original nor beyond dispute, but as he experiences them and struggles to articulate them, they take on an enormous dignity and power. If ever a man may be said to have earned his ideas, it is Yurii Zhivago.

Zhivago's opinions reflect the direction of Pasternak's yearning, the long-suppressed bias of his mind; but there is, in the novel itself, more than enough counterweight of objective presentation. Pasternak is extremely skillful at making us aware of vast historical forces rumbling behind the lives of his central figures. The Bolshevik revolution is never pictured frontally, but a series of incidents, some of them no more than a page or two in length, keep the sense of catastrophe and upheaval constantly before us—Zhivago fumbling to light an old stove during an icy Moscow winter while in the nearby streets men are shooting at each other, a callow young Menshevik "heartening" Russian troops with democratic rhetoric and meeting an ungainly death as his reward, a veteran Social Revolutionary pouring bile over the Communist leaders, a partisan commander in Siberia fighting desperately against the White armies. And as Zhivago finds himself caught up by social currents too strong for any man to resist, we remember once again Tolstoy's concern with the relationship between historical event and personal life.

Once Pasternak reaches the revolutionary period, the novel becomes a kind of spiritual biography, still rich in social references but primarily the record of a mind struggling for survival. What now matters most is the personal fate of Zhivago and his relationships with two other characters, Lara, the woman who is to be the love of his life, and Strelnikov, a partisan leader who exemplifies all of the ruthless revolutionary will that Zhivago lacks.

Zhivago himself may be seen as representative of those Russian intellectuals who accepted the revolution but were never absorbed into the Communist apparatus. That he is both a skillful doctor and a sensitive poet strengthens one's impression that Pasternak means him to be something more than an individual figure. He speaks for those writers, artists, and scientists who have been consigned to a state of permanent inferiority because they do not belong to the "vanguard" party. His sufferings are their sufferings, and his gradual estrangement from the regime, an estrangement that has little to do with politics, may well be shared by at least some of them. Zhivago embodies that which, in Pasternak's view, man is forbidden to give to the state.

Mr. Hayward reports that Pasternak has apparently referred to Turgenev's Rudin as a distant literary ancestor of Zhivago. Any such remark by a writer like Pasternak has its obvious fascination and one would like very much to know exactly what he had in mind; but my own impression is that the differences between the two characters are more striking than the similarities. Rudin, the man of the 1840s, is a figure of shapeless enthusiasms that fail to congeal into specific convictions; he is the classical example of the man who cannot realize in action the vaguely revolutionary ideas that fire his mind. Zhivago, by contrast, is a man rarely given to large public enthusiasms; he fails to achieve his ends not because he is inherently weak but because the conditions of life are simply too much for him. Yet, unlike Rudin, he has a genuine "gift for life," and despite the repeated collapse of his enterprises he brings a sense of purpose and exaltation to the lives of those who are closest to him. There is a key passage in his journal which would probably have struck Rudin as the essence of philistinism but which takes on an entirely different cast in twentieth-century Russia:

> Only the familiar transformed by genius is truly great. The best object lesson in this is Pushkin. His works are one great hymn to honest labor, duty, everyday life! Today, "bourgeois" and "petty bourgeois" have become terms of abuse, but Pushkin

forestalled the implied criticism . . . in "Onegin's Travels" we read:

Now my ideal is the housewife,
My greatest wish, a quiet life
And a big bowl of cabbage soup.

There is undoubtedly a side of Pasternak, perhaps the dominant side, which shares in these sentiments; but it is a tribute to his utter freedom from literary vanity that he remorselessly shows how Zhivago's quest for "a quiet life" ends in repeated failures and catastrophes. Zhivago's desire for "a big bowl of cabbage soup" indicates—to twist a sardonic phrase of Trotsky's—that he did not choose the right century in which to be born.

The novel reaches a climax of exaltation with a section of some twenty pages that seem to me one of the greatest pieces of imaginative prose written in our time. Zhivago and Lara, who have been living in a Siberian town during the period of War Communism, begin to sense that their arrest is imminent: not because they speak any words of sedition (Zhivago has, in fact, recently returned from a period of enforced service as doctor to a band of Red partisans) but simply because they ignore the slogans of the moment and choose their own path in life. They decide to run off to Varykino, an abandoned farm, where they may find a few moments of freedom and peace. Zhivago speaks:

But about Varykino . . . to go to that wilderness in winter, without food, without strength or hope—it's utter madness. But why not, my love! Let's be mad, if there is nothing except madness left to us. . . .

Our days are really numbered. So at least let us take advantage of them in our own way. Let us use them up saying goodbye to life. . . . We'll say goodbye to everything we hold dear, to the way we look at things, to the way we've dreamed of living and to what our conscience has taught us. . . . We'll speak to one another once again the secret words we speak at night, great and pacific like the name of the Asian ocean.

*

From this point on, the prose soars to a severe and tragic gravity; every detail of life takes on the tokens of sanctity; and while reading these pages, one feels that one is witnessing a terrible apocalypse. Begun as a portrait of Russia, the novel ends as a love story told with the force and purity of the greatest Russian fiction; yet its dependence upon the sense of history remains decisive to the very last page.

Through a ruse Zhivago persuades Lara to escape, and then he returns to Moscow. He falls into shabbiness, illness, and long periods of lassitude; he dies obscurely, from a heart attack on the streets of Moscow. Lara's fate is given in a fierce, laconic paragraph:

> One day [she] went out and did not come back. She must have been arrested in the street at that time. She vanished without a trace and probably died somewhere, forgotten as a nameless number on a list that afterwards got mislaid, in one of the innumerable mixed or women's concentration camps in the north.

Like the best contemporary writers in the West, Pasternak rests his final hope on the idea that a good life constitutes a decisive example. People remember Zhivago. His half-brother, a mysterious power in the regime who ends as a general in the war, has always helped Zhivago in the past; now he gathers up Zhivago's poems and prints them; apparently he is meant to suggest a hope that there remain a few men in the Russian hierarchy who are accessible to moral claims. Other old friends, meeting at a time when "the relief and freedom expected at the end of the war" had not come but when "the portents of freedom filled the air," find that "this freedom of the soul was already there, as if that very evening the future had tangibly moved into the streets below them."

So the book ends—a book of truth and courage and beauty, a work of art toward which one's final response is nothing less than a feeling of reverence.

☼ ISAAC DEUTSCHER: FREEDOM AND THE ASH CAN OF HISTORY

AS long as Soviet Russia remains a powerful state, and no matter how often it displays its contempt for freedom, it will exert an attraction for Western intellectuals, particularly those who have replaced the dimmed fraternal sentiments of their youth with a hardheaded valuation of industrial power. Among the French this takes the form of a rationalist dementia cut off from the domain of fact; among the British a gentlemanly tolerance for "those chaps"; among Germans a commitment to the asserted logos of History which moral experience seems unable to deflect; and among Americans a managerial camaraderie resting upon a joint esteem for the gestures of power, the wonders of technology, and bureaucratic planning (the fetishism of the plan having, in our time, replaced the fetishism of commodities).

These converging sentiments make up together what might be called a *new conciliationism* in regard to the Communist dictatorship. Among intellectuals a major symptom is the desire to add to the undisputed necessity for political coexistence an attitude that might be called moral coexistence. And since *Doctor Zhivago* has already provided a decisive test for many people—for the Communist leaders in Russia, for men out of power like the "revisionist" writers of Poland who acclaimed the book—so, through what might be called the dialectic of irritation, it has provoked Isaac Deutscher into an unusual bluntness of statement. His major charge against *Doctor Zhivago*—that its devotion to individual and liberal values is "archaic," that it "speaks the language of the dead" (though, considering their tragic history, might it not be appropriate that a great Russian poet speak the language of the dead?)—can be understood only if one realizes that Mr. Deutscher writes as a theorist who believes that the irrevocable progress of History is floating the Communist state. His assault upon Pasternak derives from a fundamental identification with the "essence," though not necessarily with each manifestation, of that progress.

At the end of his essay, in a burst of rapture Mr. Deutscher speaks of the "music of the future," the music of socialism no less, of which he hears the anticipatory chords in Khrushchev's Russia. I write from another standpoint. The "music" I hear from Russia is that of a party-state which systematically silences those who would speak for freedom. The people of Russia remain a prisoner: the leash has been lengthened, the rations are improved, but the prisoner is not free. And I do not believe that the growing wealth and strength of this jail-society assures a gradual slide into freedom, though it *may* offer new opportunities for those within Russia who want to struggle against the party monopoly of power.

*

2.

Mr. Deutscher describes *Doctor Zhivago* as a "political novel *par excellence*" and then, quite as if he were reviewing a full-scale political-social history of Communist Russia, bemoans its failure to present directly the tumultuous events of the revolutionary and postrevolutionary years. The novel does not even show us, he complains, a single bona fide Bolshevik. But if by a "political novel" (especially "*par excellence*"*!*) we mean one that focuses primarily upon a course of political happenings or upon a clash of political ideologies, then *Doctor Zhivago*, despite its occasional passages about Marxism, might better be described as an "antipolitical" novel, one that deals with the effort of a man to survive in his own being at a time when the imperious demand of politics is total.

Mr. Deutscher's critical strategy lends itself to unexpected uses: he could, for example, dismiss *The Charterhouse of Parma*, because its hero Fabrice merely glances at the central event of his time, the Battle of Waterloo, and then lives a dreamlike nonpolitical existence, even though the political events of the Napoleonic era, as Stendhal makes clear, decisively shape his life. (For that matter, Mr. Deutscher's complaints about the "coincidences" in *Zhivago* would also permit him, like recent generations of students, to dismiss Thomas Hardy's great novels in which the sense of a fate beyond human control is similarly projected through "coincidence.")

The novel Pasternak happens to have written is quite different from the one Mr. Deutscher thinks he has or should have written. Pasternak largely takes for granted the sweep of historical events and the likelihood that his Russian readers will be familiar with them. (Given their "education," it is perhaps the one thing he can take for granted.) What he wishes to impress upon his readers is the value of an independent consciousness, sometimes heroic, more often passive and helpless, yet clinging to its own terms of existence. A good many of the terrible events in Russian history of the last half-century are touched upon in the novel, either by implication or through brief presentments—and to my mind, touched upon with great force and objectivity. One thinks of the moments when Zhivago is at the front, a witness to the disintegration of the Czarist army; or later in Moscow, discovering that in times of stress the snatched pleasure of duck and vodka, because it is not shared with other men, is no pleasure at all; or still later, during the marvelously portrayed journey to the Urals, when Zhivago argues in behalf of the revolution against one of its "premature" critics, shares with ease and affection the trials of the ordinary people who are his companions on the train, and experiences, in his inner self, the meaning of a vast historical uprooting.

Here is Zhivago as a witness to the revolution:

> He realized he was a pygmy before the monstrous machine of the future; he was anxious about this future, and loved it and was secretly proud of it, and as though for the last time, as if in farewell, he avidly looked at the trees and clouds and the people walking in the streets, the great Russian city struggling through misfortune—and was ready to sacrifice himself for the general good, and could do nothing.

Mr. Deutscher charges Zhivago, as a representative of his class and/or generation, with yearning for a period (1912–1914) when Russia's middle classes "had definitely turned their back on their own radicalism of 1905," but he neglects to add that those were also years in which, perhaps mistakenly, many Russian intellectuals felt some hopes for a *liberal* development. And when he charges Pasternak with basing his "recital of the broken pledges of October . . . on a false premise," he is being less than just: for while it is true that the Bolshevik revolution did not promise to return to the climate of 1912–1914, it is also true that in its first few years it gave the intellectuals reason to hope that it would honor at least some of the freedoms Pasternak clearly had in mind when referring to the prerevolutionary years. In any case, if the point of *Doctor Zhivago* were really so preposterous as a piping for the Czarist past, the Soviet dictatorship would surely not have reacted with so sustained and intense a fury: for what damage could the book then have done, what impact could it have had? No, when the students of Moscow hailed Pasternak a few years ago, chanting a request that he read his translation of Shakespeare's Sixty-sixth Sonnet ("*And art made tongue-tied by authority*"), they saw him not as a relic of "the dead" but as a spokesman and symbol of the freedom they desired.

It is true that Zhivago's political consciousness, never more than a fragment of that complex human consciousness toward which he strives, can at no point satisfy the strict requirements of a Leninist. One of the main themes of the novel is that the Bolshevik regime, as it rapidly became monolithic and bureaucratized, gave people like Zhivago no margin for survival. As Nicola Chiaromonte has written in a moving essay (*Dissent,* Winter 1959): "What Pasternak has done is to show what is left of characters under conditions in which the very identity of the individual is threatened, and tends to be reduced to an inconsistent sequel of occasions and acts."

That is why the passage Mr. Deutscher singles out as "naïve and stilted"—the passage in which Pasternak compares the conversation of Zhivago and Lara with the dialogues of Plato—acquires in context a noble and tragic character. Loyalty to the text would require readers to be told that this passage occurs in a quick transitional section which summarizes what has been and will again be shown in dramatic fullness: that Zhivago has been ill, that he has now been reunited with Lara, that they find it possible, while living on the edge of the precipice they know awaits them, to rediscover something of the value of human existence through sharing in the spirit of sacrifice and love. But to

Isaac Deutscher, accomplice of History, all this seems "naïve," the residual sentiment of "a survivor of a lost tribe." Yes, the human tribe.

Chiaromonte's point—central for an understanding of the novel—also helps explain why Mr. Deutscher's comparison between *War and Peace* and *Doctor Zhivago* betrays both literary and political insensitivity. I happen to think, unlike other critics, that Pasternak did begin his novel with an intention of composing a story of Tolstoyan breadth. But it must have become clear to him that, if he were to write honestly, he could not compose this kind of novel about the Russia of the last decades. Pasternak began, perhaps, by desiring to capture something of the Tolstoyan freedom and spontaneity, its joy as a token of man's gratitude for existence; his characters reach for it eagerly, pathetically; but the Russia he comes to describe, whether of the War Communism years or the Stalin and post-Stalin periods, is too gray, too grim in its inhumane monolithism to permit a prolonged release of the Tolstoyan ethos. To have pretended otherwise would have been to acquiesce in the characteristic falsification of Soviet fiction.

Yet after about the first hundred pages—far from repeating, as Mr. Deutscher supposes, the usual business of the old-fashioned social novel—Pasternak radically shifts his focus and begins to compose a quite different kind of novel. The very "substance" of his imagined world, in respect to which all the other characters are observed and validated, becomes Zhivago's sense of consciousness: his sense of consciousness as the last refuge of freedom. Through his doomed yet exemplary struggle to maintain the life of contemplation, through his proud insistence upon the autonomy of his inner "organic" being, Zhivago comes to represent—and even in those moments of lassitude and demoralization that so offend Mr. Deutscher's Spartan sensibilities—everything which in human life must remain impervious to the manipulation of the party-state and its ideology.

It is for this reason that *Doctor Zhivago* is not merely a

remarkable novel in its own right but a testament for the silent and suppressed: all those who, no matter how they might reject Zhivago's ideas, share with him the yearning for the right to free reflection. It is for this reason that Zhivago, feeble broken creature that he finally becomes, still represents the "permanent revolution" of man against the total state.

Whether Pasternak confuses "the calendar of the Russian revolution" would therefore seem a secondary matter. Other great Russian novels, Dostoevsky's *The Possessed* and Turgenev's *Virgin Soil*, have also been accused, perhaps with greater justice, of violating the "calendar" of their day: a fact that in no way diminishes their value as either literature or "evidence." In any case, is this confusion quite so shocking as Mr. Deutscher claims? Outright terrorism Pasternak shows only at the end of the novel, as in the chilling paragraph which records that Lara "died somewhere, forgotten as a nameless number on a list that afterwards got mislaid, in one of the innumerable mixed or women's concentration camps in the north." What Pasternak portrays in the early twenties is the cruelty of the civil war ("White and Red atrocities rivalled each other in savagery"), the gathering fanaticism of the triumphant Communists, the agonies of personal survival. I submit that his novel shows a greater faithfulness to the essential history of our time, as it has become the crucifixion of freedom and consciousness, than all of Mr. Deutscher's dialectical turnings.

3.

About the literary merits of *Doctor Zhivago* there can of course be legitimate disagreement. But one would expect an intellectual to feel only the deepest sense of comradeship with Pasternak as a man, to be stirred to emotions of fraternity by the sight of this aging poet as he suffered in loneliness the assaults of the party-state. (Or should we congratulate Khrushchev for not having arranged his liquidation?) And here, despite Mr. Deutscher's careful statement of opposition to the witch-hunt and the banning, I find his views lamentable.

Mr. Deutscher chastises "the censors" for their "obtuseness and stupidity." But surely it is more than a matter of "censors," and something far more serious than "obtuseness." These "censors" did not act on their own, apart from the cues of Khrushchev and Mikoyan; the whole apparatus of the party-state—including the Komsomol leader who called Pasternak a pig—threw itself into the vendetta against the writer. Mr. Deutscher, faithful to his theories, must however present the matter as if it were the result of the "obtuseness" of officials out of step with History, bureaucrats who, having perhaps mislaid the calendar of the revolution, don't understand their own true interests, which Mr. Deutscher tries so patiently to explain. (One wonders, incidentally, whether the suppression of the Hungarian revolution was also due to mislaying the calendar.) *

What Mr. Deutscher does not face up to is the political significance of the Pasternak case. Pasternak, writing almost as if he too, at the end of the book, accepted Mr. Deutscher's optimistic prognosis, offered a novel that forced the regime to decide how far the "thaw" could go. The party-state answered by suppressing the book. Does this fact support Mr. Deutscher's theory about the expected gradual

* But one need not wonder for long. In *Russia in Transition* Mr. Deutscher writes: "It may be said that in October–November [1956], the people of Hungary in a heroic frenzy tried unwittingly to put the clock back, while Moscow sought once again to wind up with the bayonet, or rather the tank, the broken clock of the Hungarian Communist revolution. It is difficult to say who it was who acted the more tragic, and the more futile or hopeless role."

Calendars, clocks—the image changes, the politics remains. Like Yurii Zhivago, the people of Hungary in their quest for freedom are seen as representing the past, while the Russian tanks, however brutally, push forward the clock. No wonder that, again, Mr. Deutscher feels no overwhelming impulse to identify himself with those who fight against the tanks.

"democratization" of Russian Communism, or does it indicate that, with less violent methods, the regime stands ready to suppress fundamental disagreement and criticism, and insists upon maintaining its ideological monopoly?

Mr. Deutscher seems almost to plead with "the censors": let the senile old poet mumble his memories of the dead, he can do you no harm, Tolstoy and Dostoevsky were also Christians. But the "censors" may realize that Pasternak's version of "Christianity," because it speaks of human freedom, *is* a danger to them; and they may feel that they can manage their dictatorship without the help of Western *Besserwissers.* Or perhaps there is truth in Herbert Marcuse's remarks about the Soviet attitude toward art:

> . . . it is precisely the catastrophic element inherent in the conflict between man's essence and his existence that has been the center toward which art has gravitated. . . . The artistic images have preserved the determinate negation of the established reality—ultimate freedom. When Soviet esthetics attacks the principle of the "insurmountable antagonism between essence and existence" . . . it thereby attacks the principle of art itself.

May it not be then, that from *their* point of view, the "censors" are not so obtuse? Mr. Deutscher gives involuntary support to this possibility when he writes that, while a relic in Russia, "Zhivago still represents a powerful force" in Poland and Hungary. But the Russian "censors" know how short is the distance from Warsaw or Budapest to Moscow. And in any case, what is the logic of Mr. Deutscher's statement? If Zhivago stands for nostalgia for the *ancien régime,* and if in eastern Europe he is a threat to "the revolution," does it not follow that there may also be some ground for suppressing the book, not in Russia, but in Poland and Hungary? Mr. Deutscher will of course protest; but let him look to his own words before protesting too quickly.

*

4.

The heart of the matter is Zhivago's "archaism"—a charge that reminds one, unhappily, of Trotsky's arrogant habit of dismissing political opponents to the "ash can of history." If one believes that in their essence the Communist states embody the necessary and/or desirable future, then perhaps Zhivago is "archaic." But if one believes that the central issue of our time is freedom and that all the "old" nineteenth-century problems have acquired a new value since the rise of the total state, then Zhivago speaks for the best of the past as it relates to the future. That Pasternak is a kind of "old-fashioned" and even conservative nineteenth-century liberal I do not doubt; but if socialism is to prove something better than a cruel caricature of its own pretensions, the task of modern politics becomes that of finding a new and more humane mode of realization for the values of nineteenth-century liberalism. It becomes necessary to find a link between the values of an older generation that is represented by men like the Polish writer Marek Hlasko, who remains a rebel but has broken from Communism because, as he writes, life under Communism is "a moral atrophy."

If you have read only Mr. Deutscher and not *Doctor Zhivago* itself, you might suppose Pasternak has nothing to say about such matters. Quite the contrary! It is a main concern of his book. Does, for example, the following passage betray an esthete's "archaism" or a profound insight into characteristic vices of totalitarianism?

> Microscopic forms of cardiac hemorrhages have become very frequent in recent years. . . . It's a typical modern disease. I think its causes are of a moral order. The great majority of us are required to live a life of constant, systematic duplicity. Your health is bound to be affected if, day after day, you say the opposite of what you feel. . . . I found it painful to listen to you,

Innokentii, when you told us how you were re-educated and became mature in jail. It was like listening to a horse describing how it broke itself in.

Or is the following a "parable of a vanished generation" or a voice anticipating the democratic aspirations of tomorrow?

To conceal the failure [of forced collectivization] people had to be cured, by every means of terrorism, of the habit of thinking and judging for themselves, and forced to see what did not exist. . . . This accounts for the unexampled cruelty of the Yezhov period, the promulgation of a constitution that was never meant to be applied, and the introduction of elections that violated the very principle of free choice.

If this be "archaism," let every man who believes in freedom declare himself archaic.

5.

When a modern state exerts total control over the economy, political power becomes indistinguishable from social and economic power. If, as in Russia, the Party has a monopoly of political power, it also tends to have a monopoly of social and economic power. Democracy then becomes not a "luxury" which may be gradually expected to make its appearance, parceled out decades after the totalitarian party has seized power. It is a *sine qua non* for any socialist or "progressive" development, and its absence signifies that the people have been rendered helpless.

Hegel wrote that "The lower classes have been left more or less unorganized. And yet it is of the utmost importance that they should be organized, for only in this way can they become powerful. Without organization, they are nothing but a heap, an aggregate of atoms." This brilliant observation applies exactly to all forms of Communist society, the one major part of the world where the working class has never so much as known the experience of a legal strike, an elementary right won in the bourgeois world over a century ago.

The political outlook I have called "left authoritarianism" remains committed, with all sorts of qualifications, to what it regards as an "essential" value—the *idea*—of the Communist world. Usually this value is found in nationalized property, which is seen as an ultimate guarantor of progress. Where Marx spoke of "the categorical imperative that all conditions must be revolutionized in which man is a debased, an abandoned, contemptible being" (how archaic this sounds!), the left authoritarians prefer to speak of the tempo of Russian industrialization or the necessary unfolding of the iron laws of History. Where socialists have traditionally declared that the possibility of a humane society rests upon the capacity of men to act autonomously and freely, ceasing to be objects and becoming subjects of history, the left authoritarians put their faith in economic processes or historical abstractions acting beyond—indeed, usually against—the desires of living men.

Those who accept, wholly or in part, the left authoritarian outlook expect an orderly development, a moderate "democratization," from within the Communist world and *within the limits of its ethos and power.* It follows that, while sincerely deploring the Russian intervention, they deprecate the Hungarian revolution; that they regard the passion of a Zhivago for individual freedom as a sign of archaism. I think, however, that a commitment to democracy and/or socialism involves a belief in the need for a fundamental change of social relations in the Communist world, which means first and foremost, the collapse or destruction of the ruling party's monopoly of power. These contrasting perspectives involve far more than differences in theory or estimate: they involve the very heart of political and moral values.

What Pasternak's views about the future of the Communist world may be, I do not know. But I believe that if and when freedom is re-established in Russia, the people will regard him as one who, quite apart from political opinions, was faithful to the truth of their agony. And for that they will honor him.

PART III *Portraits and Polemics*

This section contains a group of journalistic pieces, mostly brief, which include portraits of political figures, polemics against intellectual opponents, and comments on a few central problems of the recent period.

The piece on John F. Kennedy was written a week after his assassination.

The article on President Johnson appeared in 1965, shortly after the dismal invasion of the Dominican Republic by the U.S. Marines.

Dating for the Stevenson pieces is provided in a head note preceding them.

I wrote the comment on the Goldwater movement in 1964, before the election.

The remarks on the Cold War and on "Communism Now" were both written for *Partisan Review* symposia, in 1962 and 1957 respectively.

The remaining group of reviews were all written during the period 1960–1965.

☼ ON THE DEATH OF JOHN F. KENNEDY

IT has been hard, these last few weeks, to feel much pride in being an American. Two assassinations, each ghastly in its own right and each uncovering still another side of our social pathology; callousness, maybe planned negligence, on the part of the Dallas police; fourth-grade children in the South cheering the news that a "nigger-loving" President had been murdered; subversion of the processes of law enforcement to the demands of television; recurrent efforts to gain political advantage, which neglect to consider that whoever may have killed the President, whether a Castroite fanatic or another kind, there remains the common breeding-ground of a hate-driven society, the common responsibility of governors and lunatics; and then smogs of piety about "national reconciliation" and "an era of good feeling" in American politics—it is just too much.

Only Mrs. Kennedy, in the splendor of her bearing, gave one any reason to be pleased with the human species; and it remains a question whether the style of a person can redeem the sickness of a culture.

Was Lee Oswald really the assassin? Despite the apparent weight of evidence, we cannot yet be absolutely certain. There is urgent reason to press for a complete inquiry: we should know whether the irregularities of his treatment by the police and the negligence that exposed him to murder were simply routine Texas conduct or a cover-up for something more sinister. An American Van der Lubbe? Probably not. It seems right now that Oswald was guilty, but we cannot be sure, and if possible, we should be.

In the long run, however, it hardly matters: for if not this Oswald, then another. What seems to me important is to sketch out his type—I do not pretend to describe him as an actual person, I wish rather to create a usable fiction, a "myth," as it emerges from the little we know about him and the somewhat more we know about his background and milieu.

A man who embodies the disorder of the city, an utterly displaced creature, totally and (what is more important) proudly alienated, without roots in nation, region, class. *He cannot stand it,* but what it is he cannot stand he does not know. A semi-intellectual, he picks up phrases and bits of ideology the way a derelict picks up cigarette butts on the street. In one guise he is a man of "the left" and in another of "the right": European history of the past forty years knows plenty of such political drifters and quick-change desperadoes. An absolutist of drifting, he is intelligent enough to be in rebellion, but sour, compulsive, repressed, seething with *ressentiment* in that intelligence. Liberal society cannot reach or understand him, and he, in turn, scorns it from the depths of chaos—or, as he comes to believe, from the heights of history. Dostoevsky was a friend of his.

He is not a Communist, for that requires patience and discipline, nor is he a Marxist, for that requires theoretic reflection. He exhibits, at some remove, the consequences of the *disintegration* of the Communist movement, which can no longer attract or control such desperate types, for it no longer offers them the balm of quick violence, the fantasy of sacrificial heroism, the unspeakable relief of individual action. It is of action that he dreams, a cleansing nihilist apocalypse; and he finds his true moral home not with Khrushchev or Mao, who have begun to seem bureaucratic and settled, but with a hoked-up vision of Castroism he has gotten from beguiled journalists. For him ideology is an incitement toward satisfying a need for bitter blood: he would be most at ease shooting up the streets of Caracas. It is toward the poorer, the backward, the Latin American countries that he now turns, countries, as it seems to him, where rebels have style, magnetism, blood, and manliness. And who is the "main enemy" of this smoldering upsurge? Who stands most in the way of the brilliant release, at once military and anarchic, which it promises him?

But he is also a Southerner, a poor Southern boy burning with memories of class humiliation. The South is a violent society, and as long as it is committed to racism, it must remain a violent society. That violence is visible not merely along its fringes, where the deviants and extremists gather, but also at its very center, in the power of the police and the brutality of the sheriff, as these are acquiesced in by the good citizens. Lashed together by the delusion of superiority, the whites know violence to be a potent answer to threats from the dark. And those very few who turn against this society must find it hard—so wracking is their apostasy—to avoid the extremist fevers which course through it. In the South men know how to shoot.

Now place against this emblem of our pathology still another, the one suggested by the sudden appearance of Jack Ruby. A petty grifter, he has hustled his way through life with no great success, and knows something about the harsh skills of the underworld, which he half admires, and something more about the harsh authority of the cops, which he wholly admires. He moves between these two worlds of force, sometimes landing in a racketeer union, sometimes handling bets near a race track, but always having to acknowledge the power of both worlds. If not a man of ideology he is certainly a man of principles, for he goes to shul every Friday night, he is generous to his sister, he loves the Presidents, every last one of them, and now finding himself in the manly precincts of Texas, he sports the clothing of a Southern tough. He is quick to rise in defense of the accredited pieties, even if his whole experience constitutes a denial of them. (Al Capone once issued a statement from jail denouncing Communism as an enemy of the American way of life.) Scrounging a fast buck, squirming in the interstices of society, he nevertheless quivers with patriotic righteousness. In the South men know how to shoot.

And then, the nightmare city. Its police chief explains why he had announced publicly the time the first suspect would be moved, thereby giving the second killer his opportunity: "We could have moved him earlier, but we told you fellows [reporters and TV men] 10 A.M. and we wanted to live up to it." Immortal words, filled with the spirit of our century! The law becomes an appendage of publicity, and experience the raw material for spectacle.

Yet the city survives. "Dallas," runs a headline in the November 26 New York *World-Telegram*, "Finds Solace in Wealth." And the story opens: "Talk to the people of Dallas about guilt and they tell you about their mansions, their oil wells and their riches. They pour money on their wounds."

Blessed are the rich in pocket, for they have inherited the earth.

Would it be sacrilegious to whisper that John F. Kennedy —for all his charm, his style, his intelligence—was not quite the "great president" almost everyone seems obliged to say he was? To enter this dissent in no way affects the grief every decent person feels at the President's death: after all, even not-so-great Presidents, like not-so-great human beings in general, have a right to live out the natural course of their lives.

Mr. Kennedy performed one deed for which he deserves high credit, and that is the signing of the atom test-ban treaty; even though the treaty has more symbolic than final bearing, it is valuable as it reflects the desire of almost everyone for an easing of the Cold War. But as for the rest of Mr. Kennedy's record, especially in domestic affairs, he was not a firm or innovating liberal, and what is more, he did not particularly claim to be. It was only his friends and his guests who made that claim. He confined himself far too much to legislative and bureaucratic maneuvering; he did not understand the necessity or value of trying to arouse the masses of people to a strongly felt political involvement and participation. His proposals were at best intelligent, but almost entirely insufficient. And on the crucial issue of civil rights, he lagged at first, responded only after a great mass movement of Negroes exerted heavy pressure, and then failed to understand that there are some issues on which it is better, both morally and politically, to go down fighting than to back away shrewdly.

(Mr. Norman Cousins, in a cadenced editorial, justifies this failure by noting that Abraham Lincoln was also unable to satisfy the impatient critics of his day. Well, it is just possible that Lincoln was wrong; and in any case, we might remember that Mr. Kennedy was facing the issue of Negro rights a hundred years later, when there was far less excuse for hesitation and when the impatience of the impatient had had some time in which to accumulate.)

The immediate prospect, as all observers remark, is for a period of "co-operation" and "moderation." Very good. That the shame and grief roused by the assassination may lead to some desirable consequences, is a bitter possibility. That the interval of "good feeling" will last more than a few months is a naïve assumption.

All historical experience indicates that such moments—from which, to be sure, every possible advantage for the cause of civil rights should be squeezed—do not and cannot last long. For the issues that have wracked American society these past years run too deep—the differences of social interest and ideological outlook are too strong—to allow any event, no matter how tragic, to keep them from reappearing. What has been shaping up in American society is a fundamental struggle as to its future direction, and the sad fact is that the most aggressive and determined political pressures have been coming from the right. Not merely or even primarily from the Birchers or Southern racists or conservative ideologists; in themselves these people are not too important; they matter as an advance guard, or noisy symptom, or extreme manifestation, of a deep-going fundamentalist reaction, a slow-moving and incipient counterrevolution, that has been gathering among the middle classes.

This is a rebellion against history. It is a wish to be done with those burdens that mar the enjoyment of new-found wealth and status. It is a desperately nostalgic impulse to shake off the complexities—which, in the absence of a coherent liberal leadership, have a way of emerging as the confusions—of world politics. And as anyone can testify who has spent some time in the Far West, this reaction involves an unashamed class selfishness such as we have not seen openly expressed in this country for some time, a new kind of Social Darwinism which is laced with the snobberies of greed and racism, a frigid contempt for those millions who are said, somewhere in the invisible depths, still to be suffering poverty and joblessness.

I think we should take this phenomenon with great seriousness. Today it may appear as an attachment to Goldwater, but in social range and depth it goes beyond the Goldwater movement. Signs of it could already be found in the Eisenhower following, and it will survive the possible collapse of the Goldwater boom. For a few months this sociopolitical impulse may be silenced, but it speaks too authentically for the sentiments of millions of Americans to be long suppressed.

Every issue in American politics—from civil rights to joblessness, from automation to support for colleges, from Medicare to city planning—now elicits a fundamental divergence in outlook. It cannot be helped: not all the speeches of President Johnson, nor all the columns of James Reston, can prevent it. The issue is not, as the rightist doctrinaires claim, between capitalism and socialism, but between a firm decision to pull away from modernity and social responsibility, and the inclination to move (more often, stumble) toward an enlarged welfare state.

This is a central issue in American political life, and the struggle in regard to it cannot be stilled or long postponed. It seems to me a little shocking when one hears intelligent people reduced to an American equivalent of Kremlinology and engaged in gossipy speculations as to whether "Lyndon" will shift his political stress for tactical reasons, and what "Arthur" said or didn't say. Instead, we had better do some hard thinking and make some genuine commitments.

From a liberal-left perspective there is reason for disquiet. The labor movement, facing major perils, dozes away in a state of intellectual torpor; it appeals to no segments of the unorganized, it gains no loyalties among the young, it barely makes itself heard in the discussions of national policy. The liberal movement, as a movement, has become slack, uncombative. And even the one tremendously encouraging development of the last few years, the rise of the Negroes, is for the moment balked, uncertain in perspective, a little exhausted, trapped in the dilemma that its all-too-reasonable immediate demands involve the deepest issues and problems of the American economy.

And the intellectuals? Those who are supposed to move in advance, not content with the complacence of the *status quo?* My own impression is not a happy one. In New York, as I now see it again, there is much brilliance, little direction; a great deal of talent, not much purpose. A large fraction of the writing in the advanced journals strikes me as middle-aged narcissism, a bit Alexandrian, in which the stress is upon intellectual display rather than intellectual conviction. At the very time when there are larger audiences, few American intellectuals seem to me strongly concerned with the idea of a coherent political and cultural public. Things, as the sociologists say, have become "privatized."

Intellectuals ought to be able to look beyond the moment, which means to look beyond the pieties of "national reconciliation" and toward the difficulties ahead. No one is going to be adored for saying this, but that does not make it any the less true.

☼ JOHNSON AND THE MYTH OF CONSENSUS

NOW and again we all succumb to the naïve hope that behind a public man's appearance there must be another, private reality; but anyone involved in politics of whatever kind soon comes to learn that it is a mode of life enforcing a remarkable closeness between public and private styles. What drew intellectuals to Stevenson and Kennedy was, in fact, a sense that they were "different," that they were political men who maintained some critical perspective upon themselves and therefore experienced a strain between what they were and what they had to do. Stevenson gained sympathy because he seemed to find this burden hard to bear, Kennedy won admiration because he carried the burden with such grace. Now all this may be a mere indulgent fantasy on our part, for Stevenson's notable sophistication has not kept him from playing a role at the United Nations often humiliating and sometimes deceitful. Still, for those of us who believe that self-awareness and its inevitable consequence of self-division are the marks of a civilized man, it is hard to become emotionally involved with any public figure who does not at least suggest a trace of these characteristics.

Perhaps that is why the intellectuals, while obliged to vote for Johnson, have felt so little warmth toward him. He is a totally political man, clever but not thoughtful, calculating more than reflective. He appears at once sentimental and ruthless, thin-skinned and imperious, remarkably attuned to public moods and utterly expert at the "game" of political maneuver. He is all of a piece, seemingly monolithic, not only completely *in* but totally *of* politics. Upon the devices and costs of political manipulation he is capable of looking with some irony, but toward the idea of the manipulation itself and the kind of life it entails he shows no irony whatever. For him the system of American politics is an unquestioned "given," just as the system of Russian politics must be for Brezhnev. The man is the role; the person, the function.

Within very narrow limits, this may explain why he has been so much more effective than was Kennedy in securing passage of such desirable legislation as the civil rights and education bills. (I leave aside, for the moment, the fact that Johnson won the Presidency by a far greater margin than did Kennedy.) Johnson felt no awe, no uncertainty, no fastidiousness before the mechanics of Congressional politics. Understanding it completely and accepting it gladly, he worked entirely within its limits. Sometimes he twisted arms, sometimes he waved carrots. Thereby Johnson managed to achieve more on the domestic front than his predecessor, who was neither inclined to go to the people, as in part Franklin Roosevelt had been, nor skillful at working with the politicians. The lesson seems inescapable: either be part of the machine or fight against it, but don't convey a tone of elitist superiority toward the system in whose survival you acquiesce.

Does Johnson have root convictions? The question may well be unanswerable. When he repeatedly voted in the Senate against civil rights legislation, he was no doubt sincere; when he pushed through a civil rights bill as President, he was again sincere; and it may be doubted that in the interim he was overcome by a flash of revelation. In the mind of an expert politician, the matter of right and wrong cannot be separated from an estimate of political possibilities and a measure of the conflicting forces that bring their weight to bear upon the government. What changed between Senator Johnson and President Johnson was not, or not primarily, the man Lyndon Johnson; what changed was the temper of American politics, the thrust and power of the aroused Negroes and their allies. Once there was enough pressure to make the civil rights bill a political possibility, there would soon be enough pressure to make it a political necessity; and thereby the moral problem would be transformed in nature, since now it could be quantified, it could be measured in units of gain and risk. It had become "real."

Am I being cynical? I think not. For while we may yearn for a more elevated mode of public discourse, we ought to recognize that as long as we have to function in this kind of world we would profit by thinking not merely, or so much, in the stylistic terms which encourage the Kennedy myth but also in terms of power, pressure, political coalitions. What Johnson will do in extending the welfare state, or what he can be prodded into doing, will depend no more on his personal crudeness than it would have depended, had Kennedy lived, on Kennedy's personal refinement. It will depend on what happens in the social life of the country, on which groups show strength and a serious disposition to combativeness.

This point seems especially urgent in trying to understand why Johnson has been so much more flexible and liberal in domestic than in foreign policy. I am not, of course, saying that it is all a matter of pressures within the balance of a pluralist society. Personal factors count. Johnson, no doubt, shares the simple emotional responses of the American middle class—and the working class—that the flag must not be trod upon, that Communism must be "stopped" everywhere. There is a tradition in this country of joining populism with chauvinism, and it is from a blend of the two that Johnson has been shaped politically. Probably he has also been guilty of a simple but gross miscalculation: the notion that the kind of stick-and-carrot maneuver that more or less works within a "consensus" society will also work in foreign affairs—a dangerous mistake imposing an overly simplified model of the domestic complexity upon the still more complex international scene.

Yet once allowance is made for the inclination of a man like Johnson to explode into sheer belligerent nationalism and to suppose he can handle the world as if it were Texas multiplied several times over, there is another and perhaps decisive element. The alignment of forces within the United States which makes possible a moderate if insufficient progress in domestic affairs simply breaks down when it has to confront foreign policy.

By now, measures to improve or extend welfarism are accepted by a large segment of the country. A good education bill can be passed without upsetting the balance of political or social forces and without having to conduct a struggle for popular support that might be politically damaging in the future. But the same thing is by no means true in regard to foreign policy.

Sustained dissent on foreign policy comes only from minority segments of the academic world, small groups of pacifists and some liberals. Add these together, multiply a few times out of sheer generosity, and the result is still more impressive for articulateness than power and mass support.

If, then, we recognize that in regard to foreign policy the Johnson administration is under far less popular constraint than in regard to domestic policy, and if we also bear in mind that our constitutional system allows the President very large powers in conducting external affairs, we must conclude somewhat unhappily that on problems like Vietnam and the Dominican Republic Johnson has a relatively free hand. Confronting a Medicare bill he must calculate and measure; considering a proposal to send Marines to Latin America he can act upon what he takes to be the national interest, or what may at the moment come to little more than his, or his advisers', panic and pique. And what is more, he can act with considerable assurance that his views on foreign policy, in their instinctive simplicity, are harmonious with the desires of a majority of the American people.

The result has been a worsening of a bad policy, which in principle allows the United States to cast itself in the role of policeman of the world. And the danger that ensues is not so much that of total war as it is a series of draining and interminable small wars, today in Vietnam, tomorrow in Latin America, the day after in the Near East—though it should be added that if the contingent of "hawks" keeps growing more influential and imposes upon the United States its chimerical goal of military "victory" in Vietnam, even a full-scale war with China is a possibility not to be excluded. For the United States is trying to do something in South Vietnam which may not be impossible but is certain to exact a very high political and social cost: it is trying to reverse a severe political defeat through a desperate use of military means; it is trying to blur the obvious fact that the Vietcong rests upon very considerable indigenous support; it is trying to evade the consequences of years of reactionary and stupid politics in Vietnam (support of Diem, etc.); it is trying to act in the name of a South Vietnamese nation which has all but crumbled and now consists of little more than a military apparatus; and perhaps worst of all, it is trying to do all this through systematic "management" of news, which in practice comes to little more than distortion and suppression of the dismal facts.

Yet the situation is a good deal more complicated than I have thus far allowed, and consequently a bit more hopeful. Those of us critical of American foreign policy may not have behind us the popular support which can be gained for proposals to extend domestic welfare legislation; but in a society where, alas, there is a great deal of indifference and passivity among the population at large, it becomes possible for articulate minority groups to exert—whether for good or bad—an influence disproportionate to their numerical strength. The Johnson administration, so faithful a replica of American institutional life, is enormously, even morbidly sensitive to public criticism; the President's mania for admiration and "consensus" seems almost a caricature of national character; and the result offers opportunities—though not only for "us." More seriously, there are intelligent people in Washington who realize that the continuity and self-assurance of the American political elite is greatly affected by what happens in the universities. Intellectuals, having lost much of their political bite, have gained in political influence; perhaps now, if they bite a little harder, it will be worth having the influence. Protests, teach-ins, counterproposals do not go unheard.

Consider, as a test case of what I have been saying, the invasion of the Dominican Republic. Here we faced a situation that, roughly speaking, was equivalent to the stage Vietnam was in some ten years ago—that is, a situation not yet politically hopeless. In Vietnam, thanks to French imperialism, geography, and a complex of local factors, the movement of national resistance was from the outset strongly under Communist influence, almost entirely in the North but measurably in the South. The solution that liberals and socialists have been advancing, not very effectively, for underdeveloped countries—a mixture of careful economic aid and political support for an indigenous "democratic left"—was extremely difficult to apply in the Vietnam of the fifties. For there the "democratic left" had never been strong and what there was of it had been repeatedly smashed by the Japanese, the French, the Communists, and the Diem government.

In the Dominican Republic, however, there was present a viable movement under the leadership of Juan Bosch which did aspire toward a democratic alternative to Communist and reactionary dictatorships. When Bosch, overwhelmingly chosen as President in a free election, was removed by a military junta, the United States did not stir into immediate action; that did not strike the State Department as reason for dispatching troops. At least, however, the Kennedy administration had the decency to withhold military aid and formal recognition from the junta. Johnson reversed this policy, as part of a larger shift of emphasis from the social reform promised by the Alliance for Progress to the traditional support of military regimes.

The immediate consequences we all know: the United States, so frequently declared by Adlai Stevenson, an admirer of legal niceties, violated the charter of the Organization of the American States; threw the Dominican democrats into despair; provoked the hostility and contempt of every democratic country in Latin America; and provided the Communists with a political advantage they will be exploiting for a decade.

It was vile, stupid, reactionary. And the effort at justification was insulting to ordinary human intelligence: a list of fifty-eight Communists active in Santo Domingo, without even the pretense of examining the extent of their influence, or the inner relationship of political forces in the country, or the possible consequences of sending troops. One reason the Johnson administration could resort to such shabby devices was that it assumed it would not have to face any mass opposition. Only the intellectuals would protest.

Whatever the outcome of this disaster, it is important right now to keep asking some hard questions. On what kind of information was the decision made to send troops? Did it really seem so urgent that even a day or two delay to consult the OAS countries could not have been accepted? And by what moral right does the United States government presume to choose which faction shall constitute the Dominican government? Does the "Johnson doctrine" signify that the United States is to become the policeman of the world? Will troops be dispatched to any country in which a revolution breaks out and extends beyond the limits permitted by the State Department?

For by their very nature, revolutions are ambiguous; conflicting political tendencies may join together momentarily in behalf of common ends, such as the removal of a dictator; those ends achieved, the tendencies within the revolution then come into conflict with one another. If the possibility or threat that the Communists will take over democratic revolutions—a possibility or threat that is, of course, quite real—becomes the justification for military intervention, then the United States may gain some temporary victories but in the long run will be enabling the very forces it claims to be halting.

Meanwhile, one thing is clear: the protests of intellectuals and academics seem now to matter. This should give us a modest confidence but should also serve as a warning not to exhaust whatever political credit we have. There is a destructive and at times nihilistic fringe in the essentially healthy campus protests; it takes the form, at times, of a vulgarized sort of Marxism which asserts the evils and failures of American foreign policy to be inevitable. (But if you believe that, then what is the point of demanding that the United States withdraw from Vietnam? And how do you explain the presence not only of "hawks" but of "doves," and how do you motivate your support of the "doves"? Unless of course you mean your protest simply as a maneuver to "expose," etc., etc. . . .) And disturbingly the campus protests have sometimes spilled over from entirely legitimate attacks upon United States policy in Vietnam to either an ingenuous or disingenuous support of the Vietcong.

It is a difficult position: to fight against the moral and political insanity of the "hawks" while dissociating ourselves unambiguously from the authoritarian "left." If ever there was a need in this country for a strong articulation of a true liberalism, a clear democratic radicalism, it is now. I propose that we try.

☼ STEVENSON

THIS essay was published in 1954, at a time when the McCarthyite ugliness was at its worst and most American intellectuals were placing enormous hopes on Adlai Stevenson. I argued that these hopes were misconceived and still think my argument was right. In the adulation of Stevenson I tried to analyze the dilemmas of a postwar liberalism caught between a nostalgia for political combativeness and a growing appetite for cultural gentility.

The postscript that follows the essay was written shortly after Stevenson's death in 1965. By then he was no longer the hero of the intellectuals, though some of them addressed wistful appeals to him. His record at the United Nations, as public apologist for acts it seems he privately deplored, was not an inspiring one. Yet I felt a certain sympathy for him, as a man caught in the dilemma of trying simultaneously to remain faithful to his personal convictions and fulfill what he took to be his public duty. He may never have quite been a hero, but he *had* become a figure of genuine pathos.

✡ STEVENSON AND THE INTELLECTUALS

ONLY the eggheads surrendered unconditionally. When Adlai Stevenson made his rather cryptic remark about "egghead ecstasy," he was registering a certain irritation with the cult that sprang up around his image in the intellectual world. Whether he objected from a principled dislike of hero worship or from a fear that it would hurt his chance with other, somewhat larger segments of the population, we don't know. Probably he meant both. In any case he completely captured the intellectuals, not least of all those who had declared themselves irrevocably disabused with the political life.

One wonders: why this sudden burst of uncritical enthusiasm? Surely not because Stevenson was a liberal or a New Dealer; the ideological explanation seems weakest. For if it was Stevenson's forthright liberalism that endeared him to the intellectuals, then they should have been fonder still of Truman, a man considerably more forthright. And it is common knowledge that they were not very fond of Truman: even their efforts to admire him had a way of turning into condescension.

In foreign policy Truman and Stevenson—as, for that matter, Eisenhower—had few significant differences, while in domestic policy Truman was, if anything, slightly to the left of Stevenson, who let it be known throughout the campaign that he was a moderate, sensible Democrat.

Which suggests the possibility that Stevenson won the admiration of the intellectuals not because he revived the tradition of American liberalism but because in several important ways he deviated from it.

I have recently been going through Stevenson's campaign speeches, trying to discover the secret of his success with the intellectuals. Part of the secret, I should think, must be that he so vividly symbolized their mixed feelings toward politics itself. The American intellectuals felt that their fingers had been badly burned, though by comparison with the Europeans they had merely suffered a slight singe; they were bored with crusading accents yet still enjoyed a mild idealistic lilt; they were tempted to abandon politics entirely yet felt themselves forced—indeed, trapped—into a lukewarm, gingerly participation; they wished for liberal humaneness but felt that to identify with any social class or group was outmoded, deficient in tone. And here was this remarkable man from Illinois, so charming and cultivated, so witty and so . . . well, *somewhat* weary . . . come to represent and speak for them. Roosevelt might be admired for things he had done, Stevenson was to be admired and identified with simply because of what he was.

Admired and identified with, above all, because he didn't seem really to *like* politics. His most remarkable speech—the speech of acceptance—was a prolonged exercise in ambivalence, a skillful teetering between the desire to pull out and the appetite to plunge in: I say "skillful" to suggest that he was a man both torn by doubts and shrewdly able to exploit his state of division. At times Stevenson resembled a debutante who had contracted a hasty marriage and despite the use of the most advanced precautions had been blessed with issue: and there she stands, uncomfortably holding a diaper between thumb and forefinger. Yet this stance could not have been entirely without a disingenuous element, for Stevenson was hardly a political novice. He had been in and near the Democratic Party for years, he had worked with that old Tory Frank Knox, he had served as the candidate of Jake Arvey's Illinois machine, which has never been noted for fastidiousness. Stevenson had not really "earned" his air of withdrawal and distance—he was *not* Henry Adams languidly collapsing on the Second Law of Thermodynamics. Or if he was, then one could not help taking seriously the charges of such a malicious reactionary as James Burnham that Stevenson was unfit to be President through temperamental disability.

In his introduction to his collected speeches Stevenson has written a remarkable passage about his campaign experience:

> You must emerge, bright and bubbling with wisdom and well-being, every morning at 8 o'clock, just in time for a charming and profound breakfast talk, shake hands with hundreds, often literally thousands, of people, make several inspiring, "newsworthy" speeches during the day, confer with political leaders along the way and with your staff all the time, write at every chance, think if possible, read mail and newspapers, talk on the telephone, *talk to everybody,* dictate, receive delegations, eat, with decorum—and discretion!—and ride through city after city on the back of an open car, *smiling until your mouth is dehydrated by the wind,* waving until the blood runs out of your arm, and then bounce gaily, confidently, masterfully into *great howling halls.* . . .

I have italicized what seem the key phrases: phrases of dissociation which Roosevelt would have been too shrewd to utter and Truman would never have felt any desire to. Precisely this sense of separation from his audience, as from his public self, made Stevenson seem an emblem of the intellectual condition. Under the circumstances it hardly mattered to the intellectuals what he said, just as to the bulk of the middle class it hardly mattered what Eisenhower said.

Not only could the intellectuals identify with Stevenson's public indecisions and hesitations; they could admire the spectacle of such behavior on *a higher social level* than their own. Had Stevenson really been an intellectual in the limited "professional" sense of the word, his proclamations and gestures of delicacy might have seemed annoying, since there is nothing very novel in the sight of an intellectual turning squeamish about tasks he has set himself. But for the intellectuals to see their attitudes acted out upon the public stage by a patrician who, unlike Franklin D. Roosevelt, made no effort to be anything but a patrician, by a man whose grandfather had actually been Vice-President of the United States, by a man who had married into wealth with apparent ease and out of it with obvious forbearance—this, indeed, was pleasant. In an age of "the liberal imagination" and "the new conservatism," those Siamese twins of cultural adaptation, the intellectuals themselves were beginning to cast a warm eye on that restrained yet elegant style of life which Stevenson so beautifully embodied. It seems a blunder of history that it had to be Eisenhower, a country boy turned warrior, who became President of a University graced by such figures of worldly cultivation as Gilbert Highet and Jacques Barzun. Does it take any effort of the imagination to *see* Stevenson presiding at a faculty tea in Morningside Heights?

Just as Stevenson bewitched the intellectuals by miming, from on high, their political impulses, so did he fail to attract very much enthusiasm among the workers. By and large they voted for him, but with little of the fervor they had felt for Roosevelt and Truman. At one time Roosevelt had seemed a saviour, a man who crossed the social tracks never to return. Truman was one of the plebes, and after his triumph over Dewey there was a remarkable elation in the Detroit auto plants for the workers felt, and with some reason, that they had put Truman in the White House. To some extent, the suspicion of Stevenson indicated the usual anti-intellectualism, but this could hardly have been the whole cause, since I'm told that even among those secondary United Automobile Workers officials who make an effort to avoid the more obvious forms of anti-intellectualism there was a distinct coolness toward Stevenson. He was admired for his cleverness and praised for his vocabulary, which was large for a presidential candidate; but he was clearly not one of "the people," he didn't pretend to be, he was the candidate who would rise above *mere* group interests.

Stevenson was the first of the liberal candidates in the post-Wilson era who made no effort to align himself with the plebeian tradition or with plebeian sentiments; Stevenson was the candidate whom the intellectuals, trying hard to remove plebeian stains, admired most. There is no way of "proving" this to be a causal relationship, but it would be naïve to suppose it a mere coincidence.

2.

But there were other, more important reasons. To understand why the Americans for Democratic Action, for example, was so enthusiastic about Stevenson it would be well to remember that originally it was enthusiastic about Eisenhower. This fact the ADA would as soon forget, but for its own good we should be so unkind as not to let it. After the election Arthur Schlesinger, Jr. wrote a slashing piece for *Partisan Review* about the troubles and timidities of liberals in a nation that had not chosen Stevenson; had he discussed why the ADA, in which he is a leading figure, had first proposed Eisenhower, his article would have been an act of high courage.

It may be argued that the ADA acted from ignorance,

that it did not know how mediocre and reactionary Eisenhower would prove to be. That must certainly be true. Had the ADA favored Eisenhower with full knowledge that he would soon show himself a political weakling and a captive of Big Business, it would not have been a liberal organization at all; it would have been a conservative or reactionary one. What made it, characteristically, a *liberal* organization was that it stood ready to support a man about whom it knew nothing except that he had been, it was reliably said, a competent general.

Yet there seems to me to have been a certain unconscious consistency, if not a very strong devotion to liberal principles, in the ADA endorsements of both Eisenhower and Stevenson. Consider, by way of introduction, the following points:

a) In a mild way, Eisenhower's political appeal was of the kind called "Bonapartist." Appearing at a moment of national bewilderment, when the Korean War seemed likely to continue forever and the Truman administration was shown to be shot through with corruption, Eisenhower, that stern yet homely figure, could speak as one who was not a professional "politician" yet "sound" in his views, a man alive to every need yet beyond the claim of any class or group. He was an unknown quantity, a chaste vessel into which every voter could pour his own desires. People voted for Eisenhower not merely because he promised to clean up the mess or because he satisfied the conservative moods of the new managerial strata; they chose him because he, in his stammering inscrutability, would relieve them of their burdens and take upon himself the whole intolerable weight of the nation. Traditionally, this has been the appeal of the Bonapartist leader. I do not mean to imply that Eisenhower had dictatorial ambitions, merely that he won because he was endowed, in the public eye, with the supraclass characteristics of the Bonapartist leader.

b) The favorite theory, at the moment, of American liberals about the nature of our society is advanced in economic terms by John Kenneth Galbraith ("countervailing powers") and in more general terms by Daniel Bell. The Marxist scheme of a conflict between two major classes, says Bell, does not apply very well to America: here, instead of a class struggle we have a jockeying among competing yet not incompatible power groups or interest blocs (labor, farmers, business, veterans, minority groups, the aged, etc.). Instead of ruling class and ruled we have a sharing, with desirable friction, of political power. I have argued elsewhere that Bell's theory is inadequate because it fails to recognize those patterns of subordination among interest blocs which depend upon relationships of social classes; but I fancy that neither Bell nor those who agree with him are likely to heed this criticism. The theory he advances is perfectly adjusted to, as it is a faithful reflection of, a moment of social stasis resulting from the full production of a war economy. It is a theory that replaces the image of basic social conflict with an image of controlled or controllable social competition among peer groups. Nothing is at present more likely to appeal to liberal intellectuals. Even those who have never heard of Galbraith or Bell hold similar views.

c) But if American society consists of an essentially healthy jostling among equally hearty social appetites, where do the intellectuals come in? Which is *their* interest group? They are too weak to stand independently, and at present are largely disinclined to stand in alliance with any other group. More important, what happens, given this theory of society, to the *ideal* claims and aspirations of the intellectuals, those claims and aspirations that are so deeply ingrained in their tradition? One may feel comfortable in the kind of society described by Bell but one can hardly find it a cause for enthusiasm. In the past, when radical intellectuals identified with the working class, it was with the expectation and hope that the working class, preparing the way for a new society, would abolish itself in common with all other social classes. But if today the struggle of labor, or any other social group, is merely for a little more of the contaminated swill—well, all right; but it can hardly stimulate those latent impulses toward the *ideal* which the intellectuals cannot quite (though they try hard enough) obliterate in themselves.

What happens now if we bring together these three observations? The appetite for a Bonapartist leader above classes was quite prevalent in this country in the period before the election; it was shared by the liberals, e.g., the ADA's endorsement of Eisenhower not despite but because of its ignorance of his social views. At the same time the liberal intellectuals, committed to a theory of American society that is "realistic" in the worst sense of the word, found themselves without a social place or tie, yet with an appetite for "transcending" even while retaining the theory of interest blocs. This appetite, in turn, is related to and perhaps is an aspect of that yearning for a social saviour I have previously mentioned.

A striking characteristic of Stevenson's campaign, as distinct from Roosevelt's or Truman's, was that he did not speak in the name of the poor or the workers or "one-third of the nation." The conservative press was always delighted to praise him for not indulging in Truman's "demagogy," that is, for not employing Truman's "antiplutocrat" vocabulary. Whenever Stevenson spoke before a special interest group he went out of his way to declare himself not merely *for* it, like any politician, but also *above* it—the mark of a statesman, no doubt. Somehow he, Stevenson, represented no less than "the people as a whole." In a way that he did not and could not specify, he and the Democratic Party were to provide a universal ideological binder in our society of competing yet not basically conflicting interests. Thus it was that Stevenson made it possible for the liberal intellectuals to see themselves as both realists and idealists at the same time: they could sanction a theory that American liberalism meant little more than the proper regulation of a division of the social spoils while yet invoking, through Stevenson's soaring rhetoric, a vision of that good society which once, long ago, had some actual relationship to liberal politics.

A psychological equation can now be set up: the surrender of the managerial middle class to Eisenhower is as the surrender of the intellectuals to Stevenson. But some qualifications are necessary: the middle class had no critical tradition to abandon and when it saw Eisenhower as its patron it was not far from wrong. Both groups, however, succumbed to their respective heroes with an alarmingly naïve faith, and in no way more alarming than for what it suggests of their future political behavior.

3.

It would be easy to run through Stevenson's speeches and point to the many patches of shabbiness and cant which show him to be not quite the Knight of Principle his intellectual admirers took him for. Let me cite only a few examples. Stevenson's evidently sincere devotion to civil liberties was badly compromised by his readiness to support the Smith Act and by his praise of Truman for having "put the leaders of the Communist Party in this country where they belong—behind bars" (as if *that* were any solution to the problem of Stalinism, or of civil liberties!). His advocacy of civil rights legislation was painfully qualified by his prolonged silence about the opposition of his running mate Sparkman to such legislation. His innumerable references to the split of the Republican Party into several parties seem rather cheap when one notices his refusal to face the equally obvious fact that the Democratic Party is also and indeed far more seriously split. His friendly references to the Negroes must be set against his shameful remarks in a Richmond, Virginia, speech where he placed "anti-Southernism" on a plane of equal abhorrence with "anti-Negroism." His courage in jibing at professional patrioteers at the American Legion convention is contaminated by such nonsense as his declaration that "Legionnaires are united by memories of war. Therefore, no group is more devoted to peace." (That *therefore* is priceless.) And what is one to make of his preposterous declaration that "Communist materialism" cannot be answered with "a different brand of materialism," a statement worthy of the Rev. Norman Vincent Peale; what is one to make of his utterly disingenuous remarks that the Truman administration should not be blamed for corruption since "corruption is personal and knows no party"—as if corruption might not be more indigenous to one party, or one kind of party, than another. . . .

At this point: impatient interruptions. My liberal friends cry out. After all, Stevenson was the candidate of a major party, which means he was trying to get elected. . . . No doubt. But you can't have it both ways. You can't admire Stevenson as a principled idealist and then justify his evasions on the ground that he was a candidate. I don't mean to deny that principled people have to make concessions to expediency; but the whole failure of recent liberalism has been precisely its inability to distinguish between expediency within the framework of principle and expediency that undermines and rots away principle. Sometimes one has to blink, but that doesn't mean to keep one's eyes shut.

4.

Only after the election did Stevenson reveal his full inadequacy. His round-the-world tour could be the subject of an article on the relationship between rhetoric and *realpolitik*, but here I would only say that his American admirers might at least have raised a whisper, or a whimper, of protest when he came out with praise for Chiang Kai-shek (which led one political wag to remark: *keep that man away from Madrid*). The breathless reports of Stevenson's tour in *The New Republic* have had a kind of fabulous quality, as if

Michael Straight had smuggled himself into Marco Polo's party.

More serious is Stevenson's failure to speak up with any sort of firmness against the Eisenhower administration. Here, one would think, is a golden opportunity for a liberal opposition. This administration of sanctioned mediocrity and open alliance with Big Business; this collection of moral weaklings who tremble every time McCarthy lets out his breath; this incredible group of blunderers and reactionaries—could there be a better target for liberal criticism? But Stevenson is no mere politician, he is a statesman; he is *responsible* and *restrained;* he believes in calling a spade an implement for the lifting of difficult objects.

Why does Stevenson remain silent? Because, writes Richard Rovere, he fears that "the attacks will in many parts of the world be read as a repudiation of American ends rather than as criticism of Administration means." One would think that the only possible way of reasserting "American ends" would be through a prolonged and sharp criticism of "Administration means." But that would be the way of a politician and not of a statesman who can quote from William James until the intellectuals quiver with delight. What is perhaps equally disturbing is that Mr. Rovere repeats this sort of thing in a tone of sympathetic understanding, as if to imply that we liberals, so raucous in the past, now possess a statesman too.

The only intelligent discussion of Stevenson that I have seen comes from an English journalist, G. L. Arnold, who reported on Stevenson's trip through England in *The New Leader.* This report is so germane to my remarks that I would quote at some length:

The fact is that, to put it bluntly, Stevenson struck the British as unduly anxious to conform with the prevailing American popular mood; and it so happens that this mood has few defenders here, even on the extreme Right of the Tory party, let alone among people further to the left.

[Those who heard Stevenson] had come expecting to hear and see a man who could be trusted to continue the Roosevelt-Truman inheritance in foreign policy. What they got was a more graceful and less bumbling edition of John Foster Dulles.

Again, there was his curious evasiveness about McCarthy. Admittedly he must be getting bored with having to explain that McCarthy is no Hitler, but then no one suggested that. He was simply asked for his views. They amounted to this: that McCarthy's "methods" were not perhaps all they might be, but that it was a good thing to draw attention to the Communist menace. This was not merely inadequate and evasive; it revealed a curious reluctance to say anything that might cause unpleasantness at home. . . . One can hardly suppose that Stevenson really believes McCarthy is basically doing a good job; in that case, why not say so and thus take some of the poison out of the current anti-American campaign? It is no exaggeration to say that his hearers were hoping, above all, that he would help them to project the image of a genuinely sane and liberal America. They received no assistance from him. What they got was a display of agility in ducking awkward questions.

The general consensus among the initiated was that [Stevenson] seemed a very likable kind of liberal Republican and that it was a pity he could not be included in the Eisenhower Administration. It may, of course, be that the British have an altogether mistaken view of what the Democratic Party is, and that these various puzzled reactions just show our ignorance and naivete. But, such as they are, they suggest that there is a gap between our image of American liberalism and the actual movement that goes by this name. And one begins to suspect that Mr. Stevenson's little bodyguard of friends and admirers, with their literary contacts and facilities for the projection of their views, are not altogether innocent of having allowed this gap to become so wide.

5.

Very likely, for some years to come, American socialists will have no electoral course of their own. We shall probably be confined to the basic job of advancing and clarifying our ideas as to the nature of modern society and the need for a radical social change, and to serving as a radical gadfly to the labor-liberal movement, demanding from it what is at present no small or inglorious thing: that it remain faithful, at least, to the tradition of liberalism. But for the liberal-labor movement to do this, it will have to come into increasingly frequent collision with whatever administration, of whichever party, happens to be in power. In a permanent war economy there are certain to arise grave conflicts between the needs of the bureaucratic state and the masses of trade unionists over issues ranging from civil liberties to taxation. Let but such figures as Walter Reuther and Arthur Schlesinger, Jr. stand firm in behalf of their own tradition, and they will have to invigorate their liberalism with far more critical spirit—they will have to make it more radical—than they thus far have.

Even if this were to happen, we would still be far from any basic solutions to our social problems—but then, we are far from seeing it happen. To prod and criticize, in firm but friendly terms, the dominant labor-liberal tendency is not, one must admit, an obviously exciting perspective, certainly not as exciting as that which lies open to the socialists of England, where there is a real possibility of leading a democratic transition to socialism. But it is a perspective that is likely to keep us thoroughly employed. From what we have seen of the liberals in the recent election, we need not worry that they will render criticism from the left superfluous.

☼ ADLAI STEVENSON: THE LAST, SAD YEARS

ADLAI STEVENSON was surely the most attractive human being to figure prominently in American politics since the Second World War. He was a cultivated man, in the tradition of an older America that seems almost to have disappeared. His wit was real, and it was his own. He was happily free of those delusional claims to omnipotence and omniscience which seem to overcome men of power, even in democratic republics. And for thoughtful people there was something intensely affecting in his readiness to acknowledge inner doubt, as if it were not at all a cause for shame but rather a mark of humanity.

Stevenson did not try to create a legend around his person; only his admirers did. He had the courage to enter American politics without a "lovely family": he had neither an unforgettable wife like Mamie nor a beautiful one like Jackie. He came alone, without a clan.

In underlying values and personal manner, Stevenson was a liberal man. He was ready to listen to opposing views with courtesy and attention; he believed in civilized discourse; he sought to puncture his opponent's pretensions, not to destroy his existence. But as we use the word "liberal" in this country, to signify someone more or less militantly devoted to social and economic reform, Stevenson was certainly not a liberal. Indeed, there was something both comic and pathetic in the eagerness of his intellectual admirers to remold him in the image of their desire. It was as if, in their affection for his style, they could not bear to acknowledge his distance from their belief. In some cases, however, the intellectuals were drawn to him precisely because he lacked the militant posture of the traditional American liberal: they were drawn to him because, in the increasingly conservative fifties, when the myth of social peace came to be accepted with barely a qualification, Stevenson represented what they hoped to become rather than what they had once been or might still be.

A moderately conservative man, Stevenson was prepared to accept the welfare state and some humane extensions of it. But this is no longer a matter of liberalism, only of intelligence. He had no zeal, no crusading fire, very little of the gift for reaching the ear of the masses which his far less attractive contemporary, Harry Truman, did have. And he never pretended to be anything but what he was. For the wistful delusions of his admirers he could not be held responsible.

The last years were painful, even pitiable. Stevenson at the United Nations was forced to defend precisely those aspects of American policy—the Bay of Pigs, escalation in Vietnam, invasion of the Dominican Republic—that were least defensible. He shrank in valor and manliness by choosing to repeat untruths and allowing himself to be used, quite cynically, by two presidents who needed his reputation and skill but cared little for his advice. Loyalty one can understand, even to presidents he might not have quite admired.

But there comes a time when it is loyalty to one's deepest convictions which matters most—that and nothing else.

Perhaps that time had come; perhaps it is true, as some correspondents have written, that he was preparing to resign. It would have been good. It might have helped stem, or slow, the disastrous course of President Johnson's foreign policy. Yet there is no reason to suppose that Stevenson would have taken the lead as public spokesman for the opposition, stirring the country to the outrage in the Dominican Republic, the danger in Vietnam, the distortion of the Alliance for Progress. He was not that kind of man and, what is more, he did not hold the views of those of us who criticize United States foreign policy from a radical perspective.

Still, we who would judge Stevenson for not having resigned—and I do judge him—must also consider what his choices were. He could have led the opposition? But in practice, what did that mean? For there is no real, no significant, no major opposition to which he could have turned.

The ADA: is it anything more than an agency for passing a few resolutions? The "new left": can you imagine Adlai Stevenson linking arms with Prof. Staughton Lynd, who has delivered himself in public print of a fantasy about demonstrators taking over the White House? The trade unions: can you see those intellectual eminences, George Meany and Jay Lovestone, welcoming Stevenson? The teach-ins: well perhaps, but they hardly constitute a major force within American life.

The sad part of Stevenson's last years was not merely that he lost in dignity, nor even that he allowed himself to do some very dirty work for Kennedy and Johnson. No, the sad part was that there was nowhere for him to turn, no arena of liberal criticism in which he could speak. The lack of structure, the absence of coherence, the failure in sustained controversy, which characterizes our political life also limits the opportunities available to individual leaders. They cannot do by themselves, even if they should want to, what the political system does not support. Stevenson's failure was the failure of an old-fashioned style of personal politics, the cultivated conservatism of the nineteenth century trying to cope with the realities of the twentieth.

An attractive human being is gone: we have not had very many in public life, and our present leaders do not encourage expectations of more. But let us not delude ourselves as to what Adlai Stevenson signified. He was not a man of the left, not a traditional or even new-style American liberal. He was a man who tried to act by civilized standards within the present society, and he did not succeed.

☼ THE GOLDWATER MOVEMENT

SIMPLY by winning the Republican nomination, Senator Goldwater has left a strong imprint on American politics.

Everything now shifts in his direction. The apparatus of a major party lies in the grip of his friends. The terms of public debate will be determined not by the authentic and pressing needs of the country, but by the ideological fantasias of the right wing. And the most committed and fervent political activity may be expected to come from Goldwater partisans who now can finally feel they have a cause of their own.

This last seems to me especially important. There is a new political energy surging up in this country, it is an energy of hard-bitten resentment, and it is driven by intensity of purpose at the very moment that almost all other political tendencies have become sated, slack or feeble. It provides for many Americans an ideological lure in which the imagery of nostalgia nestles against vicarious brinkmanship.

Whatever else, it ought to be clear how inadequate was the official liberalism of the last few decades. Both the Negro movement, on the one hand, and the new right wing, on the other, refuse to settle into the mild assumptions of a political equilibrium, that moderate balance in which "countervailing powers" are supposed to play off one against the other, reconcilable in their opposition. At times our society may approach this kind of equilibrium, and for certain kinds of short-range analyses, like those of Samuel Lubell, it may be useful to employ such a "model." But the realities of our social life are too rough and intractable for the politics of equilibrium to be able to contain them indefinitely. Rapid technological change, gnawing economic inequalities, a profound moral malaise, the growing discrepancy between a politics geared to diffusion and an economy requiring discipline—these are a few such realities. And they are bound to create, as they already have created, new and desperate conflicts of interest and idea. The intellectual guardians of the Goldwater movement, it is worth noting, seem not to have heard about "the end of ideology": perhaps they read the wrong magazines.

A "law" might here be advanced about recent American politics: the more housebroken the left, the more adventuresome the right. When there is not enough pressure from the liberal-labor movements upon both government and society, the right wing feels free to risk its own political course, breaking off from the moderate center to which it has usually been semiattached. For it can then calculate that even in electoral defeat it will gain power, becoming the dominant pressure upon an administration that lacks firm principles of its own.

I would venture the speculation that what crucially enabled the Goldwater movement to enter its "take-off" phase was the failure of the labor and liberal communities to cement a sufficiently strong alliance with the rising Negro movement. Once the right wing saw that the Negroes would more or less have to go it alone; once it became clear that a large fraction of even enlightened white sentiment consisted of passive sympathy, not active solidarity; once, in brief, there was no great danger that if the right wing detached itself from the political center, a resurgent Negro-labor-liberal alliance would pour into the resulting power vacuum—then the Goldwater movement was able to set out on its present course.

And a second "law": in the politics we now have in the United States, the kind and quantity of the pressure put upon the center largely determines where and what the center will be. *The Wall Street Journal* (July 14, 1964) has noted as much:

> With American political thought thus polarized between Johnson and Goldwater, the conclusion seems almost inescapable that the center of political gravity must now move rather sharply to the right. By hauling the Republican party rightward . . . Goldwater may actually have achieved some part of his dream of turning the country towards a significantly more conservative choice. . . .
>
> If Goldwater chooses to regard the Eastern financiers as his enemy, bent on control of the GOP for narrow, self-serving aims, Johnson is just as ready to hail them as new-found friends.

No foreseeable society seems likely to be so finely adjusted to the conflicting needs of its population as to preclude serious conflict and discontent. In regard to the United States today, such an expectation is sheer wishful fantasy. Conflict is inescapable, and the only question is what forms it will take and what value it will have. The tragedy of the moment is that it has been the Goldwater movement which has taken upon itself—with comic inappropriateness, but also frightening earnestness—the role of crusader. In its vocabulary, and at least part of its intent, this movement is not satisfied with a mild defense or a mild improvement of the bureaucratic and militarized welfare state. The right wing has also done something which, thus far, no other political movement in America has managed to do: it has stirred thousands of middle-class people to leave their ranch houses and enter the hustle of politics. It has made them into political activists who learn the art of attending meetings and the craft of outsitting and outvoting their more conventional opponents. It has fired them with the passions of a cause which, in the style of many demagogic movements, brings together the rhetoric of national interest with the urgencies of social selfishness. What a comedy that the notion of a "mass society" in which men flounder in apolitical passivity should be shattered by these crusaders from the barbecue pits!

The Goldwater movement is not yet fully formed: there are conflicting interests at work within it and there will be plenty of splits and transformations. Right now it seems to consist of a loose coalition between a hard reactionary core, providing muscle, ideology, and money, and a larger scatter of traditional conservatives, providing votes, emotion, and precinct committees. It is easy enough to point out the contradictions in the Goldwater platform: e.g., the promise to cut federal spending and decrease the power of national government coupled with the intent to build up still further the armed forces toward possible adventure abroad. Such contradictions are real enough, and no doubt there are a good many Goldwater partisans who manage, through the magic of sheer desire, to reconcile these perspectives in their minds. But in the long run there can be no reconciling nostalgia for *laissez faire* with lust for world domination.

Certain political commentators have been inclined to treat the Goldwater movement primarily as an emotional reflex, a revulsion from the complexities of the twentieth century. James Reston writes, for example:

> The more complicated life becomes, the more people are attracted to simple solutions; the more irrational the world seems, the more

they long for rational answers; and the more diverse everything is, the more they want it all reduced to identity.

Those who feel this way are undoubtedly attracted to Senator Goldwater, and many part-political and part-ethical movements have gone further on less. [*The New York Times,* July 21, 1964.]

Probably true, as far as it goes. A good part of the feeling behind the Goldwater movement does stem from a nostalgia for the days when Negroes knew their place, cities had not swamped the landscape, income taxes were not so oppressive, and little countries crossing the United States could be handled with gunboats. Part of the feeling behind the Goldwater movement also rests upon a sense of national frustration: if the United States is indeed as rich, powerful and good as it keeps telling itself, why then do so many countries disobey it? and why, as we edge toward omnipotence, can we not simply eradicate Communism with one swoop of our strength? *

There is more to be said than this kind of impressionistic sociology allows. For what matters is not merely the inferred *motives* of the Goldwater supporters, but the visible *meaning* of the Goldwater movement. And here the kind of assuaging sentimentalism practiced by Reston and other moderate liberals is very annoying. For it is outrageous to be told again and again that Goldwater is sincere, nice, and good. I do not believe it. The man who voted against the Civil

* One trouble with this kind of motive-probing is that it explains either too much or too little. Michael Walzer, writing from England, has a pertinent comment: "the theory of *ressentiment* has got to be stretched beyond breaking point if it is going to include the frustrated, bankrupt, embittered types who voted for Hitler; the frightened, losing-status types who, we thought, supported McCarthy; and the triumphantly egotistical, prosperous types who seem to be behind Goldwater. Barry's men, or at least some of them, are even modern and urban: how are they to be accounted for by theories which have always emphasized that right-wing politics was the anxious response of pre-modern men to the cosmopolitan and contemporary world? Dallas may be a barbarous place, but it is absolutely up-to-date barbarism. Maybe, in his own way, Goldwater has something when he talks of moral malaise."

Rights Act is not a good man. The man who said that "because Joe McCarthy lived, we are a freer, safer, and more alert nation," is not a good man. The man who in his speech at the Republican convention stirred the bestialities of racism by his innuendoes about "bullies and marauders" in the streets is not a good man. And neither is the man who, when "asked by a European reporter to comment on his policies toward Europe and Germany," replied: "I think that Germany originated the modern concept of peace through strength." [*The New York Times,* August 13, 1964.]

Muddled nostalgia, homestead economics, daydream brinkmanship all enter the Goldwater complex. But there is also a hard ideology and a precise focus of interest. No one should have any trouble in identifying these: they animate a politics of reaction. This politics rests in part on the social selfishness of large segments among the upper middle class which consciously disdain the sentiments of "welfarism" and are prepared to let the poor and the ethnic minorities stew in silence or, if noisy, be slugged into submission. This politics rests on the desire of powerful men—Ralph Cordiner is not a Midwestern automobile salesman, George Humphrey not a malaise-smitten petty bourgeois, H. L. Hunt not a bewildered storekeeper—to call a halt to social reform and then slowly to push it back. And it is a politics that rests on the dirty half-winks of racism, called euphemistically "the Southern strategy."

To insist that there is a firm reactionary intent behind the Goldwater movement is not, of course, to claim that the major centers of American big business are supporting it. Nor is it to assert that the Goldwater movement is Fascist or neo-Fascist. A segment of the business class is supporting Goldwater, and while not the crucial segment, it is, in terms of resources and perhaps even numbers, big enough. (No right-wing movement ever *begins* with the full support of big business.) And as for Fascism, obviously the Goldwater movement, like all of our native right-wing movements, diverges crucially from the patterns of European Fascism. But political phenomena must be seen not merely in their momentary appearance, but also in their potential. In and around the Goldwater movement there reside the cadres of a Fascist group; in its "culture" of social meanness, racist hostility, and chauvinist mania they find sustenance. At the moment there is no serious possibility of an American Fascism on a mass scale; but given either a depression or a group of major defeats in the Cold War, a minority segment of the Goldwater movement could well transform itself into pin-striped Fascists. That this potential simmers in American society is significant enough.

✡ THE COLD WAR

WHAT can one mean by winning or losing the Cold War? It is not as if so complex an historical development were undertaken by plan or intent, with a set of clear goals that would allow us to measure the extent to which they have been realized. The Cold War began as a result of a great many interlocking causes, such as national interests asserted and threatened, imperial ambitions among the victors in the last war, ideological conflicts both profound and factitious, etc. The struggle between the two sides will continue, I think, through the lifetime of everyone reading these lines, though the forms it will take are impossible to predict.

If the aim of the West was to destroy the Communist societies, then the Cold War has been lost. It begins to seem that the Communist dictatorship, like any other kind of political system resting on an industrialized economy, can achieve some measure of internal stability. How long this stability will last no one can say with assurance; but Russian Communism, apparently past the worst ordeals of industrialization and no longer subject to the crises produced by Stalinist terrorism, is reaching a point of development and inner modification somewhat like that of capitalism in the advanced Western countries.

To say this is not, of course, to approve of or be reconciled to the Communist regime. Stabilization does not necessarily imply a good society or a gradual evolution toward democracy, as the theorists of inevitable progress suppose. It merely signifies that we had better expect to face the Communist threat for a long time, relying not upon "inherent" upheavals of the historic process but upon our own intelligence and radical powers of renewal to meet that threat. I believe, or at least hope, that even in a society with a rising standard of living the problem of dictatorship cannot be long evaded; I expect that this will bring severe conflicts within Russia; but these conflicts will have to be endured and worked out by those living under the dictatorship, for there is no longer any possibility, as there was never any desirability, of external intervention.

If the Western aim was to "roll back" Russian might in Europe, then the Cold War has been lost. Given the world in which we live—"I too dislike it"—nothing short of atomic war can now remove the hold of Russia upon its satellites, and no sane person can propose to launch such a war. In the present epoch there is emerging a new kind of imperialism, largely ideological in nature, which seems likely to be as persistent and pernicious as the older kinds, and quite as great a possible incitement to war as the arms race.

If the Western aim was to check Communist expansion in Asia or Africa, then the issue remains in doubt, though the prospects are gray. The political *appeal* of Communism in some of the Asian countries seems to have declined, yet its political *power* remains considerable. The reasons for this power are familiar: Communism provides deracinated intellectuals with an ideology through which to release their ambition, distress, ideals, envy, and need for a synthetic world outlook; it gives a technic of struggle to nationalist movements which in their own right have little more than a grievance and a mystique; it capitalizes on the deep hostility toward the white man; it carries itself with the posture of victory; and it seems to offer, as in some desperately inhumane and probably inefficient way it does offer, a quick road to industrialization.

Can all this be countered by the West, even a West led by democratic radicals? I doubt it. We must resign ourselves to the likelihood that the *ressentiment* of the underdeveloped countries, a development that would have occurred if there were not a single Communist on the globe, will have to run its course and in doing so will find a ready partner in the Communist movement: a model of success, a source of language, a pattern of economics.

Still, much could be done to minimize the painfulness of this event and to enable the political elites of the underdeveloped countries to hasten their intellectual independence. The problem goes far deeper than providing more economic aid —much as that is needed—or even greater "understanding." For one thing, the West needs the kind of political leaders it now totally lacks in all of its parties, conservative, liberal, and socialist: men who can grasp something of the psychology of desperation and the dynamic of romanticism. For another, if the West is to become a source of attraction for the underdeveloped countries and regain some political charisma in the world struggle, it needs a sharply radical turn in its own social life. Meanwhile, the best we can hope for is larger quantities of economic aid to those countries like India where there is a solid democratic tradition, and a diplomacy clever enough to realize that in some countries and at certain historical moments a "neutralism" short of total dependence on Russia or China constitutes a piece of good fortune.

If the aim of the West was to prevent Europe from succumbing to Communist domination, then the Cold War has probably been won. In the West European countries the Communist parties may still get almost as many votes as they did ten years ago, but they have lost in *élan*, youthfulness, militancy, and the power to cripple national existence. Despite the Berlin crisis, the long-range trend in Europe is toward stabilization of the current political division, and this implies a serious check to the expansionist ambitions of Communism. The socioeconomic recovery of Western Europe is a major and, on the whole, a hopeful fact of the postwar years: it means that in a number of countries with the highest level of political culture there remain opportunities for experiment and initiative, even where these are not being exploited at the moment.

Obviously it is desirable that the United States reorient its policies to help movements of social reform, especially in the underdeveloped countries. But this is not quite so easy as many liberals suppose. Far more is needed than money, good will or even a new set of "images" for America abroad. The Kennedy administration has been unimpressive in this respect, as in so many others, and not because some of its technical projects (e.g., in Latin America) are unworthy of support but because it has not thought out the implications, or shown a willingness to face the risks, of presenting a new "image" to the world.

A new image requires a new substance, and a new substance means first of all a sharp turn leftward *at home*. One reason the New Deal aroused strong feelings throughout the world was that Roosevelt, despite his frequent opportunism, was at several crucial points ready to fight against his domestic opponents. He aligned himself with, or took advantage of, significant mass movements and sentiments, so that the dynamism of American political life in the thirties came to seem an earnest of our intentions. By contrast, Kennedy works almost entirely through a slick bureaucratic style: he is committed to the politics of caution and compromise. One trouble with his administration is that it is too damned clever, too clever in the manner of Irish ward politics and too clever in the manner of Harvard intellectual parties. It fails to understand that there are times when a good hard fight, even if momentarily lost, is of greater political and educative value than brilliant but confusing maneuvers. (Perhaps, however, it doesn't see much to fight about.) It proposes to create political images of America through a rhetoric with little risk: no one is fooled, nor much impressed. At home all this approach does is to incite the far right just enough to give it a new confidence and aggression. In foreign policy there have been some sensible achievements, apart from the Cuban disaster, but these tend to lose their meaning and impact if they are not articulated in the context of a full-scale political position.

There are other, more complex difficulties. "Identify," you say, "with the movements and leaders of change throughout the world"—but this cannot mean the same thing now that it might have fifteen years ago. We are paying the price for an immediate past of sluggishness, cowardice, and reaction. A liberal foreign policy in 1947 or 1952 might have had notable consequences, while the apparently same policy transferred to the sixties might cause hardly a ripple. The intentions could be as good, the terms of application the same; but the context has changed, usually for the worse. Too many things have settled in the underdeveloped countries, and partly this is due to the conduct of both Russia and the United States, partly to the predictable weaknesses of the leaders of the new nations. Any policy of trying to "identify with the movements and leaders of change throughout the world" must therefore be more radical and even desperate than it would have had to be ten or fifteen years ago, and that is something the administration does not care to face. In all fairness it should be added that the possibilities for such a policy have seriously narrowed: there are a number of countries in which one can hardly find any "movements and leaders of change." And what could have been done in and/or for Indochina, Algeria, and Cuba some years ago can no longer be done today, just as what might still be done in Latin America will be impossible fifteen years from now. Prescriptions depend not merely on a general diagnosis but also on exact observation of the stage the illness has reached.

The domestic situation is less favorable than in the late forties for a turn toward an aggressively liberal foreign policy. The American people have been systematically lied to about the realities of world politics; there is a growing cynicism about the value of foreign aid; and a new articulate minority, the extreme right wing, which is the only political movement in America with crusading spirit and energy, stands ready to fight any signs of generosity in foreign affairs. To cope with all this, we would have to have an administration prepared to educate, proselytize, and do harsh political battle: that is, prepared to face immediate losses in behalf of long-range goals.

Is a genuinely liberal turn possible? Yes. Likely? No. I am impatient with half-baked Marxists who "deduce" the impossibility of a major shift in foreign policy from the fact that capitalism still prevails in this country; experience has shown that under sufficient pressure and need social systems can display unprecedented flexibility and break past their earlier limits of response. But I suspect those critics are right who say that the administration, in its suave "pragmatism" and canny politicking, will not have the courage to act.

The liberals, too, need the courage of revaluation. If the United States were to become a nation supporting "movements and leaders of change," then all the usual endorsements of nonintervention would have to be reconsidered. To favor any kind of intervention in regard to, say, a rightist dictatorship in the Dominican Republic undercuts the ground of a principled opposition to intervention in regard to a "leftist" dictatorship in Cuba. Now the Cuban invasion and the role of the United States in that fiasco were ghastly blunders, stupid and reactionary; they showed how deeply entrenched were the forces of the political right in Washington, quite apart from any change of administration. Yet unless one believes that the Castro dictatorship deserves moral or political support, a point of view favoring help to "movements and leaders of change" in, say, Paraguay or Haiti forces one to surrender any principled opposition to a similar policy in Cuba. It then becomes, crucially, a matter of the political wisdom and nature of the intervention.

I am committed to the "position" of democratic socialism, that is, to the idea of a society in which the values of democratic participation and fraternity will have suffused its major economic and political institutions. To say this, however, is to speak in terms of a large historical span extending a century into the past and perhaps a century into the future. One must in honesty admit that such a commitment does not necessarily signify that "we" have answers to particular problems better than those advanced by other people. Between the historic "position" and particular proposals of socialists there is some connection, of course, but not necessarily a clear or direct one.

The "position" of democratic socialism remains for me a valid and inspiriting one; but to have this "position" does not, alas, provide one with automatic answers to problems of the Cold War, disarmament, stopping Communism, nationalizing industry, etc., any more than an acceptance of the Sermon on the Mount necessarily provides answers to specific moral problems. Unfortunately, democratic socialism is today weak in regard to the problems of the moment, first because it is caught up in a deep and absorbing crisis of intellectual "position," second because in many countries it has declined into little more than an agency of liberal reform, and third because some of our immediate problems do not permit quick or complete solutions by anyone.

The right wing of socialism displays intelligence and skill, in some countries, at working out limited social improvements, but it has virtually ceased to pretend that it speaks in the name of a major historical transformation. The left wing wishes to recapture the spirit of transcendence which characterized socialism in its early days, yet cannot find specific political proposals toward that end which would also be relevant to the conditions of mid-twentieth century society. Behind these difficulties lies a deeper and more pervasive intellectual crisis. Serious partisans of democratic socialism are troubled by the fact that there seems to be a dissociation, or at least there is no longer an assured connection, between their animating sentiments and their formulated program. They can no longer take it for granted that the one presupposes the other, and in such a crisis it is hard to step forward with a voice of certainty. Nevertheless, the perspective of democratic socialism remains a central hope in the increasingly collectivist world in which we live, the one way of escaping the insufferable choice between capitalism and Communism. In that fundamental sense, it is sure to be profoundly important during the years ahead, as a permanent possibility of escape from the dilemmas of the Cold War; but at any given moment, unfortunately, this will not assure it of adequate power to shape the actual course of events.

There are three attitudes toward the Cold War that I would reject:

The uncompromising "anti-Communist crusade" which would subordinate every social interest and intellectual divergence to Western power and which, if pushed to its logical conclusion, may well lead to nuclear war;

the campaign for unilateral disarmament which bases itself on moral absolutes and barely troubles to estimate the power consequences that might follow from an adoption of its proposals;

the sociological analysis which foresees a convergence between East and West in the direction of a highly bureaucratic and authoritarian society, so that, in the name of an historical possibility that is admittedly a real one, it fails to take into account, or act upon, the life-and-death differences between the Communist dictatorships, softened as they may be, and the Western democracies, marred as they may be.

My sense of it is that radical intellectuals must try to maintain a point of view which acknowledges the stake they have in preserving Western democracy while exercising a maximum of political independence. This means that one cannot pretend to be neutral or indifferent in regard to the world struggle. I want, for example, to see a policy which prevents Berlin from succumbing to Communist encirclement while yet avoiding nuclear war. Between the West and "ourselves" there is, not a full identity of interest, but a sharing of certain limited goals, the realization of which requires us to depend upon Western power and also to put forward a variety of radical proposals. Thus, within this complex perspective, I would propose that, no matter what other nations do, the United States refrain from a resumption of nuclear testing—that seems to me both a moral obligation and a way of regaining the political initiative from the Communists. I would also support proposals for "phased" disarmament by the West as a means of trying to break the arms deadlock.

The conflict between East and West is almost certain to continue for a long time. What we can try to do is to affect Western policy toward a stress upon progressive economic and political ends, rather than dangerous displays of military strength.

✡ COMMUNISM NOW

DURING the past two decades most Western liberals and socialists have tried to grapple with the problem of Russian society by constructing a model of a unique phenomenon called totalitarianism. Naturally, the best political analysts have focused on what seemed unprecedented in Russian and German totalitarianism: the role of terror as an integral element of this new society; the terrifying power of ideology as both the mental equivalent of terror and a means for dominating the total life of man; the extreme atomization of social life, so that classes tend to become pulverized into a passive and anonymous mass; the consolidation of a ruling elite which appropriates to itself not merely a variety of goods or a monopoly of power but the very possession of the state and of its citizens.

Now, if we take as typical of this approach Hannah

Arendt's *Origins of Totalitarianism* and Orwell's *1984*, we see that both books, whatever their faults and "exaggerations," did us a moral and intellectual service by insisting that totalitarianism was not merely an extension of monopoly capitalism, Russian expansionism, Leninist dictatorship, man's inherent sinfulness, or anything else. To one or another extent, such elements were present in the totalitarian regimes, but what made them so powerful and frightening was their break with old traditions, be they good or bad traditions; precisely, that is, the extent to which they embodied that which is distinctively new in the totalitarian ethos. That no actual society behaved quite like the one Arendt described or Orwell imagined is hardly a cogent criticism of their books, for the value of a model depends partly on its not pretending to take into account fluctuations of local events.

If I now suggest that a possible conclusion from the recent Russian changes is that this model of totalitarianism—let us agree to call it the political model—is no longer sufficient, I do not mean to suggest that it has lost its usefulness. There is a sense in which the very difficulties encountered on the analytic plane require that we stress all the more strongly the moral premises that were often the stimulant toward constructing this model. Yet it does begin to seem that the political model of totalitarianism needs to be supplemented, and drawn into a tension, with more traditional forms of socioeconomic analysis.

The implicit assumption of Arendt, Orwell, and other such writers is that totalitarianism is a society which has achieved a kind of stasis, even if one of systematized chaos; a society that has established an equilibrium between the flow of terror that is essential to its existence and the energies that make possible the permanence of this terror. In this respect, however, Orwell may have been shrewder than Arendt, since he anticipated a gradual slackening of both ideological and social hysteria in the totalitarian unfuture, a diminution of that ferocious intensity which has until now characterized all of totalitarian society and which Arendt so dramatically seized upon as a dominant factor of its existence. But while Orwell anticipated a gradual decline from fanaticism into torpor, he did not suppose that the decline might affect the continued employment of active terror. He did not consider that the energies making for terror might gradually run down and that, partly because of the consequences of forced industrialization, the practice of terror might be replaced by a policy of terror in reserve.

Similarly, the political model did not adequately prepare us for the possibility of the rise, not of a new bourgeoisie (for if the term is used with any exactness, there is no bourgeoisie in Russia), but of habits of life that we generally associate with the bourgeoisie. Terror, since it cannot safely be confined to a chosen sector of the population, must frighten the rulers too, and more, it must weary them. In Khrushchev and his successors we see representatives of those members of the ruling stratum who, just because they are the products and survivors of Stalinism, now want to relax a little and savor their privileges: they express a political equivalent of the psychology of the *nouveau riche.* The big question is whether a touch of relaxation will stimulate an appetite for a great deal more of freedom, and whether the immediate social impulses of the Russian rulers toward their own brand of "moderation" will not come into a major clash with their basic political interests, which require above all else the continued iron domination of the party.

The political model of totalitarianism has given us an extremely acute sense of the quality of Russian society and has helped us maintain a moral response; but now, without abandoning it, we should recognize that there have been factors at work in molding Russian society which cannot be accounted for in terms of this model and are not peculiar to totalitarianism. Most notably, of course, there has been the rapid process of industrialization which does not insure any progress or liberalization, as certain new apologists for Communism claim, but which does make possible new social and political forms within totalitarianism.

So that while the concept of the "mass society," which lies behind the work of Arendt and other writers, remains extremely valuable, it now becomes necessary to bring to bear the methods of class and institutional analysis in order to understand the repressed social formations, the hidden class alignments and struggles, that exist beneath the surface of Russian life. Between the theory of mass society and the methods of class analysis there may be a conceptual clash, but the reality of Russian society requires, I think, an eclectic employment of both.

One of the theoretical possibilities that needs to be considered is that a convergence is taking place in the characters of the major societies in the world. Just as totalitarianism is becoming a trifle "liberal," so the liberal world has been showing impulses in the direction of totalitarianism, or at least authoritarianism. To some extent this convergence—a convergence, I had better say, is not an identity—is the result of a universal breakdown of values; perhaps to a greater extent, it is the result of an uncontrolled socioeconomic process closely related to, yet not quite the same as, the growth of industrialization.

This process, which is as difficult to label as it is easy to observe, involves the increasing helplessness of individual man, the loss of energy and direction among traditional social movements, the lessening of distinctions between political and economic power, the triumph of the state in every area of economics and culture, the "machinization" of life—and *perhaps* a partial solution in the future of those material problems that were the occasion for, but not the true motive behind, the rise of socialism. It may be that a worldwide solution to the problem of hunger is inseparable from at least a serious effort to solve other, less tangible problems; and in a sense it would be reassuring to think so. But if we are honest we should face the possibility—it is surely no more than that—of a general trend toward a society that would be a sort of low-pressured, usually nonterroristic yet essentially unfree authoritarianism, a society that might provide men with food, television, and houses of a kind but would not permit or encourage them to achieve true human status.

It would be pleasant to learn that this is merely a bad dream of my own.

One of the mildly amusing aspects of the Russian problem is that the issues debated by Marxists fifteen or twenty years ago have a way of cropping up once more among people who haven't the faintest notion that they are repeating old and weary polemics. For years the anti-Stalinist left used to debate the question: Does Russia need a political reform within the regime or a deep-going social revolution that would transform class and institutional relations? Today this seemingly abstruse question has acquired a new seriousness. The impulse among certain intellectuals to effect a rapprochement with the Russian regime will find as its rationale the claim that all Russia needs is a reform from on high, a gradual dripping down of moderate quantities of democracy. Trotsky's unfortunate theory that Russia was a corrupted "workers' state" will now become popular among people who never heard of it and who will now advance it without any of his redeeming revolutionary passion.

But is not a reform of totalitarianism a contradiction in terms? Given the existence of a statified economy, serious political changes *are* socioeconomic changes; the establishment of political democracy in Russia, far from being a desirable adornment or improvement, would involve the profoundest shifts in class relations and social power.

Whether one can speak of a ruling class in Russia that has gained the stability of the bourgeoisie in the early capitalist era, is not an immediately vital question. What is important is that Russian society, far from being a mere deformation of the socialist ideal, is an exploitative class society, and that in this society political domination is the means toward economic oppression. The ruling class or stratum, which functions through the party but is not confined to it, establishes the conditions and relations of production; it enjoys a mode of existence that sets it apart from other social classes; it determines the way in which the surplus national product is to be used, and does so with a freedom and ruthlessness no capitalist class has ever been able to command. So that if one identifies Stalinism with certain political characteristics that are not essential to this society, one can say that the recent changes involve the dissolution of Stalinism; but if one identifies Stalinism with a system of social relations, a totalitarian collectivism, then it makes sense to speak of Russia today as Stalinism without Stalin. For the essence of the recent changes is an effort to re-establish the authority of the dominant strata of the Communist party, that is, to consolidate and "legitimate" the position of the ruling class by repudiating the system of personal rule that helped bring it into being.

The death of political Stalinism leaves the vulgar kinds of anti-Stalinism without a future. Just as it will become harder to oppose Russian power, so will it become harder to oppose the intellectual claims of its apologists. Analytically this will require more flexibility; morally, a greater intransigence. Most of all, it will require a greater political independence, a greater readiness to think radically than most American intellectuals have recently shown. For now we shall no longer have Stalin helping us.

✡ ON THE CAREER AND EXAMPLE OF C. WRIGHT MILLS

C. WRIGHT MILLS was a man who, in Malraux's phrase, wished to "put a scar upon the map." He had little charm and less loveliness; one could not easily imagine him relaxing into ease or wisdom. He was a man of power, an intensely personal kind of power, which came down upon one like a fist, hard and good-humored. Though himself a dedicated intellectual, he felt a certain contempt—mixed with uneasy admiration—toward most of the New York intellectuals, for what he wanted above all was that his opinions, his desires should *matter* in this world, and he had become convinced that most of the people writing for the serious magazines had surrendered the hope of power or influence and settled into a routine of brilliant display.

He left his scar upon the map. The sociologists he stirred to fear and anger by smashing their neat conceptual models and by insisting upon the wildness, speed, and passion of modern history; the intellectuals of the anti-Communist left with whom he worked for a time as a guerrilla ally but against whom he turned when he suspected them of resignation and defeat; the graduate students whom he excited into contempt for the trivialities of the academy—all responded not merely, perhaps not even primarily, to his writings, but to his personal force. Even his enemies paid him that tribute.

For perhaps a decade I was a friend, or at least a steady intellectual collaborator, of Mills. I found him difficult, exhausting, and exciting, a man whose pressure of will seldom let up and often forced other people, even those who loved him as I could not, into the resistance of self-defense. But neither in our period of closeness nor later, when we quarrelled politically, could one doubt his strength, his trusting energy and confidence. Everything he had—talent, personal life, restlessness, ambition—he threw into the effort to create for himself a unified style of life, one that would bring together thought and action, power and reflection, as few intellectuals seemed capable of doing.

Mills first became known in the intellectual world at about the time Dwight Macdonald was publishing his lively radical magazine *Politics*. At this time, directly after World War II and all the disillusionments that followed it, the intellectual left was beginning to fall apart. Old ideologies were shattered, new ones not in sight. Only Macdonald's personal zest as editor of *Politics* created the possibility—perhaps the illusion—of preserving some sort of left-wing community. Into this depressing scene there suddenly barged the bear-like figure of Mills, a radical neither hardened by dogma nor softened by defeat, an American marvelously unscarred by history, an academic brilliantly equipped in his field yet also blessed with a journalistic gift. Here was a new friend, a new ally—who could not be drawn to him? He had little taste, it is true, for those semico-operative ventures that New York intellectuals recurrently improvise; he was a loner, a one-man work gang who had learned about Max Weber from Hans Gerth at Wisconsin and, as we supposed, had inherited from the atmosphere of his youth something of the wobbly's high-spirited rebelliousness and the muckraker's zeal for exposure.

Mills once explained to me that of the three proclaimed goals of the French Revolution he understood the appeal of liberty and equality well enough, but had very little sense of fraternity. He was right; and it is this failure of imagination—a symptom of his larger failure to appreciate the value of men working together in a bond of harmony and closeness—which kept him from fully grasping the historical significance of the socialist movement as a human enterprise. But if one could learn not to tax him on this score—and what was the point of it?—Mills made a marvelous intellectual ally, a native American radical who could speak both with indigenous accents and high sophistication. When some of us started *Dissent* in 1953 he would not join the venture ("no editorial boards for me"), but no sooner were we attacked by the ex-radicals than he came charging to our defense. Both attitudes, the fundamental apartness and the intense moment of solidarity, were characteristic of him.

That was the beginning. The end was sad and painful. In 1957 Mills came back from a trip to Europe and asked me to visit him. I went with anxiety and foreboding, for I had already heard rumors that he was in a state of manic exaltation, working up a new political outlook which would pit him against his old friends. Two or three minutes after we began talking, he started to pound away: he had discovered reasons for hope in the East European world, he was impressed by the industrial achievements of the Communist nations, he regarded the intransigent anti-Communism of his old friends as obsolete (soon he would be calling us the "futilitarians of the left"), and he wanted to see a new alignment of "the left," a sort of informal Popular Front that would include intellectuals who were to one or another extent sympathetic to the Communist bloc.

We sat together for hours in a shabby lunchroom on Amsterdam Avenue, under a garish blue light and to the background of popular "Spanish" music. He kept hammering away and I retreated into silence. I felt that sense of despair which comes over one at losing the possibility of communication with a person one has intensely valued over the years. It seemed to me that he no longer talked, as once he had; he exhorted and pronounced, he sloganized in outline form, as if he had suffered an apocalyptic seizure. And there was little I could say.

Let there be no misunderstanding. Mills was not a convert to Communism. Nor was it news to me that things were changing rapidly and importantly in the Communist countries, or that democrats and socialists could now find friends in those countries—but among the intellectuals who were beginning, however hesitantly, to oppose the authoritarian structure of the regime. Where we differed was in our historical estimate of how far the dictatorships could be expected to relax, and far more important, in our moral-political response to the contending forces in the East European countries. My instinctive solidarity went out to those intellectuals in Poland who, whatever their enforced vocabulary, were really liberals and socialists at heart, while Mills identified himself less with the living men who spoke for freedom in Eastern Europe than with the historical process, as he took it to be, which would transform the Communist countries into societies closer to the image of our desire.

To me Mills's new outlook was an intellectual disaster. To him, my resistance to that outlook must have seemed like the conservatism of a radical who fears to surrender fixed positions. We parted, tense and distraught, each certain that far more than a personal disagreement was at stake. This kind of break between people who cared about politics can be as wracking as a personal separation between two people who have shared some part of their lives. In its miniature way, our split represented a development that is certain to become more sizable during the next several years. When Mills wrote his pamphlet, *The Causes of World War III*, in 1958, I reviewed it in caustic terms; he replied with heat; and we never saw one another again.

Between these two moments—roughly, between 1946 and 1957—Mills did his most valuable and distinguished work. All of his important books (*White Collar, Character and Social Structure, The Power Elite*) contain brilliant sections and chapters displaying Mills's gift for the destruction of the myths of social accommodation that had grown up during the late forties and early fifties. All of them are valuable for puncturing the fantasies of social harmony and universal prosperity which had become accepted currency among social scientists and journalists. All are distinguished by Mills's keen notation of the troubledness of American life, a troubledness which it had become the special task of many of his colleagues to deny. And all of them are marked by a gift for improvising social generalizations on a secondary level, that is, not on the world-historical scale of a Marx or Weber but on the scale of a theorist trying to observe a society in the closeness and detail of its motion.

Yet none of Mills's books, nor the posthumous collection of essays in *Power, Politics and People*, achieves the classical stature, the absolute rightness of description, which one finds in the Lynds' *Middletown* or Cash's *The Mind of the South* or Myrdal's *An American Dilemma*. And the reason is not that Mills was less gifted than these writers—though it is certainly true that he lacked their capacity for the particular detail, the concrete observation, which brings a social analysis to life. (Mills knew this, and at one point in the mid-fifties he read Balzac voraciously in the hope of discovering the secret of narrative specification.)

Mills failed to achieve the finished performance of a Lynd, a Cash, or a Myrdal because he had undertaken a task more difficult than they had. He could not accept the static assumptions of many sociologists, who proposed to fix the lineaments of society almost as if it were an unchanging presence, or who, in effect, gave up the wish to grasp the idea of modern society and contented themselves with observations, often useful, on its detailed manifestations. The suprahistorical impulse which makes a good part of contemporary sociology seem so limited to outsiders, Mills fought against and, on the whole, with good effect. The tendency of certain ex-radicals in the sociological profession to describe American society in terms of more or less balanced interest groups rather than of contending classes and power formations, Mills also resisted. He kept reminding his colleagues and the world at large about the realities of power in America; he kept insisting that the ideal pattern of the democratic polity was very far indeed from the truth about the relationships of power. And he was right.

But his dilemma was that in trying to work up a sociology that would be both realistic and radical, he lacked a full-scale theory of his own. He might have fallen back upon Marxism, which had the strength of a major tradition and an imposing, if deceptive, coherence. But he could not accept the traditional pictures of Marxism; they grew increasingly at variance with modern industrial society: there was no revolutionary proletariat, no class polarization in the sense predicted by Marx. The Marxist method remained a powerful one, but the social axioms that accrued to the Marxist tradition seemed to him largely obsolete. Inevitably, the result was that his best work is tentative, improvisatory, a straining toward a new theoretical synthesis he desired but could not find. Had he been content to follow along the ruts of orthodox Marxism his work would have possessed greater internal coherence than it did, but it would not have been so closely related to the actualities of American society as it now and again is. *The Power Elite*, his most important book, played an enormously useful role in reminding people that, quite apart from the formal political structure, there exists in America a hierarchy of socioeconomic power closely dependent on ownership and wealth, income, and property; but with its unfinished conception of a triad of power elites, military, industrial, and political, it does not offer an entirely satisfactory picture of either the internal composition of the rulers or their relationship to the political process.

The collection of essays recently put together by Irving Louis Horowitz (*Power, Politics and People,* Oxford University Press) is characterized by similar strengths and weaknesses. Mills's best pieces are his earlier ones: strictly sociological studies but with a political sharpness that rescues them from academicism. There is a devastating critique of Lloyd Warner's work on social class, a sharp attack on James Burnham's managerial theories, a brilliant paper on "The Professional Ideology of Social Pathologists." Mills was at his best as a freewheeling critic, corrosively analytical, for whom radicalism served as a strategy for puncturing deceptions but had not yet become a burdensome quest for intellectual synthesis.

His later pieces seem to me sharply to decline in quality. For all his objection to "abstract empiricism" in sociology, what becomes evident is that he himself had little gift for social observation: he was not a good reporter.

Another major weakness of his later work is due to the fact that he was turning away from sociology and toward politics. Each of these disciplines has its own requirements, its own standards, its own modes of procedure. Mills knew a great deal about sociology, but not very much about politics; he failed to see that the style of abstraction appropriate to one is not at all appropriate to the other; and he failed to grasp that the factors of time, immediacy, and limited choice are far more stringent in political analysis than in sociological delineation. (For example, to offer a long-range description of the causes of the Cold War, be it correct or incorrect, in terms of the fundamental tendencies of European society is not yet to cope with the immediate *political* problem of the division of Berlin. One of the things that so badly marred Mills's *Causes of World War III* was inability or unwillingness to confront this distinction.)

The two pamphlets Mills wrote in the last years of his

life, one on World War III and the other on Cuba, mark the nadir of his intellectual career. They are scandalous not because they are pamphlets designed for a large audience—there is a tradition of pamphleteering which serious people should not scorn. These writings are scandalous because they are so shoddy in thought and method, so crowded with rhetorical wind, so grandiose in pretension and feeble in documentation, and so coy in their evasions (I have in mind especially the shameful equivocations about the Hungarian revolution in *Causes* and the narrative trickery, so unworthy of a man like Mills, employed in the Cuba pamphlet).

In his last years Mills became the idol of an international political tendency, the authoritarian left. He won the admiration of Castroite partisans and young people in search of charismatic revolution to replace the tarnished images of Khrushchevite Russia and Maoist China. The sad truth is that he deserved the admirers he won: perhaps he even deserved to have Mr. Horowitz edit his book of essays.

I prefer to remember another Mills: a man of great seriousness if only fragmentary achievement, a natural rebel at a time when most intellectuals were taking to cover, a keen and ambitious mind that had the courage to undertake too much. This Mills, in the prime of his life and achievement, deserves every honor as an example of the intellectual who stands alone, firm in his freedom, speaking with strength and critical urgency. Compared to the shilly-shallying of his academic colleagues, this Mills seems a giant. For if it is true that some of them can point to work more neatly rounded and firmly structured than the achievement of Mills, what is the measure of their success against the tragic power of his failure?

☼ BOURBON ON THE ROCKS

IN America we have become accustomed to thinking of the reactionary as a small-town primitive marked by the pathos of cultural obsolescence and moral fright. Historically, there is much to be said for this image. But in James Burnham we have something rather new, an American reactionary on the French style: the "aristocratic" intellectual who makes no pretense to humaneness, gladly proclaims his chauvinism, breathes a frigid contempt for the plebes, and indulges in public fantasies of imperial grandeur. It should be said in his behalf that Burnham's public career has been temperamentally consistent, even if ideologically distraught: he has always been a cold-blooded snob, first as a Trotskyist, then as herald of the "managerial revolution," and lately as geopolitical strategist in charge of World War III for the *National Review.* Though sophisticated enough to go through the motions of intellectual complexity, he is driven by an urge toward apocalyptic crudeness; and all those who will not plunge with him into preparations for atomic *fin du mondisme* he regards as "confused" or "muddled" or "weak" liberals, mere patsies for the oncoming Communist hordes, and more to be despised than pitied. Whatever his ultimatistic obsession of the moment (and there have been quite a few), he finds it hard to repress a well-bred snarl for those men of humane doubts who refuse to go along with him each time he discovers a new mission.

To whom, one wonders, is his strange book (*Suicide of the West,* John Day) addressed?—this rodomontade blending academic hauteur with fanatic shrillness, which announces, as if it were a fact beyond dispute, that the West has been seized by a lemminglike impulse toward collective suicide, for which liberalism provides the ideological rationale; that American foreign policy (perhaps because deprived of its bodily essences?) is suspiciously soft on Communism; that the boundaries of "civilization" are being steadily contracted under assault from barbarians; that the Welfare State corrodes American freedom and character; and that the streets of our cities are menaced by dark-skinned hoodlums.

The conservative faithful have heard it all before, though hardly from so cultivated a source; and surely the literate public is not likely to respond to this odd yoking of Ortega y Gasset and General Jack D. Ripper. But after a time I found an answer to my question: the book will serve admirably as a tip sheet, a Barnes & Noble handbook, for campus conservatives, those little-league Goldwaters looking for debater's points with which to stun liberal professors. Here they can learn that some liberals (those who do not wish to invade Cuba) shamefully prefer Peace to Freedom, and that liberal theory is beset by an inherent conflict between its devotion to popular sovereignty, which can sometimes lead to popular tyranny, and its devotion to minority rights, which can sometimes lead to social immobility.

(Hardly a problem for Burnham, however, who is not very infatuated with either term of this dilemma.)

Most of the book is devoted to an agonizingly slow description of liberalism, as if Burnham had been traumatized by too much exposure to dimwitted students. You can learn here that the ADA is a liberal bulwark, that Arthur Schlesinger, Jr. and Eleanor Roosevelt are representative liberals, that most liberals are internationalist in outlook—red-hot news that will just shake up everyone at Bob Jones University. A curious result of this baby talk, however, is that the American liberal emerging from Burnham's pages seems far more principled, tough-spirited, and intellectually coherent than he is likely in fact to have been these past few decades; for Burnham will have nothing to do with the qualifications and modulations of political reality, and as a result the fact that the distance between most American liberals and most American conservatives has recently been lessening, never appears in his pages. He's a black-and-white man; and he stands for white.

The true qualities of his book come out in a sentence here, a passage there. In a section worthy of Josiah Bounderby, he mocks those liberals who wish to erase such symptoms of social pathology as Skid Row, for "Skid Row is the end of the line; and there must be an end of the line somewhere." He deplores the "deterrence" strategy held by official United States opinion as "a gigantic bluff," for—believe me, I'm quoting accurately—"the purpose of the entire strategic nuclear force is not at all to be used." (*I don't say we wouldn't get our hair mussed up . . .*) He is troubled by the double standard of liberalism, its tendency to excuse methods employed by underdogs which it would condemn if used by oppressors. Writing about the treatment of Negroes by Southern cops, he remarks: "The truncheons of hard-pressed police struggling to preserve the minimum elements of public order against unloosed chaos become [for liberals] Satanic pitchforks. . . ." This concern for impartiality leads Burnham to notice that "There has never been a liberal protest against the outrages committed by the South African Negroes."

The author of *Suicide of the West* is a versatile, many-sided figure. Professor James Burnham, mellow sage of conservatism, notes that not all human troubles can be eradicated and that, sad as it may be, we had better reconcile ourselves to the likelihood that other peoples will continue to suffer hunger. Fighting Jim Burnham, last of the individualists, remarks that he has no objection to social security, but resents the Welfare State's imposition of *automatic* social security and wishes it would allow citizens a choice of voluntary systems. (Whether he favors a similar voluntary arrangement in regard to the draft, he does not say.) Sir James, Leftenant General in His Majesty's forces, bemoans the loss of those "splendid fighting men . . . the Gurkhas, Sikhs, Senegalese and Berbers . . . not the least of the grievous losses that the West has suffered from the triumph of decolonialization." Old African Pioneer Burnham, looking Voerward, decries independence in East Africa as "the occasion when native black men, who have neither spun nor reaped, can take for nothing or next to nothing many of those splendid farms and ranches that the knowledge, effort, foresight, administrative ability, and capital of Europe-sprung white men have slowly brought into being. . . ." And most spectacularly, behind a mountain of maps, Chief of Staff Burnham, fighting grimly to stiffen the jellied spine of the West, counts off the loss of our forts and our ports:

> The great harbor of Trincomalee, commanding the western flank of the Bay of Bengal, southeast Asia and the Strait of Malacca, ceases to be a Western strategic base. Gone too are the mighty ports of Dakar and Casablanca, looming over the Atlantic passage. Of the guardian bases of the north African littoral, southern flank of Europe, only Mers-el-Kebir remains. . . .

And yet, and yet, am I perhaps unjust? Is there not still another James Burnham, a good man with a kindly wink, a cheerful nod, for the lowest orders? Movingly he tells us about two Negroes—"cheerful, pleasant fellows" of course —whom he sees regularly in New York and who work at collecting piles of old paper-board boxes. Their IQs "were almost out of sight" (would a mere liberal bother to take the IQs of Negro peddlers?) but they "could handle the work they were doing." And then Mayor Wagner, a "leading liberal politician," came along to demand that the state lift the minimum wage to $1.50 an hour. This "rise in the minimum wage," Burnham discovered, "would most certainly throw those two chaps out of their jobs." As it now is, "with their wives going out some as part-time maids and the older children running a few policy tickets," these Negroes can survive. But satisfy the liberal's "ideological abstraction," raise the minimum wage for those hundreds of thousands of New Yorkers living on a semistarvation level, and "my friends," Burnham sadly concludes, will become "bums and delinquents."

It is touchingly humane, this little story, and it leads me to another which Burnham in his modesty has failed to mention.

There are times—we all know them—when everything seems too much. The generals will not take advice on how to start atomic confrontations, Washington keeps knuckling under to the Reds, the Welfare State won't let us set up a private Social Security system or buy TVA, and even some of those chaps at the *National Review* may not be so very bright. Wearied and harassed, our hero goes back to the Old Plantation, where order still prevails and, since it is an organic society, everyone knows his place. At the spacious entrance he is greeted by George, the grinning house-servant, who brings a mint julep and a happy smile: "We'z all glad to have you back, Marse James, moughty nice to have you back." You, reader, corrupted by "ideological abstractions" of liberalism, may suppose that George is unfree, a chattel slave. But the truth is that Marse James looks after George and speaks of him feelingly as "my friend." And you know—that George is a happy man. A happy man, suh.

✡ THE EUROPEAN AS REVOLUTIONARY

"EVEN before I emerged from childhood, I seem to have experienced, deeply at heart, that paradoxical feeling which was to dominate me all through the first part of my life: that of living in a world without any possible escape, in which there was nothing for it but to fight for an impossible escape. I felt repugnance mingled with wrath and indignation, toward people whom I saw settled comfortably in this world. How could they not be conscious of their captivity, of their unrighteousness?"

These ringing sentences open Victor Serge's memoirs of his life as a European revolutionist (*Memoirs of a Revolutionary, 1901–1941*, translated and edited by Peter Sedgwick, Oxford University Press). Few Americans could, in good faith, say as much: perhaps none but a handful of jail-hardened militants at the outer edge of the Negro movement who have chosen alienation from American society as a badge of honor. But in the Europe of the past seventy-five years it was possible for thousands of men to speak as Serge did, without seeming vain or histrionic. Bourgeois intellectuals and half-educated proletarians, they declared themselves enemies of society, rejected its pleasures and corruptions, and fought a bitter war against its very existence. Nothing quite like this had occurred in the Western world since the rise of apocalyptic sects in the Middle Ages; even in the French Revolution few, if any, of the major figures regarded themselves so completely as men beyond the margin.

Anyone unable to imagine the social and moral pressures which drove some of the best Europeans to a life of estranged rebellion, is immediately disqualified from understanding twentieth-century history. This includes, I suspect, most Americans, even those who are well-educated; the historical sense does not flourish among us. But for readers who do wish to grasp the special qualities of recent European experience, who want to see at close range how the pressures of inherited evil produced a systematic extremism, Serge's memoirs are indispensable. Here in a nervous impressionistic style—Serge was a master of the historical vignette—is a classical account of the European as revolutionist.

Turning back to his youth among the Belgian anarchists, where he encountered a demiworld of intellectual desperadoes "athirst for the absolute"; tracing his involvement during the twenties in the Communist movement and his early adherence to the Trotskyist opposition, as a result of which he suffered a near-fatal exile to Central Asia; and completing his account with the fall of Paris, a flight to Mexico, where he died in 1947, and final years of loneliness, during which he drove himself to those lacerating intellectual reconsiderations that were the common fate of all the more thoughtful radicals who had survived Hitler and Stalin—Serge, as he tells this story of revolt, wandering, heresy, and defeat, seldom stoops to self-apology or romantic nostalgia. He regards his life with a mixture of authority and detachment, aware of his own self both as a theater for the clash of political forces and as an independent organism with desires and frustrations. He is quite free of that masochistic, Koestlerian sourness which mars the confessions of so many ex-Communists. It is as if he were saying: this was the experience of a committed man, so it was and so, perhaps, it had to be.

Serge was never a Marxist theoretician, neither in the imposing sense one associates with the names of Trotsky and Bukharin, nor in the pompous style of the routine Communist functionary. He was primarily an observer, a superior journalist from whose books there emanates the heat and turmoil of historical immediacy. For Serge the social photograph was always more important than the social theory, and as a consequence the world of early Communism which he sketches in his best chapters comes to seem a credible *human* world, full of variety and conflict, illustrating the usual range of conduct from heroism to venality, and very far indeed from that static demonology which certain theorists like to attribute to Communism.

Trotsky, though he liked Serge, condescended toward him. Serge, felt Trotsky, was a literary dilettante who, while utterly devoted to the cause of socialism, would not become a disciplined follower of the Trotskyist or any other left-wing party. In the sense that Trotsky meant it, Serge was indeed a dilettante, but that is precisely a major source of his strength as a memoirist: he cared about nuances, textures, and quirks of experience, he refused to dissolve men into historical forces. In addition to the *Memoirs* he has left several other works that deserve to be remembered, most notably *L'An I de la révolution russe*, a firsthand account of early Bolshevik Russia that cries out for a complete translation (parts appeared in an American Trotskyist journal some years ago), and *The Case of Comrade Tulayev*, an exciting novel about Russia during the years of the Stalinist terror, which has recently been published in paperback.

The *Memoirs* themselves are rich with historical portraits, some of famous men and others of figures quite forgotten, such as the Old Bolshevik, Boris Eltsin, whom Serge met after both had been exiled by Stalin and who "would make tea, like the old student he was, and at last smile, bright-eyed, and say: 'Tonight I read a page of Hegel over again: it's a tremendous stimulant for the mind.' " If, as I have said, reading this book makes it difficult to sustain the demonological view of modern Russian history, it also convinces one, since the evidence comes from a man who never became a professional anti-Bolshevik, that a strong element of authoritarianism lay at the very heart of Leninist doctrine and practice. This was not the only element, nor was its triumph inevitable, but strong it certainly was. What Serge writes on this theme remains quite to the point: "It is often said that 'the germ of Stalinism was in Bolshevism at its beginning.' Well, I have no objection. Only, Bolshevism also contained many other germs. . . . To judge the living man by the death germs which the autopsy reveals in a corpse—and which he may have carried in him since his birth—is this very sensible?"

The most vivid pages in these *Memoirs* sketch the darkening of Russian life during the twenties as the dictatorship consolidated its power and Stalinism edged toward terror. In 1926 Serge encountered a former Chekist, Konstantinov, notorious for brutality. Now, himself in opposition to Stalin, Konstantinov "unveils his secret" to Serge and it is a scene worthy of Dostoevsky:

"The secret is that everything has been betrayed. From the years that Lenin was alive, treason had wormed its way into the Central Committee. He knows the names, he has the proofs. . . . He whispers the names of foreigners, of the most powerful capitalists, and of yet others, which have an occult significance for him. He specifies a city beyond the Atlantic. I follow his chain of reasoning with the secret uneasiness that one feels in the presence of some lunatic logician. And I observe that he has the inspired face of a madman."

Here, in a personal syndrome, is the madness which later will be transformed into the system of bureaucratic slaughter.

This is a book with the mark of sincerity, the sincerity of a man who paid for his knowledge but who emerged from disenchantment still glowing with the idealism of his youth. I find it a rare and lovely thing, and if I were teaching twentieth-century history in an American university, I would ask my students to read this book as a way of reaching to the inner quality of a crucial modern experience.

✡ MADNESS, VISION, STUPIDITY

TOWARD the end, Whittaker Chambers seems to have gone a little mad. It is not hard to understand why, and if one brings to life a fraction of the imaginativeness we all so devoutly accord to literature, it is even possible to sympathize with his condition.

Chambers felt himself to be a man burdened with a vision. He treasured a note André Malraux had sent him after the appearance of *Witness:* "You are one of those who did not return from Hell with empty hands." (Whether Malraux remarked on the value of what Chambers brought back or the possibility that after a conspiratorial-ideological debauch it might be a nice touch of modesty to return with "empty hands," Chambers does not say.) He, Chambers, knew—perhaps he alone knew—the nature and magnitude of the Communist threat. He knew—perhaps he alone knew—that it was symptomatic of a far deeper malaise in Western society, which could be traced back to the rise of secular humanism in the Renaissance: the devil's work. And everywhere about him he saw evidence of fatty social degeneration: a society hurtling itself into prosperous suicide, insensitive to its moral premises, and unaware that it stood at the point of collapse such as the Roman Empire faced shortly before . . . well, such analogies never being very precise, let's just say, shortly before the Roman Empire fell. Like most aspirants to prophecy, Whittaker Chambers was fond of this notion.

Nobody understood the contemporary crisis as Chambers did, and it was an understanding that made it no easier for him to bear his cross. The intellectuals he knew to be hopeless, carriers of heresy and decay. Socialists, ultimately, were allies of Communism, even if, in mere fact, they perished resisting it; liberals were socialists in disguise, sapped by Marxism; and as for most American conservatives, they were either timid liberals or spokesmen for petty selfishness. Chambers wrote for the *National Review*—a man harassed by a vision must write somewhere—but he seems to have felt it lacking in disinterested grandeur; nor was he impressed with William Buckley's spiritual credentials. And one can allow Chambers the credit of supposing that he would have been disdainful of the sharpers who led the Goldwater campaign.

What Chambers really yearned for was to discard his soiled American self and appear—reincarnate, in ascetic leanness—as a twentieth-century Dostoevsky. Then he would speak for the mysteries of the faith, excoriate the materialist West, and proclaim a holy war against the Moscow anti-Christ (in which, despite his distaste for modern technology, "I suspect the argument must be completed by the Bombs"). Historical action often takes the form of repetitive impersonation, and all public gesture involves a risk of parody; but what a hopelessly ridiculous piece of miscasting Chambers subjected himself to! He had the ambition to prophecy, but not the calling. He knew, like most half-educated Americans, either too much or too little: too much for mere demagogy, too little for clear analysis. And besides, how could Dostoevsky be an American, or an American be Dostoevsky? The question seems to have haunted Chambers: which may be one reason he felt so lonely, misunderstood, and paranoid. To harbor a vision of the apocalypse is never comfortable; to harbor it on a farm in Maryland could drive even a saint mad. And a saint he was not.

Everything about Chambers—his grandiose solemnity, his stunning pretentiousness, his oracular incompetence—was appalling: everything but his stubborn conviction that we live in an age of apocalypse and a cluster of personal qualities which come through in *Cold Friday* (Random House), a posthumous collection of his articles, notes, and diaries. To grant Chambers any virtue, even a trace of humanity, is to risk a hissing of anger from certain liberals who need to see him as the complete contemporary villain. But why? If such people encountered Chambers in a novel, say in Trilling's *Middle of the Journey*, they would insist on granting him complexity of motive and shading of character.

Cold Friday has some well-written pages displaying Chamber's intense feeling for the natural world, also some testimony of his close and sustaining family life. If one can break past the crust of pontification, there is a man to be found in the book: not perhaps a very likable man but one who has had his share of suffering. Most of the time, Chambers does his best to keep the reader from making this discovery.

As for the vision of apocalypse he struggled so hard to maintain, that is not highly regarded in this country. Few of our intellectuals share this vision; not many try to understand it. We like to behave as if the United States were exempt from the terrors of modern history, and perhaps, by some turn of fate, it will prove to be. But not all the evidence is in yet, and even if we emerge from this epoch far luckier than we probably deserve, it can at least be argued that American intellectuals have a moral obligation to share with the rest of humanity an awareness of what the twentieth century has meant. And without a sense of apocalypse, how can one truly respond to the experience of this century?

Yet *Cold Friday* shows that even with a sense of apocalypse one can fail to respond. To recognize the presence of an unprecedented historical disaster is not yet to understand its causes or nature. Chambers was the kind of writer who by instinct and training reduced everything to melodrama. It was a gift of sorts, enabling him to present political struggles in a shocking chiaroscuro but disabling him for serious thought. In saying this I do not mean that he had wrong or even detestable ideas; I mean, literally, that he could not think. Chambers had an infuriating contempt for the customary rules of evidence; he was seldom able to connect one link in a sequence of argument to another; he preferred the stupefying power of assertion, the lordly rights of the man who has "returned from hell."

A few instances:

1) "If God exists, a man cannot be a Communist, which begins with the rejection of God. But if God does not exist, it follows that Communism, or some suitable variant of it, is right."

This nonsense Chambers first advanced in *Witness*; he was repeatedly challenged and answered; the statement is false in fact, inept in logic, impudent in morals, and unchristian in spirit. Yet he repeats it again and again, without the faintest effort to reason or argue, adding only the insidious qualification, "some suitable variant of [Communism]," to take care of the liberals.

2) With the air of a man who has just heard Pascal deliver a *pensée*, Chambers describes a conversation with a Passionist monk to whom he poured out his worries about the viability and virility of the West. "Who says," replied this Father Alan, "that the West deserves to be saved?" Chambers was overwhelmed, struck dumb by this "Verey flare" of illumination.

What is this "West" that is to be saved? The Salk vaccine or Jim Crow, anesthesia or torture, Shakespeare or Spillane, the seven-hour day or child labor? Why must some undifferentiated entity be saved or not saved? Precisely who among mortals is to take upon himself the presumption of answering this kind of question about the culture of mankind? And if the West is judged unworthy of salvation (which, in my distance from orthodoxy, I had always supposed was God's business, not Chambers's or Father Alan's), where but from the tradition of the West can one draw the values for something better? But if that is so, then at least part of "the West" deserves to be saved.

3) "You cannot replace God with Point Four. If you fed the starving millions four square meals a day and studded their primitive lands with automated factories, men would still die of despair."

No ordinary person, only a special kind of besotted ideologue, could say anything so stupid. Can one put under the same rubric the despair of a Brazilian peasant watching his children starve and the despair of a well-fed American who finds life aimless? Suppose the Brazilian peasant, suddenly lifted to plenty, were then to learn the malaise of a sophisticated New Yorker: he might indeed die of despair (which, by the way, even in New York is not quite so easy), but it would be for entirely new reasons and would therefore have entirely new political and social repercussions. In respect to social stability, prospects of democracy, the threat of Communism, and the personal life of the peasant, a very great deal would have changed. In any case, who proposes to *replace* God with Point Four? Whatever men in Latin America may have lacked—bread, health, minimal dignity—has surely not been caused by the absence of God or His accredited representatives.

To argue against foolishness can make one feel somewhat

foolish; but I suppose it is necessary, since Chambers has his representative significance. He was perhaps the most dramatic example we have recently had in America of the intellectual *manqué* hungering for prophecy and power, the journalist of ideological melodrama, the man who fancies himself a mixture of Ivan and Alyosha Karamazov, but more nearly resembles their buffoonish half-brother Smerdyakov.

PART IV *Premises and Reconsiderations*

✡ IMAGES OF SOCIALISM

DURING the past several decades, the experience of socialists who try to think, like that of conservatives and liberals who try to think, has been one of steady intellectual crisis. When several of us formed *Dissent* in 1953, it was a tacit premise of our enterprise that the traditional Marxist ideology, even in the democratic, anti-Stalinist version to which some of us had been attached, was no longer tenable—or, at the least, it required a sustained re-examination. Such things are easy to say, but hard to do. We had no illusion that we could reconstruct a new and shiny political system for socialists, we doubted that it would be a good thing to do even if it were possible, and we were entirely certain that we lacked the equipment to undertake such a task. But what Lewis Coser and I did attempt to do in the following essay was to provide, so to speak, an agenda of concerns, a pointer in the direction we wanted to go. Necessarily the essay is fragmentary: that is its nature. Necessarily it is argumentative: most often with itself or with the ideas we once held, ideas that hover over it, shadowlike. Still, it has served for a few of us as a statement of principles during the years since its composition.

"GOD," said Tolstoy, "is the name of my desire." This remarkable sentence could haunt one a lifetime, it reverberates in so many directions. Tolstoy may have intended partial assent to the idea that, life being insupportable without some straining toward "transcendence," a belief in God is a psychological necessity. But he must also have wanted to turn this rationalist criticism into a definition of his faith. He must have meant that precisely because his holiest desires met in the vision of God he was enabled to cope with the quite unholy realities of human existence. That God should be seen as the symbolic objectification of his desire thus became both a glorification of God and a strengthening of man, a stake in the future and a radical criticism of the present.

Without sanctioning the facile identification that is frequently made between religion and socialist politics, we should like to twist Tolstoy's remark to our own ends: *socialism is the name of our desire.* And not merely in the sense that it is a vision which, for many people throughout the world, provides moral sustenance, but also in the sense that it is a vision which objectifies and gives urgency to their criticism of the human condition in our time. It is the name of our desire because the desire arises from a conflict with, and an extension from, the world that is; nor could the desire survive in any meaningful way were it not for this complex relationship to the world that is.

At so late and unhappy a moment, however, can one still

specify what the vision of socialism means or should mean? Is the idea of utopia itself still a tolerable one?

1.

The impulse to imagine "the good society" probably coincides with human history, and the manner of constructing it—to invert what exists—is an element binding together all pre-Marxist utopias. These dreamers and system-makers have one thing in common: their desire to storm history.

The growth of the modern utopian idea accompanies the slow formation of the centralized state in Europe. Its imagery is rationalistic, far removed from the ecstatic visions that accompany the religiously inspired rebellions agitating feudal society in its last moments. As the traditional patchwork of autonomous social institutions in Western Europe was replaced, in the interests of efficiency, by an increasingly centralized system of rule, men began to conceive of a society that would drive this tendency to its conclusion and be governed completely by rationality. But not only the increasing rationality of political power inspired the thinking of social philosophers; they were stirred by the growth of a new, bourgeois style of life that emphasized calculation, foresight and efficiency, and made regularity of work an almost religious obligation.

As soon as men began to look at the state as "a work of art," as "an artificial man, created for the protection and salvation of the natural man" (Hobbes, *Leviathan*), it took but one more step to imagine that this "work of art" could be rendered perfect through foresight and will. Thomas Campanella, a rebellious Calabrian monk of the seventeenth century, conceived in his *City of the Sun* of such a perfect work of art. In Campanella's utopia, unquestionably designed from the most idealistic of motives, one sees the traits of many pre-Marxist utopias. Salvation is *imposed,* delivered from above; there is an all-powerful ruler called the

Great Metaphysicus (surely no more absurd than the Beloved Leader); only one book exists in the City of the Sun, which may be taken as an economical image of modern practice: naturally, a book called Wisdom. Sexual relations are organized by state administrators "according to philosophical rules," the race being "managed for the good of the commonwealth and not of private individuals. . . ." Education is conceived along entirely rationalistic lines, and indeed it must be, for Campanella felt that the Great Metaphysicus, as he forces perfection upon history, has to deal with recalcitrant materials: the people, he writes in a sentence that betrays both his bias and his pathos, is "a beast with a muddy brain."

And here we come upon a key to utopian thought: the galling sense of a chasm between the scheme and the subjects, between the plan, ready and perfect, and the people, mute and indifferent. (Poor Fourier, the salesman with phalanxes in his belfry, comes home daily at noon, to wait for the one capitalist, he needs no more than one, who will finance utopia.) Intellectuals who cannot shape history try to rape it, either through actual violence, like the Russian terrorists, or imagined violence, the sudden seizure of history by a utopian claw. In his City of the Sun Campanella decrees—the utopian never hesitates to decree—that those sentenced to death for crimes against the godhead, liberty, and the higher magistrates are to be rationally enlightened, before execution, by special functionaries, so that in the end they will acquiesce in their own condemnation. Let no one say history is unforeseen.

Two centuries after Campanella, Etienne Cabet, a disciple of Robert Owen and Saint-Simon, envisaged the revolutionary dictatorship of Icar, an enlightened ruler who refuses to stay in power longer than is necessary for establishing the new society; he no doubt means it to wither away. Meanwhile Icaria has only one newspaper, and the republic has "revised all useful books which showed imperfections and it has burned all those which we judged dangerous and useless."

The point need not be overstressed. The utopians were not—or not merely—the unconscious authoritarians that malicious critics have made them out to be. No doubt, some did harbor strong streaks of authoritarian feeling which they vicariously released through utopian images; but this is far from the whole story. Robert Owen wanted a free co-operative society. Decentralization is stressed in Morelly's utopia, *Floating Islands.* The phalanxes of Fourier are to function without any central authority and if there must be one, it should be located as far from France as possible, certainly no nearer than Constantinople.

But it is not merely a question of desirable visions. In the most farfetched and mad fantasies of the utopians there are imbedded brilliant insights. The same Fourier who envisaged the transformation of brine into an agreeable liquid and the replacement of lions and sharks by mildly domestic "anti-lions" and "antisharks" also writes with the deepest understanding of the need for both the highest specialization of labor in modern society and the greatest variety and alternation of labor in order to overcome the monotony of specialization.

The authoritarian element we find in the utopians is due far less to psychological malaise or power-hunger (most of them are genuinely good people) than to the sense of desperation that frequently lies beneath the surface of their fantasying. All pre-Marxist utopian thinking tends to be ahistorical, to see neither possibility nor need for relating the image of the good society to the actual workings of society as it is. For Fourier it is simply a matter of discovering the "plan" of God, the ordained social order that in realizing God's will ensures man's happiness. (Socialism for Fourier is indeed the name of his desire—but in a very different sense from that which we urge!) The imagined construction of utopia occurs *outside* the order or flux of history: it comes through fiat. Once utopia is established, history grinds to a standstill and the rule of rationality replaces the conflict of class or, as the utopians might have preferred to say, the conflict of passions. In his *Socialism, Utopian and Scientific* Frederick Engels describes this process with both sympathy and shrewdness:

Society presented nothing but wrongs; to remove these was the task of reason. It was necessary, then, to *impose this upon society from without* by propaganda and, whenever possible, by the example of model experiments. These new social systems were foredoomed as utopian; the more completely they were worked out in detail, the more they could not avoid drifting off into pure phantasies. . . .

We can leave it to the literary small fry to solemnly quibble over these phantasies, which today only make us smile, and to crow over the superiority of their own bald reasoning, as compared with such "insanity." As for us, we delight in the stupendously great thoughts and germs of thought that everywhere break out through their phantastic covering. . . . (Emphasis added.)

Given the desire to impose utopia upon an indifferent history, a desire which derives, in the main, from a deep sense of alienation from the flow of history, it follows logically enough that the utopians should for the most part think in terms of elite politics. Auguste Comte specifies that in the "Stage of Positive Science," society is to be ruled by an elite of intellectuals. The utopia to be inaugurated by the sudden triumph of reason over the vagaries and twists of history—what other recourse could a lonely, isolated utopian have but the elite, the small core of intellect that, like himself, controls and guides? Saint-Simon, living in the afterglow of the French Revolution, begins to perceive the mechanics of class relations and the appearance for the first time in modern history of the masses as a decisive force. But in the main our generalization holds: reformers who lack some organic relationship with major historical movements must almost always be tempted into a more or less benevolent theory of a ruling elite.

2.

Utopia without egalitarianism, utopia dominated by an aristocracy of mind, must quickly degenerate into a vision of useful slavery. Hence, the importance of Marx's idea that socialism is to be brought about, in the first instance, by the activities of a major segment of the population, the workers. Having placed the drive toward utopia not beyond but squarely— perhaps a little too squarely—within the course of history, and having found in the proletariat that active "realizing" force which the utopians could nowhere discern on the social horizon, Marx was enabled to avoid the two major difficulties of his predecessors: ahistoricism and the elite theory. He had, to be sure, difficulties of his own, but not these.

Marx was the first of the major socialist figures who saw the possibility of linking the utopian desire with the actual development of social life. By studying capitalism both as an "ideal" structure and a "real" dynamic, Marx found the sources of revolt within the self-expanding and self-destroying rhythms of the economy itself. The utopians had desired a revolt against history but they could conduct it, so to speak, only from the space-platform of the imaginary future; Marx gave new power to the revolt against history by locating it, "scientifically," within history.

The development of technology, he concluded, made possible a society in which men could "realize" their humanity, if only because the brutalizing burden of fatigue, that sheer physical exhaustion from which the great masses of men had never been free, could now for the first time be removed. This was the historic option offered mankind by the Industrial Revolution, as it is now being offered again by the Atomic Revolution. Conceivably, though only conceivably, a society might have been established at any point in historical time which followed an equalitarian distribution of goods; but there would have been neither goods nor leisure enough to dispense with the need for a struggle over their distribution; which means bureaucracy, police, an oppressive state; and in sum, the destruction of egalitarianism. Now, after the Industrial Revolution, the machine might do for all humanity what the slaves had done for the Greek patriciate.

Marx was one of the first political thinkers to see that both industrialism and the "mass society" were here to stay, that all social schemes which ignored or tried to controvert this fact were not merely irrelevant, they weren't even interesting.* It is true, of course, that he did not foresee—he could not—a good many consequences of this tremendous historical fact. He did not foresee that "mass culture" together with social atomization (Durkheim's *anomie*) would set off strong tendencies of demoralization working in opposition to those tendencies that made for disciplined cohesion in the working class. He did not foresee that the rise of totalitarianism might present mankind with choices and problems that went beyond the capitalist/socialist formulation. He did not foresee that the nature of leisure would become, even under capitalism, as great a social and cultural problem as the nature of work. He did not foresee that industrialism would create problems which, while not necessarily insoluble, are likely to survive the span of capitalism. But what he did foresee was crucial: that the great decisions of history would now involve masses of men, that the "stage" upon which this struggle would take place had suddenly, dramatically been widened far beyond its previous dimensions.

And when Marx declared the proletariat to be the active social force that could lead the transition to socialism, he was neither sentimentalizing the lowly nor smuggling in a

* In an excellent review of T. S. Eliot's *Notes Towards the Definition of Culture* (*The Kenyon Review*, Summer 1949) William Barrett puts his finger on the central weakness of all those who, like Eliot, cling to an "elite" theory of culture: "Anyone who wants to meditate about the history of culture would do well to walk any afternoon in the vicinity of Times Square. Where do all these crowds come from? How do they fill their day? What is to be done with them?"

theory of the elite, as many of his critics have suggested. Anyone who has read the chapter in *Capital* on the Working Day or Engels's book on the conditions of the English workers knows that they measured the degradation of the workers to an extent precluding sentimentality. As for the idea of the proletariat as an elite, Marx made no special claim for its virtue or intelligence, which is the traditional mode of justifying an elite; he merely analyzed its peculiar *position* in society, as the class most driven by the workings of capitalism to both discipline and rebellion, the class that come what may, utopia or barbarism, would always remain propertyless.

There is another indication that Marx did not mean to favor an elite theory by his special "placing" of the proletariat. His theory of "increasing misery"—be it right, wrong or vulgarized—implied that the proletariat would soon include the overwhelming bulk of the population. The transition to socialism, far from being assigned to a "natural" elite or a power group, was seen by Marx as the task of the vast "proletarianized" majority.

Concerned as he was with the mechanics of class power, the "laws of motion" of the existing society, and the strategy of social change, Marx paid very little attention to the description of socialism. The few remarks to be found in his early work and in such a later book as *The Critique of the Gotha Program* are mainly teasers, formulations so brief as to be cryptic, which did not prevent his disciples from making them into dogmas. An interesting division of labor took place. Marx's predecessors, those whom he called the "utopian socialists," had devoted themselves to summoning pictures of the ideal future perhaps in lieu of activity in the detested present; Marx, partly as a reaction to their brilliant daydreaming, decided to focus on an analysis of those elements in the present that made possible a strategy for reaching the ideal future, and in the meantime, why worry about the face of the future, why create absurd blueprints? As a response to Fourier, Saint-Simon, and Owen there was much good sense in this attitude; given the state of the European labor movements in the mid-nineteenth century it was indispensable to turn toward practical problems of national life (Germany) and class organization (England). But the Marxist movement, perhaps unavoidably, paid a price for this emphasis.

As the movement grew, the image of socialism kept becoming hazier and hazier, and soon the haziness came to seem a condition of perfection. The "revisionist" Social Democrat Eduard Bernstein could write that the goal is nothing, the movement everything; as if a means could be intelligently chosen without an end in view! In his "State and Revolution" Lenin, with far greater fullness than Marx, sketched a vision of socialism profoundly democratic, in which the mass of humanity would break out of its dumbness, so that cooks could become cabinet ministers, and even the "bourgeois principle of equality" would give way to the true freedom of nonmeasurement: "from each according to his ability and to each according to his need." But this democratic vision did not sufficiently affect his immediate views of political activity, so that in his crucial pamphlet "Will the Bolsheviks Retain State Power?" written in 1917, Lenin, as if to brush aside the traditional Marxist view that the socialist transformation requires a far greater popular base than any previous social change, could say that "After the 1905 Revolution Russia was ruled by 130,000 landowners. . . . And yet we are told that Russia will not be able to be governed by the 240,000 members of the Bolshevik Party—governing in the interests of the poor and against the rich."

What happened was that the vision of socialism—would it not be better to say the *problem* of socialism?—grew blurred in the minds of many Marxists because they were too ready to entrust it to History. The fetishistic use of the word "scientific," than which nothing could provide a greater sense of assurance, gave the Marxist movement a feeling that it had finally penetrated to the essence of History, and found there once and for all its true meaning. The result was often a deification of History: what God had been to Fourier, History became to many Marxists—a certain force leading to a certain goal. And if indeed the goal was certain, or likely enough to be taken as certain, there was no need to draw up fanciful blueprints, the future would take care of itself and require no advice from us. True enough, in a way. But the point that soon came to be forgotten was that it is we, in the present, who need the image of the future, not those who may live in it. And the consequence of failing to imagine creatively the face of socialism—which is not at all the same as an absurd effort to paint it in detail—was that it tended to lapse into a conventional and lifeless "perfection."

3.

Perfection, in that image of socialism held by many Marxists—the image, that is, which emerged at the level of implicit belief—was one of a society in which tension, conflict, and failure had largely disappeared. It would be easy enough to comb the works of the major Marxists in order to prove this statement, but we prefer to appeal to common experience, to our own knowledge and memories as well as to the knowledge and memories of others. In the socialist movement one did not worry about the society one wanted; innumerable and, indeed, inconceivable subjects were discussed but almost never the idea of socialism itself, for History, Strategy and The Party (how easily the three melted into one!) had eliminated that need. Socialism was the Future—and sometimes a future made curiously respectable, the middle-class values that the radicals had violently rejected now being reinstated, unwittingly, in their vision of the good society. There could hardly be a need to reply to those critics who wondered how some of the perennial human problems could be solved under socialism: one *knew* they would be. In effect, the vision of socialism had a way of declining into a regressive infantile fantasy, a fantasy of protection.

Our criticism is not that the Marxist movement held to a vision of utopia: that it did so was entirely to its credit, a life without some glimmer of a redeeming future being a life cut off from the distinctively human. Our complaint is rather that the vision of utopia grew slack and static. Sometimes it degenerated into what William Morris called "the cockney dream" by which efficiency becomes a universal solvent for all human problems; sometimes it slipped off, beyond human reach, to the equally repulsive vision of a society in which men become rational titans as well-behaved and tedious as Swift's Houyhnhnms. Only occasionally was socialism envisaged as a society with its own rhythm of growth and tension, change and conflict.

Marx's contribution to human thought is immense, but except for some cryptic if pregnant phrases, neither he nor his disciples have told us very much about the society in behalf of which they called men into battle. This is not quite so fatal a criticism as it might seem, since what probably mattered most was that Marxism stirred millions of previously dormant people into historical action, gave expression to their claims and yearnings, and lent a certain form to their desire for a better life. But if we want sustained speculations on the shape of this better life we have to turn to radical mavericks, to the anarchists and libertarians, to the Guild Socialists. And to such a writer as Oscar Wilde, whose *The Soul of Man Under Socialism* is a small masterpiece. In his paradoxical and unsystematic way Wilde quickly comes to a sense of what the desirable society might be like. The great advantage of socialism, he writes, is that it "would relieve us from that sordid necessity of living for others which, in the present condition of things, presses so hard upon almost everybody." By focusing upon "the unhealthy and exaggerated altruism" which capitalist society demands from people, and by showing how it saps individuality, Wilde arrives at the distinctive virtue of Socialism: that it will make possible what he calls Individualism.

4.

We do not wish to succumb to that which we criticize. Blueprints, elaborate schemes do not interest us. But we think it may be useful to suggest some of the qualities that can make the image of socialism a serious and mature goal, as well as some of the difficulties in that goal:

Socialism is not the end of human history, as the deeply held identification of it with perfection must mean. There is no total fulfillment, nor is there an "end to time." History is a process which throws up new problems, new conflicts, new questions; and socialism, being within history, cannot be expected to solve all these problems or, for that matter, to raise humanity at every point above the level of achievement of previous societies.* As Engels remarked, there is no final synthesis, only continued clash. What socialists want is simply to do away with those sources of conflict which are the cause of material deprivation and which, in turn, help create psychological and moral suffering. Freedom may then mean that we can devote ourselves to the pursuit of more worthwhile causes of conflict. The hope for a conflictless society is reactionary, as is a reliance upon some abstract "historical force" that will conciliate all human strife.

The aim of socialism is to create a society of co-operation, but not necessarily, or at least not universally, of harmony. Co-operation is compatible with conflict, is indeed

* In his book *Entretiens* the French surrealist André Breton records a dialogue in which he, Diego Rivera, and Leon Trotsky took part. Trotsky, writes Breton, "suffered visibly when one of us stopped to caress pre-Columbian pottery; I still see the look of blame he fixed on Rivera when Rivera stated that the art of design had declined since the epochs of the cave, and how he exploded one evening when we let ourselves go by speculating out loud that once the classless society was installed, new causes of bloody conflict—that is, causes other than economic—might not fail to appear. . . ." Breton, to be sure, like most surrealists, is rather too liberal with other people's blood, but that apart, his implied criticism of Trotsky has a point.

inconceivable without conflict, while harmony implies a stasis.

Even the "total abolition" of social classes, no small or easy thing, would not or need not mean the total abolition of social problems.

In a socialist society there would remain a whole variety of human difficulties that could not easily be categorized as social or nonsocial; difficulties that might well result from the sheer friction between the human being and society, *any* society—from, say, the process of "socializing" those recalcitrant creatures known as children. The mere existence of man is a difficulty, a problem, with birth, marriage, pain, and death being only among the more spectacular of his crises. To be sure, no intelligent radical has ever denied that crises would last into a socialist society, but the point to be stressed is that with the elimination of our major material troubles, these other problems might rise to a new urgency, so much so as to become *social* problems leading to new conflicts.

5.

But social problems as we conceive of them today would also be present in a socialist society.

Traditionally, Marxists have lumped all the difficulties posed by critics and reality into that "transitional" state that is to guide, or bump, us from capitalism to socialism, while socialism itself they have seen as the society that would transcend these difficulties. This has made it a little too easy to justify some of the doings of the "transitional" society, while making it easier still to avoid considering not what socialism *will* be like, but what our image of it should be. Without pretending to "solve" these social problems as they might exist under socialism, but intending to suggest a bias or predisposition, we list here a few of them:

*

A. BUREAUCRACY

Marxists have generally related the phenomenon of bureaucratism to social inequality and economic scarcity. Thus, they have seen the rise of bureaucracy in Leninist Russia as a consequence of trying to establish a workers' state in an isolated and backward country which lacked the economic prerequisites for building socialism. Given scarcity, there arises a policeman to supervise the distribution of goods; given the policeman, there will be an unjust distribution. Similarly, bureaucratic formations of a more limited kind are seen as parasitic elites which batten upon a social class yet, in some sense, "represent" it in political and economic conflicts. Thus bureaucratism signifies a deformation, though not necessarily a destruction, of democratic processes.

This view of bureaucratism seems to us invaluable. Yet it would be an error to suppose that because a class society is fertile ground for bureaucracy, a classless society would automatically be free of bureaucracy. There are other causes for this social deformation; and while in a socialist society these other causes might not be aggravated by economic inequality and the ethos of accumulation as they are under capitalism, they would very likely continue to operate. One need not accept Robert Michels's "Iron Law of Oligarchy" in order to see this. (Michels's theory is powerful but it tends to boomerang: anyone convinced by it that socialism is impossible will have a hard time resisting the idea that democracy is impossible.) Thus the mere presence of equality of wealth in a society does not necessarily mean an equality of power or status: if Citizen A were more interested in the politics of his town or the functioning of his factory than Citizen B, he would probably accumulate more power and status; hence, the *possibility* of misusing them. (Socialists have often replied, But why should Citizen A want to misuse his power and status when there is no pressing economic motive for doing so? No one can answer this question definitively except by positing some theory of "human nature," which we do not propose to do; all we can urge is a certain wariness with regard to any theory which discounts in advance the possibility that noneconomic motives can lead to human troubles.) Then again, the problem of sheer size in economic and political units is likely to burden a socialist society as much as it burdens any other society; and large political or economic units, because they require an ever increasing delegation of authority, often to "experts," obviously provide a setting in which bureaucracy can flourish. But most important of all is the sheer problem of representation, the fact that as soon as authority is delegated to a "representative" there must follow a loss of control and autonomy.

Certain institutional checks can, of course, be suggested for containing bureaucracy. The idea of a division of governmental powers, which many Marxists have dismissed as a bourgeois device for thwarting the popular will, would deserve careful attention in planning a socialist society, though one need not suppose that it would have to perpetuate those elements of present-day parliamentary structure which do in fact thwart the popular will. Similarly, the distinction made in English political theory, but neglected by Marxists, between democracy as an expression of popular sovereignty and democracy as a pattern of government in which the rights of minority groups are especially defended, needs to be taken seriously. In general, a society that is pluralist rather than unitary in emphasis, that recognizes the need for diversification of function rather than concentration of authority—this is the desired goal.

And here we have a good deal to learn from a neglected branch of the socialist movement, the Guild Socialists of England, who have given careful thought to these problems. G. D. H. Cole, for example, envisages the socialist society as one in which government policy is a resultant of an interplay among socioeconomic units that simultaneously cooperate and conflict. Cole also puts forward the provocative idea of "functional representation," somewhat similar to the original image of the Soviets. Because, he writes, "a human being, as an individual, is fundamentally incapable of being represented," a man should have "as many distinct, and separately exercised, votes, as he has distinct social purposes or interests," voting, that is, in his capacity of worker, consumer, artist, resident, etc.*

But such proposals can hardly be expected to bulk very large unless they are made in a culture where the motives for private accumulation and the values sanctioning it have significantly diminished. If, as we believe, the goal of socialism is to create the kind of man who, to a measurable degree, ceases to be a manipulated object and becomes a motivated subject, then the growth of socialist consciousness must prove an important bulwark against bureaucracy. A society that stresses co-operation can undercut those prestige factors that make for bureaucracy; a society that accepts conflict, and provides a means for modulating it, will encourage those who combat bureaucracy.

B. PLANNING AND DECENTRALIZATION

Unavoidably, a great deal of traditional socialist thought has stressed economic centralization as a prerequisite for planning, especially in the "transitional" state between capitalism and socialism. Partly, this was an inheritance from the bourgeois revolution, which needed a centralized state; partly, it reflected the condition of technology in the nineteenth century, which required centralized units of production; partly, it is a consequence of the recent power of Leninism, which stressed centralism as a means of confronting the primitive chaos of the Russian economy but allowed

* A serious objection to this idea is that it seems to put a premium on "activity," so that the good socialist citizen who prefers to raise begonias may be relegated to a secondary status by comparison with the one who prefers to attend meetings. Cole seems to follow in the unattractive tradition of "the life of the member" party, whereby the movement swallows up the whole life of those who belong to it. (Cf. *In the Twilight of Socialism,* by Joseph Buttinger.)

it to become a dogma in countries where it had no necessary relevance. Whatever the historical validity of these emphases on centralism, they must now be abandoned. According to the famous economist Colin Clark, the new forms of energy permit an economical employment of small decentralized industrial units. Certainly, every impulse of democratic socialism favors such a tendency. For if mass participation—by the workers, the citizens, the people as a whole—in the economic life of the society is to be meaningful, it must find its most immediate expression in relatively small economic units. Only in such small units is it possible for the nonexpert to exercise any real control.

From what we can learn about Stalinist "planning," we see that an economic plan does not work, it quickly breaks down, if arbitrarily imposed from above and hedged in with rigid specifications which allow for none of the flexibility, none of the economic *play*, that a democratic society requires. Social planning, if understood in democratic terms—and can there really be social planning, as distinct from economic regulation, without a democratic context?—requires only a loose guiding direction, a general pointer from above. The rest, the actual working out of variables, the arithmetical fulfillment of algebraic possibilities, must come from below, from the interaction, co-operation and conflict of economic units participating in a democratic community.

All of this implies a considerable modification of the familiar socialist emphasis on nationalization of the means of production, increase of productivity, a master economic plan, etc.—a modification but not a total rejection. To be sure, socialism still presupposes the abolition of private property in the basic industries, but there is hardly a branch of the socialist movement, except the more petrified forms of Trotskyism, which places any high valuation on nationalization of industry *per se*. Almost all socialists now feel impelled to add that what matters is the use to which nationalization is put and the degree of democratic control present in the nationalized industries. But more important, the idea of nationalization requires still greater modification: there is no reason to envisage, even in a "transitional" society, that all basic industries need be owned by the state. The emphasis of the Guild Socialists upon separate Guilds of workers, each owning and managing their own industries, summons no doubt a picture of possible struggles within and between industries; all the better! Guilds, co-operatives, call them what you will—these provide possible bulwarks against the monster Leviathan, the all-consuming state, which it is the sheerest fatuity to suppose would immediately cease being a threat to human liberty simply because "we" took it over. The presence of numerous political and economic units, living together in a tension of co-operation-and-conflict, seems the best "guarantee" that power will not accumulate in the hands of a managerial oligarchy—namely, that the process already far advanced in capitalist society will not continue into socialism. Such autonomous units, serving as buffers between government and people, would allow for various, even contradictory, kinds of expression in social life.* The conflicts that might break out among them would be a healthy social regulator, for while the suppression of conflict makes for an explosive accumulation of hostility, its normalization means that a society can be "sewn together" by noncumulative struggles between component groups. And even in terms of "efficiency," this may prove far more satisfactory than the bureaucratic state regulation of Communist Russia.

Only if an attempt is made to encompass the total personality of the individual into one or another group is conflict likely to lead to social breakdown. Only then would conflicts over relatively minor issues be elevated into "affairs of state."

* In the famous "trade union" dispute between Lenin and Trotsky that took place in the early 1920s, Lenin clearly understood, as Trotsky did not, that even, and particularly, in a workers' state—or, as Lenin more realistically called it, a deformed workers' state—the workers need agencies of protection, in this case trade unions, against this "own" state. That the dispute remained academic is another matter.

So long as the dogma of "total allegiance"—a dogma that has proven harmful in both its Social Democratic and Leninist versions—is not enforced, so long as the individual is able to participate in a variety of groupings without having to commit himself totally to any of them, society will be able to absorb a constant series of conflicts.

Nor would the criterion of efficiency be of decisive importance in such a society. At the beginning of the construction of socialism, efficiency is urgently required in order to provide the material possibility for a life of security and freedom. But efficiency is needed in order, so to speak, to transcend efficiency.

Between the abstract norms of efficiency and the living needs of human beings there may always be a clash. To speak in grandiose terms, as some anarchists do, of Efficiency vs. Democracy is not very valuable, since living experience always requires compromise and complication. All one can probably say is that socialists are not concerned with efficiency as such but with that type of efficiency which does not go counter to key socialist values. Under socialism there are likely to be many situations in which efficiency will be consciously sacrificed, and indeed one of the measures of the success of the socialist society would be precisely how far it could afford to discard the criterion of efficiency. This might be one of the more glorious ideas latent in Engels's description of socialism as a "reign of freedom."

These remarks are, of course, scrappy and incomplete, as we intend them to be, for their usefulness has a certain correlation with their incompleteness; but part of what we have been trying to say has been so well put by R. H. S. Crossman that we feel impelled to quote him:

The planned economy and the centralization of power are no longer socialist objectives. They are developing all over the world as the Political Revolution [the concentration of state powers] and the process is accelerated by the prevalence of war economy. The main task of socialism today is to prevent the concentration of power in the hands of *either* industrial management *or* the state bureaucracy—in brief, to distribute responsibility and so to enlarge freedom of choice. This task was not even begun by the Labour Government. On the contrary, in the nationalized industries old managements were preserved almost untouched. . . .

In a world organized in ever larger and more inhuman units, the task of socialism is to prevent managerial responsibility degenerating into privilege. This can only be achieved by increasing, even at the cost of "efficiency," the citizen's right to participate in the control not only of government and industry, but of the party for which he voted. . . . After all, it is not the pursuit of happiness but the enlargement of freedom which is socialism's highest aim.

C. WORK AND LEISURE

No Marxist concept has been more fruitful than that of "alienation." As used by Marx, it suggests the psychic price of living in a society where the worker's "deed becomes an alien power." The division of labor, he writes, makes the worker "a cripple . . . forcing him to develop some highly specialized dexterity at the cost of a world of productive impulses. . . ." The worker becomes estranged from his work, both as process and product; his major energies must be expended upon tasks that have no organic or creative function within his life; the impersonality of the social relationships enforced by capitalism, together with the sense of incoherence and discontinuity induced by the modern factory, goes far toward making the worker a dehumanized part of the productive process rather than an autonomous human being. It is not, of course, to be supposed that this is a description of a given factory; it is a "lead" by which to examine a given factory. This theory is the starting point of much speculation on the nature of modern work, as well as upon the social and psychological significance of the industrial city; and almost all the theorizing on "mass culture," not to mention many of the efforts to "engineer" human relations in the factory, implicitly acknowledge the relevance and power of Marx's idea.

But when Marx speaks of alienation and thereby implies the possibility of nonalienation, it is not always clear whether he has in mind some precapitalist society in which men were presumably not alienated or whether he employs it as a useful "fiction" derived by a process of abstraction from the observable state of society. If he means the former, he may occasionally be guilty of romanticizing, in common with many of his contemporaries, the life of precapitalist society; for most historians of feudalism and of that difficult-to-label era which spans the gap between feudalism and capitalism, strongly imply that the peasant and even the artisan was not quite the unalienated man that some intellectuals like to suppose. Nonetheless, as an analytical tool and a reference to future possibilities, the concept of alienation remains indispensable.

So long as capitalism, in one form or another, continues to exist, it will be difficult to determine to what degree it is the social setting and to what degree the industrial process that makes so much of factory work dehumanizing. That a great deal of this dehumanization is the result of a social structure which deprives many men of an active sense of participation or decision-making and tends to reduce them to the level of controlled objects, can hardly be doubted at so late a moment.

We may consequently suppose that in a society where the democratic ethos had been reinforced politically and had made a significant seepage into economic life, the problem of alienation would be alleviated. But not solved.

In his *Critique of the Gotha Program* Marx speaks of the highest stage of the new society as one in which "the enslaving subordination of individuals in the division of labor has disappeared, and with it also the antagonism between mental and physical labor; labor has become not only a means of living, but itself the first necessity of life. . . ." Remembering that Marx set this as a *limit* toward which to strive and not as a condition likely to be present even during the beginning of socialism, let us then suppose that a society resembling this limit has been reached. The crippling effects of the division of labor are now largely eliminated because people are capable of doing a large variety of social tasks; the division between physical and mental labor has been largely eliminated because the level of education has been very much raised; and —we confess here to being uncertain as to Marx's meaning —labor has become "the first necessity of life." But even now the problem of *the nature of work* remains. Given every conceivable improvement in the social context of work; given a free and healthy society; given, in short, all the desiderata Marx lists—even then there remains the uncreativeness, the tedium, what frequently must seem the meaninglessness, of the jobs many people have to perform in the modern factory.

It may be said that in a socialist society people could live creatively in their leisure; no doubt. Or that people would have to do very little work because new forms of energy would be developed; quite likely. But then the problem would be for men to find an outlet for their "productive impulses" not in the way Marx envisaged but in another way, not in work but in leisure. Except for certain obviously satisfying occupations, and by this we do *not* mean only intellectual occupations, work might now become a minor part of human life. The problem is whether in any society it would now be possible to create—given our irrevocable commitment to industrialism—the kind of "whole man" Marx envisaged, the man, that is, who realizes himself through and by his work. Which is not to say that there wouldn't be plenty of room for improvement over the present human condition.

It is not as a speculation about factory life in a socialist society that this problem intrigues us, but rather as an entry into another problem about which Marx wrote very little: what we now call "mass culture." Socialists have traditionally assumed that a solution to economic problems would be followed by a tremendous flowering of culture; and this may happen, we do not know. But another possible outcome might be a population of which large parts were complacent and self-satisfied, so that if hell is now conceived as a drawing room, utopia might soften into a suburb. In any case, we are hardly likely to feel as certain about the cultural consequences of social equality as Trotsky did when he wrote in *Literature and Revolution* that under socialism men might reach the level of Beethoven and Goethe. This seems implausibly romantic, since it is doubtful that the scarcity of Beethovens and Goethes can be related solely to social inequality; and what is more it does not even seem very desirable to have a society of Beethovens and Goethes.

Between the two extreme forecasts there is the more likely possibility that under socialism a great many people would inevitably engage in work which could not release "a world of productive impulses" but which would be brief and light enough to allow them a great deal of leisure. The true problem of socialism might then be to determine the nature, quality, and variety of leisure. Men, that is, would face the full and terrifying burden of human freedom, but they would be more prepared to shoulder it than ever before.

6.

"The past and present," wrote Pascal, "are our means; the future alone our end." Taken with the elasticity that Pascal intended—he surely did not mean to undervalue the immediacy of experience—this is a useful motto for what we have called utopian thinking, the imaginative capacity for conceiving of a society that is qualitatively better than our own yet no mere fantasy of static perfection.

Today, in an age of curdled realism, it is necessary to assert the utopian image. But this can be done meaningfully only if it is an image of social striving, tension, conflict; an image of a problem-creating and problem-solving society.

In his *Essay on Man* Ernst Cassirer has written almost all that remains to be said:

*

A Utopia is not a portrait of the real world, or of the actual political or social order. It exists at no moment of time and at no point in space; it is a "nowhere." But just such a conception of a nowhere has stood the test and proved its strength in the development of the modern world. It follows from the nature and character of ethical thought that it can never condescend to accept the "given." The ethical world is never given; it is forever in the making.

Some time ago one could understandably make of socialism a consoling day-dream. Now, when we live in the shadow of defeat, to retain, to will the image of socialism is a constant struggle for definition, almost an act of pain. But it is the kind of pain that makes creation possible.

☼ AUTHORITARIANS OF THE LEFT

WRITTEN in 1954 with Lewis Coser, this essay initiated a strand of thought and polemic which keeps recurring in our writing, as indeed throughout this book. In a century that has given rise to totalitarianism, it is inevitable that there should develop among some intellectuals a variety of rationales for the support—be it crude or subtle—of dictatorial regimes. Few intellectuals can bring themselves to justify the idea of totalitarian dictatorship as such; those who wish to attach themselves emotionally and politically to a Communist regime need to rationalize their choice in the name of some "higher" objective, such as Historical Progress or Economic Development. (The intellectuals who supported Nazi and Fascist dictatorships engaged in similar maneuvers.)

One of the most prevalent styles of justification has been

the politics of authoritarian elitism, which tends to dismiss the value of democratic processes, brushes off as utopian the claim that the mass of ordinary people must be free to participate and choose in the political process, and sees one or another benevolent ruling party as an agent of history acting "in behalf" of humanity. Such modes of thought can be found along the entire intellectual spectrum: on the right, among figures like James Burnham, with their snobbish and pseudoaristocratic elitism; in the center, among bureaucratic liberals and disillusioned New Dealers, who narrow the arena of political decision-making to a small circle of "key men"; and on the left, where there has been active a group of writers led by Paul Sweezy, Isaac Deutscher, and the late Paul Baran, who offer a variety of sophisticated apologias for the Communist regimes.

During the last twelve or fifteen years I have felt obliged to keep up a running attack on this political outlook, especially in its leftist manifestations: partly because it has exerted some influence among radical youth in the United States, partly because democratic radicals have a special hygienic obligation, and partly because the defense of democratic values seems to me the central task for intellectuals in the contemporary world. My strong impression is that, as the Communist societies abandon outright terror but remain one-party dictatorships, the issues raised in the following essay will become more and more crucial. So let me say to the reader: this polemic is not one of those hair-splitting disputes that occur among radicals (as among all other political tendencies), it concerns the most fundamental problems of political and moral life. I wish the essay were written a bit more gracefully; the references to "Stalinism" should not be too troublesome, since Stalinism is not so distant a political phenomenon and in any case it is possible to substitute the term "Communism"; but I remain utterly convinced that what we wrote here is urgent, and not merely for socialists or radicals, but for persons of almost every political inclination.

THE original impetus of nineteenth-century socialism was—with some familiar, significant exceptions—profoundly democratic. Marx and Engels, though not they alone, looked toward an awakening of the masses of humanity from the stupor of centuries. Their aim was to transform passive objects into articulate subjects. The high level of economic development they desired had meaning for them not as a "final end"—they were never economic fetishists—but as a means by which to approach the one truly human goal: the humanization of humanity.

Once, however, it became clear that socialism had failed to achieve power, all the "old crap," as Marx had bluntly called it, again rose to the surface of intellectual life. The idea of democratic autonomy, the hope for human self-realization was now dismissed as utopian. Among many intellectuals there spread once more—it had never really been absent—an implicit contempt for the masses of human beings, whom they regarded primarily as creatures to be controlled and manipulated.

And this was true for many radicals as well. Living as we do in an historical moment when the old socialist passion has died out and a new one has not yet come to life, all the temptations for succumbing to the prevalent trends of authoritarian thought are particularly strong. Imperceptibly, many radicals have come to accept the moral terms of their adversaries. Benevolent manipulation now strikes them as the only "realistic" alternative to malevolent manipulation. But if that is the best radicalism can do, then it has no further reason for existence.

2.

A century ago Jacob Burckhardt predicted that the coming age would be the age of the "great simplifiers." He could hardly have had Marxism in mind—but he might as well have. During its early flowering Marxism was one of the most complex and hence *unfinished* constructs of the human intelligence. Now, in the postliberal world, the simplifiers have taken command.

We are thinking of that "left" tendency, amorphous in personnel but easily located intellectually, which grants most of the criticisms made of Russian Stalinism (that it is brutal, inhuman, dictatorial) but then finds a rationale or a half-defense for it in the name of Historical Necessity or in the world-wide drive toward industrialization or in the need for raising, by whatever means, the level of production or in the claim, true enough, that capitalism is a decadent society. Everything admirable in Marx's thought—his intellectual complexity, his humanist passion, his philosophical flexibility—is neglected in behalf of a simplistic economic determinism which measures human progress by little more than production statistics. This mode of thought is represented by Paul Sweezy in the *Monthly Review*, where it comes closest to an apologia for the Russian regime. It finds another variant in the "orthodox" Trotskyist groups which see in the fact that Stalinism destroys bourgeois property relations a proof of its "progressiveness." Frederick Schuman and I. F. Stone occasionally express ideas that fall within this orbit of thought. And while Isaac Deutscher cannot at all be identified with this intellectual tendency, he provides it, no doubt unintentionally, with the most subtle and persuasive arguments.

Marx spoke of "the categorical imperative that all conditions must be revolutionized in which man is a debased, an enslaved, an abandoned, a contemptible being." The intellectual tendency of "left authoritarianism" prefers to speak of the tempo of Russian industrialization. Marx said that the great evil of capitalism was that it "alienated" man from his work and from his self. "Left authoritarianism" prefers to neglect the question of whether the economic expansion it finds so admirable in Russia has led to an increase or decrease in the "alienation" of the Russian workers and intellectuals. Marx insisted that societies must be seen in their social totality, he called his *Capital* a study in *political* economy, he measured the claims of societies by their concrete human consequences. "Left authoritarianism," eager to find some ground for declaring Russian society "progressive" or for anticipating its "democratization," must abstract the element of industrial productivity from its social context.

In his book *Socialism* Paul Sweezy defines socialism as "a system which disallows private property." That is all: we neither omit nor suppress anything from his statement. Whether in a system which "disallows private property" man might still be "a debased, a contemptible being" (and what else has he been forced to become in Russia?) does not seem to concern Sweezy at all. For him the dialectic of property is simple: private is bad, public good.

Along the same lines Sweezy writes that "the outstanding achievement of socialism in the Soviet Union has been the victory in the war against Nazi Germany. . . . It is the Soviet Union's military success in the war against Germany which more than anything else has convinced the world that socialism really works. This is a fact which historians of the future may well rank in importance along with the October Revolution." Russia won the war; hence Stalinism really works. (How? Toward what end? In whose interest?) A series of curious parallels follows from this coarsely "pragmatic" argument: In 1920 Lenin lost the war to Poland; hence Leninism didn't *really* work. Hitler almost conquered Europe; hence Hitlerism almost *really* worked, and indeed for a short time may *really* have worked.

Nor is Mr. Sweezy more sensitive with regard to human freedom. "The restrictions on liberty which are characteristic of Soviet Russia," he writes, "are far less symptomatic of the time than the crisis of liberty in the United States." All one needs to know about Sweezy as a socialist or simply a democrat can be gleaned from the exquisite delicacy of that word "restriction."

Now there is no way of *proving* that Sweezy's view of what socialism means is wrong. Socialism being a kind of society that has never yet existed on this planet, he would seem to have as much right to define it in his way as we in ours. But if he defines it as equivalent to the mere abolition of private property and if he then casts this definition within an argument justifying or minimizing the destruction of freedom in Russia, it must be said that not only does his view run counter to almost every strand of the Marxist tradition but far more important, it projects a vision of the future that is utterly detestable. When a writer provides an eccentric variation to a commonly agreed upon statement of a social goal, this may tell us almost nothing about the goal, but it does tell us a good deal about the writer. And in this instance what matters is not the writer personally, but the kind of thought he expresses, reducing the socialist ideal to the prison-world of *1984*.

3.

Perhaps the greatest achievement of the Marxian theory of economics, one that is likely to resist all attack, was that it rejected the fetishistic view that economic processes were analogous to natural processes, and instead proceeded to interpret economic relations as one aspect of the total existential relations among men. Economic categories, Marx insisted, could not be understood outside of the social relations which flourished at a given historical moment. But to the writers who, in one or another way, speak for "left authoritarianism" all this has become meaningless. They care for economic plans, technological advances, production figures—in their eyes these in themselves are sufficient to demonstrate the viability and/or the "progressiveness" of Russian society. Unwittingly they revert to the very fetishism against which Marx struggled. But with this difference: *the fetishism of the plan is substituted for the fetishism of the commodity.*

4.

Twenty, even ten years ago it was possible to argue with a Stalinist or a fellow traveler. If one could convince him that oppression, terror, and misery dominated Russian life, one might break him from his loyalties. Today, however, the tough new "realist" is totally impervious to such argument, for his half-hidden loyalty to Stalinist thinking is based not on a humanitarian illusion but on a sympathetic identification with precisely the most brutal features of Russian politics. A terrifying change has taken place: a change not in ideas but in values. For the new kind of fellow traveler all that matters is that in Russia there is nationalized economy, or that there has been a rise in its productive level or that (on the bones of millions) "social stability" has been established.

Thus Arthur K. Davis, who is one of the purer specimens of "left authoritarianism," writes in the *American Sociological Review* that freedom is

> a subjective feeling of personal well-being which results from the objective fact of living in an effectively functioning society . . . a number of concrete patterns of societal organization can meet this abstract definition of freedom: *It is entirely possible that among them is . . . the totalitarian community—once the latter has been stabilized or routinized.* (Emphasis added.)

Here we have entered the realm of "left" Newspeak: freedom equals slavery, slavery equals freedom. What, one wonders, would Mr. Davis make of Marx's view that "the kingdom of freedom actually begins only where drudgery, enforced by hardship and by external purposes, ends; it thus lies, quite naturally, beyond the sphere proper of material production." To Marx the root *is* man, to Mr. Davis and his cothinkers it is an "effectively functioning society." And here we come to another central trait of the political tendency we are trying to describe: its fatal attraction to power, power as lure, power as virtue, power as the one ultimate, undeniable reality of life.

5.

A somewhat more subtle argument focuses upon the future. Instead of simply asserting that "what is is right," the writers who express one or another element of "left authoritarianism" imply that "what will be will be right." This worship of the putative success of the future is often evident in the work of writers who might be ashamed to argue that present might is right; they forget that the present is merely the future of the past. They will admit without hesitation the flaws in the social structure of Russia but these flaws weigh rather lightly for them in the balance of History, since they prepare—apparently, by their very accumulation—for the glories of tomorrow.

Yet it is just as dubious to defend the rightness of the future because it is the future, as to defend the rightness of the present because it is "given." A moral-political judgment takes on value only when argument is made as to *why* present or future is "right." If that is not done, judgment succumbs to the mere acceptance of the "factuality of facts," whether in the past or future; that is to say, judgment declines into justification.

The burden of moral-political choice cannot be shifted to a defenseless future. Marx felt that "the people cannot really be happy until it has been deprived of illusory happiness by the abolition of religion"—but now we witness a displacement of religious feelings onto the abstraction of History. By shifting the responsibility onto History (as, for example, in the argument that the horrors of Stalinism may be justified by the need for industrialization in backward countries) it becomes possible to avoid political-moral responsibility. In this way the Religion of History can be made to serve as a more flexible apologia for the acceptance of "the given" than can any other-worldly religious system. One is reminded of Kierkegaard's biting comment on Hegel: "His work is full of syntheses, while life is full of choices."

6.

Why have intellectuals become more receptive to authoritarian modes of thought? We cannot even attempt a full answer here, but what seems most important is the argument from failure. Democratic socialism has been defeated: it did not work: it cannot work: it is wrong. No one goes through a process of thought quite so simple, yet as a description of an intellectual development it may be adequate.

But more. The old image of the intellectual as a man on the margin no longer quite holds, neither under Stalinism nor capitalism. Many of those who might once have been forced to the painful necessity of functioning in the interstices of society have now found an honored place close to its summit. The bureaucratized and militarized modern state must use ideology, and for this it needs specialists in the manipulation of opinion, intellectuals who can create bonds of loyalty. These new specialists in human manipulation have learned that only force counts, only toughness wins; they often feel a violent horror of speculative thought, an almost complete cynicism toward anything that does not proceed from the already given. But while this may partly explain the general tendency, there still remains the minority of exceptions, those who continue to feel alienated from society and turn to *the other side.* Here, to provide further analysis, we would have to enter the realms of individual psychology and biography—which we are not prepared to do. Suffice it to say that many of the intellectuals who do turn to a full or partial sympathy toward Stalinism seek there a continuation, a logical fulfillment of the authoritarian patterns of their own world.

For many of the intellectuals who grew up under the influence of Stalinism and who have shaken off its formulas without abandoning its modes of thought, the ideology of "left authoritarianism" provides an extremely comfortable outlook. It no longer speaks to them in the name of liberty, mass spontaneity, the proletariat; "all that," and the social and emotional risks accompanying it, can be assigned to the romantic past. At the same time, however, "left authoritarianism" preserves and enlarges a cynical element of the traditional fellow-traveling outlook by connecting it with the most up-to-date and sophisticated theories of managerial and bureaucratic society: let the eggs be broken as they will, the omelet will still be made. It permits them to be indifferent to human values while retaining their faith in Dnieperstroi. It thus has become the perfect philosophy for those who have lost faith in *both* capitalism and socialism.

Some years ago George Orwell, in an essay on James Burnham, foresaw this phenomenon with the same sensitiveness as that with which he saw so much else:

> If one examines the people who, having some idea of what the regime is like, are strongly Russophile, one finds that, on the whole, they belong to the "managerial" class of which Burnham writes. That is, they are not managers in the narrow sense, but scientists, technicians, teachers, journalists, broadcasters, bureaucrats, professional politicians: in general middling people who feel themselves cramped by a system that is still partly aristocratic, and are hungry for more power and more prestige. . . . Burnham, although the English Russophile intelligentsia would repudiate him, is really voicing their secret wish to destroy the old, equalitarian version of socialism and usher in a hierarchical society where the intellectual can at last get his hands on the whip.

*

7.

The most outwardly impressive (especially for those to whom "economics" always seems more impressive than anything else)—the most outwardly impressive argument of "left authoritarianism" is the argument from industrialization. It is here that Isaac Deutscher, while in intention clearly distinct from the political tendency we are describing, provides it with its most sophisticated rationale.

An essential element of "left authoritarianism" is the idea that the expansion of productive forces is "progressive" or at least potentially "progressive." Now it may readily be granted that a certain expansion of productive capacities is a *necessary* condition for the emergence of a more humane society. But it is a gross error to assume that for attaining such a society the mere expansion of productive forces is a *sufficient* condition. What matters most is the relationship between the expansion of productive forces and the quality of the consciousness that accompanies it.

Nothing can be more misleading than the analogy which so occupies Isaac Deutscher, the analogy between the bourgeois and socialist revolutions. Bourgeois society could develop without the direct political rule of the bourgeoisie; socialism cannot develop without the democratic rule of the workers or, if you will, the people. Much could be done *for* the bourgeois, everything must be done *by* the socialist working class. Nor is this a matter of schematic dogmatism: it inheres in the very idea of socialism. The working class can attain social power only if and when it forms itself through its own organs of self-determination, only if and when it creates its own institutions capable of assuming the burden of a new society. Hence as long as the working class, as in present-day Russia, is prevented from achieving an awareness of its own distinctiveness, it cannot be said to have the capacity for ordering society.

A society like that in Russia which prevents the free and spontaneous organization of the workers cannot therefore be said to facilitate the achievement of socialism. Totalitarian society breaks up human and social bonds, it destroys the ties of fraternity that are a precondition for socialist values; it reduces the masses to a heap, an aggregate of atoms. Clearly, then, the meaning of industrialization in twentieth-century Stalinism cannot be adduced from nineteenth-century capitalism.

Nor is this significantly changed by the fact that Marxist writings have been utilized in the Russian state ideology. Just as medieval schoolmen used elements of the Greek tradition, and the Bible was used as a text by the inquisitors, so Marx, distorted, mutilated, and disfigured, has become a text from which the regime can, at convenience, extract citations. The masses, on the other hand, have been prevented, by the atomization and suppression to which the regime subjects them, from testing the truth at the core of the Marxist argument: that only in and through their own concerted action can men achieve the removal of hateful social conditions. To see in the cynical manipulation of Marxist terms by the state bureaucracy a means for the perpetuation of socialist consciousness is an ideological parallel to the view that the Stalinist regime performed the distasteful task of primitive accumulation "for" the workers.

Few of the social-cultural advantages which industrialization has traditionally brought to the West have yet appeared in Stalinist Russia. It is easy enough to say that industrialization prepares the ground for democracy, but to say this is to view the relationship of economy to politics abstractly rather than to examine the *concrete* way in which Russian industrialization has been purchased at a catastrophic cost to human consciousness.

Historically, the early phases of industrialization in the West were accompanied by sharp and, in the main, open social struggle. From this process of social struggle rather than as an automatic corollary of industrialization, the great democratic triumphs which we associate with the nineteenth century were won. They came not simply because England was being industrialized; they came because the industrialization was accompanied by a rich social history in which a vast growth of human awareness took place.

In Russia things have been entirely different. Here the course of social history during the period of industrialization has witnessed the destruction of those very rights, both civil and human, which are generally pointed to as the justification for the horrors of English industrialization. No free intelligentsia, for example, has been able to appear in Stalinist Russia as it did in nineteenth-century England, fiercely criticizing the repellent features of society and developing an independent attachment to democratic norms. Imagine merely what a Dickens could do for and to present-day Russia! It is precisely the absence of any *possibility* of a Dickens in present-day Russia which suggests how false and facile is the analogy between the process of industrialization in bourgeois society and in Stalinist society.

When it is sometimes argued that it is not inconceivable that the Russian bureaucracy might be induced to give up *some* of its privileges, one is ready to agree—though the problem is at present so hypothetical as to be virtually irrelevant. No ruling class has ever, of course, remained free from the pressure of change, all ruling classes have to some degree felt the need to adjust themselves to new conditions. The real question, however, is whether a ruling class has ever voluntarily given up its *essential* privileges, i.e., its ruling position. For this phenomenon, we submit, there are no historical precedents.

Would the disappearance of some privileges and some abuses, together with the continuation of the basic social and human relationships that characterize Russian society today, be sufficient to give the Russian regime a clean bill of socialist or democratic health? Those who are prepared to answer this question, however gingerly, in the affirmative may be said to be "left authoritarians." Here, precisely, lies the test. For it is not inconceivable that the standard of living may rise in Russia. Nor is it inconceivable that the Russian terror will be lessened, or at least regularized and "normalized." Not very much can be expected, since the pressure of the international conflict is likely to keep the regime from making too many concessions—and for the international situation the Russian regime bears, of course, a strong responsibility. But even if certain economic concessions and improvements were to be granted, even if a "relaxation" were to take place within the tension of totalitarianism, the one thing that seems beyond crediting is that the regime would grant, or would grant without the most terrific pressure *against* it, any significant political and social rights.

Which leads us to another point requiring clarification. If the distasteful characteristics of Russian society stemmed primarily from distortions within the sphere of consumption (that is, in the distribution of goods), then indeed changes in this sphere would amount to a change in the essential structure of society. But that is not the case.

The party secretaries and executives, the Red Directors and Soviet managers do not just "live better"—though they certainly and grossly do that too. They control the means of production and the means of coercion. Differentials in the sphere of consumption are only the most obvious symbols of differentials in the sphere of social and political power, as well as in the process of production. To be sure, in classical capitalism the bourgeoisie controlled the means of production because of the private ownership of each individual entrepreneur in his share of the social means of production, but such private ownership is by no means the only way a ruling class has asserted its dominion. The ruling classes of classical India and China did *not* individually own the chief means of production, the land.

The Russian bureaucracy controls the means of production not by right of private property but by holding in its hands the state, the levers of political and social and economic power. It commands them not individually but collectively. The difference involved may be to a limited extent compared—though comparisons are always hazardous—with that between a nineteenth-century entrepreneur and a modern corporation. The heads of many modern corporations do not themselves own a share in them, they derive their power essentially from an ability to control, which is partly based on the incapacity for action of the nominal owners, the often atomized and powerless stockholders. *Mutatis mutandis,* Russian society may be compared to a vast corporation. The bureaucracy does not individually own, it collectively controls—and hence prevents all other strata from participation in decision-making. Individual members of the bureaucracy, like individual entrepreneurs, may run the risk of elimination from its ranks, but the bureaucracy as such is a self-perpetuating ruling class whose power is defined by its relation to the means of production, i.e., by its relation to the state. Far from being a parisitic excrescence on a healthy body, it is an integral element of a corrupt social structure.

When Marx spoke of the increase of productive forces as a prerequisite for socialism, he had in mind—one can say this with some assurance—not an isolated development in one or another country but a general or "universal" development of, at least, the Western world. He had in mind, as well, a growth of social consciousness which he assumed to be parallel with the process of bourgeois industrialization—but which our experience has shown not at all parallel with Stalinist industrialization. From Marx's point of view the overall development of productive forces was "progressive" because it made *possible* a society of plenty and leisure. But today we have reached on a world level a degree of productive expansion sufficient for beginning the construction of a world socialist economy. This is not to say that many areas of the world, taken in isolation, possess the economic prerequisites for the flowering of a socialist economy; it is simply to say that if the world-wide productive forces could now be utilized in a socially constructive manner it would be possible to hasten appreciably the industrialization of the backward areas. So that what counts now is the political-social use of the productive forces already available. It therefore seems possible that if we lived in a sane and fraternal world the problem of raising the economic and cultural level of Asia could be solved without having to subject it to all the horrors of primitive accumulation which characterized the English experience.

With regard to this problem, as with regard to many others, politics in the twentieth century primes economics. Political and moral values—and choices—have assumed crucial relevance precisely to the degree that economic and technological problems appear to become manageable.

Hence, the process of primitive accumulation in Russia and/or China cannot be judged in terms analogous to the primitive accumulation of the bourgeois world. For where the bourgeois accumulation was the opening to a new level of social consciousness, the Stalinist accumulation is the conclusion to the failure of the world-wide socialist movement and the destruction of its consciousness.

It is sometimes said that the Stalinists have at least brought millions of previously dormant people into modern history. But this is merely a less troubled way of remarking that modern totalitarian movements, both Stalinist and Fascist, have to employ, even as they rigidly channel, the energies of the masses. What is not said is *how* these previously dormant millions are brought into modern history. For they are brought not as subjects learning to act autonomously but as objects being manipulated.

Marx did not say: economic levels determine human consciousness. He said: social existence determines human consciousness. Between the first and second of these statements there is the difference between vulgarity and insight. And if it is indeed social existence that determines human consciousness, it may well be asked: what kind of human consciousness, what quality of life, can follow from the social existence that Stalinism imposes upon its peoples?

✡ THIS AGE OF CONFORMITY

(*Notes on an endless theme, or, A catalogue of complaints*)

WHEN this essay first appeared in 1954, it aroused a quantity of anger, hostility and irritation. Understandably so: it was a scatter-shot polemic, meant to strike a wide variety of targets.

The early fifties were not a happy time in American life. Eisenhower was President, the perfect emblem of the torpor and mediocrity that had settled upon the country. McCarthy was running wild; the Korean war was bloody and ugly; the possibility of a world war seemed intensely real. And the intellectuals were not, as a rule, distinguishing themselves through a militant defense of freedom. One could really have supposed that the country had settled into a prolonged state of reaction and malaise, and those few of us who took a strongly critical stand could hardly avoid a feeling of isolation.

Thanks to the Negro revolution, a new generation of student rebels, the hopeful tone introduced by the Kennedy administration, and a complex of changes in international politics, there has been a significant improvement in our domestic life since the late fifties. Nevertheless I am eager for "This Age of Conformity" to be read, first because it is a contribution—not objective, not from the coolness of distance—to a critical history of one of the least glorious periods in American intellectual life, and second because it may help illuminate the struggles of a decade ago for a younger generation not especially keen on historical memory.

Polemics bring unexpected consequences, and by the late fifties "the age of conformity" had become a gratingly familiar phrase in American journalism. In 1960 I therefore found myself noting ruefully:

"There are gray moments when I charge myself with some small responsibility for the endless chatter about 'conformity' that has swept the country. Six years ago, when McCarthyism was at its worst and the response of many intellectuals somewhat less than heroic, I wrote a sharp polemic for *Partisan Review* called 'This Age of Conformity.' Much of what appeared there still seems to me true, but I could not know that, unintentionally, I was helping to make the outcry against conformity into a catchword of our conformist culture. . . .

"Intellectuals used to complain that society ignored or rejected their ideas; they could hardly have imagined what might happen when, for ends of its own, society learned to 'adapt' those ideas. During the past few decades the most remarkable trait of American culture has been neither conformity nor conservatism, not even its truly astonishing dullness; it has been an unprecedented capacity for assimilating—and thereby depreciating—everything on its own terms, both lavish praise and severe attacks.

"Assaults upon mass culture become an indispensable element of culture: the spice for the stew. *One idea seems as good as another, since none seems to matter very much*—

this amiably nihilistic version of *chacun à son goût* is the most authentic sentiment of the age. . . ."

INTELLECTUALS have always been partial to grandiose ideas about themselves, whether of an heroic or masochistic kind, but surely no one has ever had a more grandiose idea about the destiny of modern intellectuals than the brilliant economist Joseph Schumpeter. Though he desired nothing so much as to be realistic and hard-boiled, Schumpeter had somehow absorbed all those romantic notions about the revolutionary potential and critical independence of the intellectuals which have now and again swept through the radical and bohemian worlds. Marx, said Schumpeter, was wrong in supposing that capitalism would break down from inherent economic contradictions; it broke down, instead, from an inability to claim people through ties of loyalty and value. "Unlike any other type of society, capitalism inevitably . . . creates, educates and subsidizes a vested interest in social unrest." The intellectuals, bristling with neurotic aspirations and deranged by fantasies of utopia made possible by the very society they would destroy, become agents of discontent who infect rich and poor, high and low. In drawing this picture Schumpeter hardly meant to praise the intellectuals, yet until a few years ago many of them would have accepted it as both truth and tribute, though a few of the more realistic ones might have smiled a doubt as to their capacity to do *all that.*

Schumpeter's picture of the intellectuals is not, of course, without historical validity, but at the moment it seems spectacularly, even comically wrong. And wrong for a reason that Schumpeter, with his elaborate sense of irony, would have appreciated: he who had insisted that capitalism is "a form or method of economic change and not only never is but never can be stationary," had failed sufficiently to consider those new developments in our society which have changed the whole position and status of the intellectuals. Far from creating and subsidizing unrest, capitalism in its most recent stage has found an honored place for the intellectuals; and the intellectuals, far from thinking of themselves as a desperate "opposition," have been enjoying a return to the bosom of the nation.

2.

In 1932 not many American intellectuals saw any hope for the revival of capitalism. Few of them could support this feeling with any well-grounded theory of society; many held to a highly simplified idea of what capitalism was; and almost all were committed to a vision of the *crisis* of capitalism which was merely a vulgarized model of the class struggle in Europe. Suddenly, with the appearance of the New Deal, the intellectuals saw fresh hope: capitalism was not to be exhausted by the naïve specifications they had assigned it, and consequently the "European" policies of the Roosevelt administration might help dissolve their "Europeanized" sense of crisis. So that the more American society became Europeanized, adopting measures that had been common practice on the Continent for decades, the more the American intellectuals began to believe in . . . American uniqueness. Somehow, the major capitalist power in the world would evade the troubles afflicting capitalism as a world economy.

The two central policies of the New Deal, social legislation and state intervention in economic life, were not unrelated, but they were separable as to time; in Europe they had not always appeared together. Here, in America, it was the simultaneous introduction of these two policies that aroused the enthusiasm, as it dulled the criticism, of the intellectuals. Had the drive toward bureaucratic state regulation of a capitalist economy appeared by itself, so that one could see the state becoming a major buyer and hence indirect controller of industry, and industries on the verge of collapse being systematically subsidized by the state, and the whole of economic life being rationalized according to the long-run needs, if not the immediate tastes, of corporate economy—had all this appeared in isolation, the intellectuals would have reacted critically, they would have recognized the trend toward "state capitalism" as the danger it was. But their desire for the genuine social reforms that came with this trend made them blind or indifferent to the danger. Still, one may suppose that their enthusiasm would have mellowed had not the New Deal been gradually transformed into a permanent war economy; for whatever the theoretical attractions of the Keynesian formula for salvaging capitalism, it has thus far "worked" only in times of war or preparation for war. And it was in the war economy, itself closely related to the trend toward statification, that the intellectuals came into their own.

Statification, war economy, the growth of a mass society and mass culture—all these are aspects of the same historical process. The kind of society that has been emerging in the West, a society in which bureaucratic controls are imposed upon (but not fundamentally against) an interplay of private interests, has need for intellectuals in a way the earlier, "traditional" capitalism never did. It is a society in which ideology plays an unprecedented part: as social relations become more abstract and elusive, the human object is bound to the state with ideological slogans and abstractions—and for this chore intellectuals are indispensable, no one else can do the job as well. Because industrialism grants large quantities of leisure time without any creative sense of how to employ it, there springs up a vast new industry that must be staffed by intellectuals and quasi-intellectuals: the industry of mass culture. And because the state subsidizes mass education and our uneasy prosperity allows additional millions to gain a "higher" education, many new jobs suddenly become available in the academy: some fall to intellectuals. Bohemia gradually disappears as a setting for our intellectual life, and what remains of it seems willed or fake. Looking upon the prosperous ruins of Greenwich Village, one sometimes feels that a full-time Bohemian career has become as arduous, if not as expensive, as acquiring a Ph.D.

Bohemia, said Flaubert, was "the fatherland of my breed." If so, his breed, at least in America, is becoming extinct. The most exciting periods of American intellectual life tend to coincide with the rise of Bohemia, with the tragic yet liberating rhythm of the break from the small town into the literary roominess of the city, or from the provincial immigrant family into the centers of intellectual experiment. Given the nature of contemporary life, Bohemia flourishes in the city—but that has not always been so. Concord too was a kind of Bohemia, sedate, subversive and transcendental all at once. Today, however, the idea of Bohemia, which was a strategy for bringing artists and writers together in their struggle with and for the world—this idea has become disreputable, being rather nastily associated with kinds of exhibitionism that have only an incidental relationship to Bohemia. Nonetheless, it is the disintegration of Bohemia that is a major cause for the way intellectuals feel, as distinct from and far more important than what they say or think. Those feelings of loneliness one finds among so many American intellectuals, feelings of damp dispirited isolation which undercut the ideology of liberal optimism, are partly due to the breakup of Bohemia. Where young writers would once face the world together, they now sink into suburbs, country homes and college towns. And the price they pay for this rise in social status is to be measured in more than an increase in rent.

It is not my purpose to berate anyone, for the pressures of conformism are at work upon all of us, to say nothing of the need to earn one's bread; and all of us bend under the terrible weight of our time—though some take pleasure in learning to enjoy it. Nor do I wish to indulge in the sort of good-natured condescension with which Malcolm Cowley recently described the younger writers as lugubrious and timid long-hairs huddling in chill academies and poring over the gnostic texts of Henry James—by contrast, no doubt, to Cowley's own career of risk-taking. Some intellectuals, to be sure, have "sold out" and we can all point to examples, probably the same examples. But far more prevalent and far more insidious is that slow attrition which destroys one's ability to stand firm and alone: the temptations of an improved standard of living combined with guilt over the historical tragedy that has made possible our prosperity; one's sense of being swamped by the rubbish of a reactionary period together with the loss of those earlier certainties that had the advantage, at least, of making resistance easy. Nor, in saying these things, do I look forward to any sort of material or intellectual asceticism. Our world is neither to be flatly accepted nor rejected: it must be engaged, resisted and—who knows, perhaps still—transformed.

All of life, my older friends often tell me, is a conspiracy against that ideal of independence with which a young intellectual begins; but if so, wisdom consists not in premature surrender but in learning when to evade, when to stave off, and when to oppose head on. Conformity, as Arthur Koestler said some years ago, "is often a form of betrayal which can be carried out with a clear conscience." Gradually we make our peace with the world, and not by anything as exciting as a secret pact; nowadays Lucifer is a very patient and reasonable fellow with a gift for indulging one's most legitimate desires; and we learn, if we learn anything at all, that betrayal may consist of a chain of small compromises, even while we also learn that in this age one cannot survive without compromise. What is most alarming is not that a number of intellectuals have abandoned the posture of iconoclasm: let the *Zeitgeist* give them a jog and they will again be radical, all too radical. What is most alarming is that the whole idea of the intellectual vocation—the idea of a life dedicated to values that cannot possibly be realized by a commercial civilization—has gradually lost its allure. And it is this, rather than the abandonment of a particular program, which constitutes our rout.

Lionel Trilling has addressed himself to some of these problems; his perspective is sharply different from mine. Mr. Trilling believes that "there is an unmistakable improvement in the American cultural situation of today over that of, say, thirty years ago," while to me it seems that any comparison between the buoyant free-spirited cultural life of 1923 with the dreariness of 1953, or between their literary achievements, must lead to the conclusion that Mr. Trilling is indulging in a pleasant fantasy. More important, however, is his analysis of how this "improvement" has occurred: "In many civilizations there comes a point at which wealth shows a tendency to submit itself, in some degree, to the rule of mind and imagination, to apologize for its existence by a show of taste and sensitivity. In America the signs of this submission have for some time been visible. . . . Intellect has associated itself with power, perhaps as never before in history, and is now conceded to be in itself a kind of power." Such stately terms as "wealth" and "intellect" hardly make for sharp distinctions, yet the drift of Mr. Trilling's remarks is clear enough—and, I think, disastrous.

It is perfectly true that in the government bureaucracy and institutional staff, in the mass-culture industries and the academy, intellectuals have been welcomed and absorbed as never before. It is true, again, that "wealth" has become far more indulgent in its treatment of intellectuals, and for good reasons: it needs them more than ever, they are tamer than ever, and its own position is more comfortable and expansive than it has been for a long time. But if "wealth" has made a mild bow toward "intellect" (sometimes while picking its pocket) then "intellect" has engaged in some undignified prostrations before "wealth." Thirty years ago "wealth" was on the defensive, and twenty years ago it was frightened, hesitant, apologetic. "Intellect" was self-confident, aggressive, secure in its belief or, if you wish, delusions. Today the ideology of American capitalism, with its claim to a unique and immaculate destiny, is trumpeted through every medium of communication: official propaganda, institutional advertising and the scholarly writings of people who, until a few years ago, were its major opponents. Marx-baiting, that least risky of occupations, has become a favorite sport in the academic journals; a whining genteel chauvinism is widespread among intellectuals; and the bemoaning of their own fears and timidities a constant theme among professors. Is this to be taken as evidence that "wealth" has subordinated itself to "intellect"? Or is the evidence to be found in the careers of such writers as Max Eastman and James Burnham? To be sure, culture has acquired a more honorific status, as restrained ostentation has replaced conspicuous consumption: wealthy people collect more pictures or at least more modern ones, they endow foundations with large sums—but all this is possible because "intellect" no longer pretends to challenge "wealth."

What has actually been taking place is the absorption of large numbers of intellectuals, previously independent, into the world of government bureaucracy and public committees; into the constantly growing industries of pseudo culture; into the adult education business, which subsists on regulated culture anxiety. This process of bureaucratic absorption does not proceed without check: the Eisenhower administration dismissed a good many intellectuals from government posts. Yet it seems likely that such stupidity will prove temporary and that one way or another, in one administration or another, the intellectuals will drift back into the government: they must, they are indispensable.

Some years ago C. Wright Mills wrote an article in which he labeled the intellectuals as "powerless people." He meant, of course, that they felt incapable of translating their ideas into action and that their consequent frustration had become a major motif in their behavior. His description was accurate enough; yet we might remember that the truly powerless people are those intellectuals—the new realists—who attach themselves to the seats of power, where they surrender their freedom of expression without gaining any significance as political figures. For it is crucial to the history of the American intellectuals in the past few decades—as well as to the relationship between "wealth" and "intellect"—that whenever they become absorbed into the accredited institutions of society they not only lose their traditional rebelliousness but to one extent or another *they cease to function as intellectuals.* The institutional world needs intellectuals *because* they are intellectuals but it does not want them *as* intellectuals. It beckons to them because of what they are but it will not allow them, at least within its sphere of articulation, either to remain or entirely cease being what they are. It needs them for their knowledge, their talent, their inclinations and passions; it insists that they retain a measure of these endowments, which it means to employ for its own ends, and without which the intellectuals would be of no use to it whatever. A simplified but useful equation suggests itself: the relation of the institutional world to the intellectuals is as the relation of middle-brow culture to serious culture. The one battens on the other, absorbs and raids it with increasing frequency and skill, subsidizes and encourages it enough to make further raids possible—at times the parasite will support its victim. Surely this relationship must be one reason for the high incidence of neurosis that is supposed to prevail among intellectuals. A total estrangement from the sources of power and prestige, even a blind unreasoning rejection of every aspect of our culture, would be far healthier if only because it would permit a free discharge of aggression.

I do not mean to suggest that for intellectuals all institutions are equally dangerous or disadvantageous. Even during the New Deal, the life of those intellectuals who journeyed to Washington was far from happy. The independence possible to a professor of sociology is usually greater than that possible to a writer of television scripts, and a professor of English, since the world will not take his subject seriously, can generally enjoy more intellectual leeway than a professor of sociology. Philip Rieff, a sociologist, has caustically described a major tendency among his colleagues as a drift from "science" to "policy" in which "loyalty, not truth, provides the social condition by which the intellectual discovers his new environment." It is a drift "from the New School to the Rand Corporation."

There is, to be sure, a qualitative difference between the academy and the government bureau or the editorial staff. The university is still committed to the ideology of freedom, and many professors try hard and honestly to live by it. If the intellectual cannot subsist independently, off his work or his relatives, the academy is usually his best bet. But no one who has a live sense of what the literary life has been and might still be, either in Europe or this country, can accept the notion that the academy is the natural home of intellect. What seems so unfortunate is that the whole *idea* of independence is losing its traditional power. Scientists are bound with chains of official secrecy; sociologists compete for government research chores; foundations become indifferent to solitary writers and delight in "teams"; the possibility of living in decent poverty from moderately serious literary journalism becomes more and more remote. Compromises are no doubt necessary, but they had better be recognized for what they are.

Perhaps something should be said here about "alienation," a subject on which intellectuals have written more self-humiliating nonsense than on any other. Involved, primarily, is a matter of historical fact. As Philip Rahv has put it: "During the greater part of the bourgeois epoch . . . [writers] preferred alienation from the community to alienation from themselves." Precisely this choice made possible their strength and boldness, precisely this "lack of roots" gave them their speculative power. Almost always, the talk one hears these days about "the need for roots" veils a desire to compromise the tradition of intellectual independence, to seek in a nation or religion or party a substitute for the tenacity one should find in oneself. Isaac Rosenfeld's remark that "the ideal society . . . cannot afford to include many deeply rooted individuals" is not merely a clever *mot* but an important observation.

It may be that the issue is no longer relevant; that, with the partial submission of "wealth" to "intellect," the clash between a business civilization and the values of art is no longer as urgent as we once thought; but if so, we must discard a great deal, and mostly the best, of the literature, the criticism, and the speculative thought of the twentieth century. For to deny the historical fact of "alienation" (as if that would make it any the less real!) is to deny our heritage, both as burden and advantage, and also, I think, to deny our possible future as a community.

Much of what I have been describing here must be owing to a feeling among intellectuals that the danger of Stalinism allows them little or no freedom in their relations with bourgeois society. This feeling seems to me only partly justified, and I do not suffer from any inclination to minimize the Stalinist threat. To be sure, it does limit our possibilities for action—if, that is, we still want to engage in any dissident politics—and sometimes it may force us into political alignments that are distasteful. But here a crucial distinction should be made: the danger of Stalinism may require temporary expedients in the area of *power* such as would have seemed compromising some years ago, but there is no reason, at least no good reason, why it should require compromise or conformity in the area of *ideas*, no reason why it should lead us to become partisans of bourgeois society, which is itself, we might remember, heavily responsible for the Stalinist victories.

3.

"In the United States at this time liberalism is not only the dominant but even the sole intellectual tradition." This sentence of Lionel Trilling's contains a sharp insight into the political life of contemporary America. If I understand him correctly, he is saying that our society is at present so free from those pressures of conflicting classes and interests which make for sharply defined ideologies, that liberalism colors, or perhaps the word should be bleaches, all political tendencies. It becomes a loose shelter, a poncho rather than a program; to call oneself a liberal one doesn't really have to believe in anything. In such a moment of social slackness, the more extreme intellectual tendencies have a way, as soon as an effort is made to put them into practice, of sliding into and becoming barely distinguishable from the dominant liberalism. Both conservatism and radicalism can retain, at most, an intellectual recalcitrance, but neither is presently able to engage in a sustained practical politics of its own; which does not mean they will never be able to.

The point is enforced by looking at the recent effort to affirm a conservative ideology. Russell Kirk, who makes this effort with some earnestness, can hardly avoid the eccentricity of appealing to Providence as a putative force in American politics: an appeal that suggests both the intensity of his conservative desire and the desperation behind the intensity. Peter Viereck, a friskier sort of writer, calls himself a conservative, but surely this is nothing more than a mystifying pleasantry, for aside from the usual distinctions of temperament and talent it is hard to see how his conservatism differs from the liberalism of Arthur Schlesinger, Jr. For Viereck conservatism is a shuffling together of attractive formulas, without any effort to discover their relationship to deep *actual* clashes of interest: he fails, for example, even to consider that in America there is today neither opportunity nor need for conservatism (since the liberals do the necessary themselves) and that if an opportunity were to arise, conservatism could seize upon it only by acquiring a mass, perhaps reactionary dynamic, that is, by "going into the streets." And that, surely, Mr. Viereck doesn't want.

If conservatism is taken to mean, as in some "classical"

sense it should be, a principled rejection of industrial economy and a yearning for an ordered, hierarchical society that is not centered on the city, then conservatism in America is best defended by a group of literary men whose seriousness is proportionate to their recognition that such a politics is now utterly hopeless and, in any but a utopian sense, meaningless. Such a conservatism, in America, goes back to James Fenimore Cooper, who anticipates those implicit criticisms of our society which we honor in Faulkner; and in the hands of serious imaginative writers, but hardly in the hands of political writers obliged to deal with immediate relations of power, it can become a myth which, through abrasion, profoundly challenges modern experience. As for the "conservatism" of the late Senator Taft, which consists of nothing but liberal economics and wounded nostalgia, it lacks intellectual content and, more important, when in power it merely continues those "statist" policies it had previously attacked.

This prevalence of liberalism yields, to be sure, some obvious and substantial benefits. It makes us properly skeptical of the excessive claims and fanaticisms that accompany ideologies. It makes implausible those "aristocratic" rantings against democracy which were fashionable in some literary circles a few years ago. And it allows for the hope that any revival of American radicalism will acknowledge not only its break from, but also its roots in, the liberal tradition.

At the same time, however, the dominance of liberalism contributes heavily to our intellectual conformity. Liberalism dominates, but without confidence or security; it knows that its victories at home are tied to disasters abroad; and for the *élan* it cannot summon, it substitutes a blend of complacence and anxiety. It makes for an atmosphere of blur in the realm of ideas, since it has a stake in seeing momentary concurrences as deep harmonies. In an age that suffers from incredible catastrophes it scoffs at theories of social apocalypse—as if any *more* evidence were needed; in an era convulsed by war, revolution, and counterrevolution it discovers the virtues of "moderation." And when the dominant school of liberalism, the school of *realpolitik*, scores points in attacking "the ritual liberals," it also betrays a subterranean desire to retreat into the caves of bureaucratic caution. Liberalism as an ideology, as "the haunted air," has never been stronger in this country; but can as much be said of the appetite for freedom?

Sidney Hook discovers merit in the Smith Act: he was not for its passage but doubts the wisdom of its repeal. Mary McCarthy, zooming to earth from never-never land, discovers in the American war economy no less than paradise: "Class barriers disappear or tend to become porous; the factory worker is an economic aristocrat in comparison to the middle-class clerk. . . . The America . . . of vast inequalities and dramatic contrasts is rapidly ceasing to exist." Daniel Boorstin—he cannot be charged with the self-deceptions peculiar to idealism—discovers that "the genius of American politics" consists not in the universal possibilities of democracy but in a uniquely fortunate geography which, obviously, cannot be exported. David Riesman is so disturbed by Veblen's rebelliousness toward American society that he explains it as a projection of father-hatred; and what complex is it, one wonders, which explains a writer's assumption that Veblen's view of America is so inconceivable as to require a home-brewed psychoanalysis? Irving Kristol writes an article minimizing the threat to civil liberties and shortly thereafter is chosen to be public spokesman for the American Committee for Cultural Freedom. And in the Committee itself, it is possible for serious intellectuals to debate—none is *for* McCarthy—whether the public activities of the Wisconsin hooligan constitute a serious menace to freedom.

One likes to speculate: suppose Simone de Beauvoir and Bertrand Russell didn't exist, would not many of the political writers for *Commentary* and *The New Leader* have to invent them? It is all very well, and even necessary, to demonstrate that Russell's description of America as subject to "a reign of terror" is malicious and ignorant, or that de Beauvoir's picture of America is a blend of Stalinist clichés and second-rate literary fantasies; but this hardly disposes of the problem of civil liberties or of the justified alarm many sober European intellectuals feel with regard to America. Between the willfulness of those who see only terror and the indifference of those who see only health, there is need for simple truth: that intellectual freedom in the United States is under severe attack and that the intellectuals have, by and large, shown a painful lack of militancy in defending the rights which are a precondition of their existence.*

It is in the pages of the influential magazine *Commentary* that liberalism is most skillfully and systematically advanced as a strategy for adapting to the American *status quo*. The magazine has been more deeply preoccupied, or preoccupied at deeper levels, with the dangers to freedom stemming from people like Freda Kirchwey and Arthur Miller than the dangers from people like Senator McCarthy. In March 1952 Irving Kristol, then an editor of *Commentary*, could write that "there is one thing the American people know about Senator McCarthy: he, like them, is unequivocally anti-Communist. About the spokesmen for American liberalism, they feel they know no such thing. And with some justification." In September 1952, at the very moment when McCarthy had become a central issue in the presidential campaign, Elliot Cohen, the senior editor of *Commentary*, could write that McCarthy "remains in the popular mind an unreliable, second-string blowhard; his *only* support as a

* It must in honesty be noted that many of the intellectuals least alive to the problem of civil liberties are former Stalinists or radicals; and this, more than the vast anti-Marxist literature of recent years, constitutes a serious criticism of American radicalism. For the truth is that the "old-fashioned liberals" like John Dewey and Alexander Meiklejohn, at whom it was once so fashionable to sneer, have displayed a finer sensitivity to the need for defending domestic freedoms than the more "sophisticated" intellectuals who leapt from Marx to Machiavelli.

great national figure is from the fascinated fears of the intelligentsia." (My emphasis.) As if to blot out the memory of these performances, Nathan Glazer, still another editor, wrote an excellent analysis of McCarthy in the March 1953 issue; but at the end of his article, almost as if from another hand, there again appeared the magazine's earlier line: "All that Senator McCarthy can do on his own authority that someone equally unpleasant and not a Senator can't, is to haul people down to Washington for a grilling by his committee. It is a shame and an outrage that Senator McCarthy should remain in the Senate; yet I cannot see that it is an imminent danger to personal liberty in the United States." It is, I suppose, this sort of thing that is meant when people speak about the need for replacing the outworn formulas and clichés of liberalism and radicalism with *new ideas.*

4.

To what does one conform? To institutions, obviously. To the dead images that rot in one's mind, unavoidably. And almost always, to the small grating necessities of day-to-day survival. In these senses it may be said that we are all conformists to one or another degree. When Sidney Hook writes, "I see no specific virtue in the attitude of conformity or nonconformity," he is right if he means that no human being can, or should, entirely accept or reject the moral and social modes of his time. And he is right in adding that there are occasions, such as the crisis of the Weimar Republic, when the nonconformism of a Stefan George or an Oswald Spengler can have unhappy consequences.

But Professor Hook seems to be quite wrong in supposing that his remark applies significantly to present-day America. It would apply if we lived in a world where ideas could be weighed in free and delicate balance, without social pressures or contaminations, so that our choices would be made solely from a passion for truth. As it happens, however, there are tremendous pressures in America that make for intellectual conformism and consequently, in this tense and difficult age, there are very real virtues in preserving the attitude of critical skepticism and distance. Even some of the more extreme antics of the professional "bohemians" or literary anarchists take on a certain value which in cooler moments they might not have.*

What one conforms to most of all—despite and against one's intentions—is the *Zeitgeist*, that vast insidious sum of pressures and fashions; one drifts along, anxious and compliant, upon the favored assumptions of the moment; and not a soul in the intellectual world can escape this. Only, some resist and some don't. Today the *Zeitgeist* presses down upon us with a greater insistence than at any other moment of the century. In the 1930s many of those who hovered about the *New Masses* were mere camp-followers of success; but the conformism of the party-line intellectual, at least before 1936, did sometimes bring him into conflict with established power: he had to risk something. Now, by contrast, established power and the dominant intellectual tendencies have come together in a harmony such as this country has not seen since the Gilded Age; and this, of course, makes the temptations of conformism all the more acute. The carrots, for once, are real.

Real even for literary men, who these days prefer to meditate upon symbolic vegetables. I would certainly not wish to suggest any direct correlation between our literary assumptions and the nature of our politics; but surely some of the recent literary trends and fashions owe something to the more general intellectual drift toward conformism. Not, of course, that liberalism dominates literary life, as it dominates the rest of the intellectual world. Whatever practical interest most literary men have in politics comes to little else

* It may be asked whether a Stalinist's "nonconformism" is valuable. No, it isn't; the Stalinist is anything but a nonconformist; he has merely shifted the object of his worship, as later, when he abandons Stalinism, he usually shifts it again.

than the usual liberalism, but their efforts at constructing literary ideologies—frequently as forced marches to discover values our society will not yield them—result in something quite different from liberalism. Through much of our writing, both creative and critical, there run a number of ideological motifs, the importance of which is hardly diminished by the failure of the men who employ them to be fully aware of their implications. Thus, a major charge that might be brought against some New Critics is not that they practice formal criticism but that they don't; not that they see the work of art as an object to be judged according to laws of its own realm but that, often unconsciously, they weave ideological assumptions into their writings.* Listening recently to Cleanth Brooks's lecture on Faulkner, I was struck by the deep hold that the term "orthodox" has acquired on his critical imagination, and not, by the way, on his alone. But "orthodox" is not, properly speaking, a critical term at all, it pertains to matters of religious or other belief rather than to literary judgment; and a habitual use of such terms can only result in the kind of "slanted" criticism Mr. Brooks has been so quick, and right, to condemn.

Together with "orthodox" there goes a cluster of terms which, in their sum, reveal an implicit ideological bias. The word "traditional" is especially tricky here, since it has legitimate uses in both literary and moral-ideological contexts. What happens, however, in much contemporary criti-

* This may be true of all critics, but is most perilous to those who suppose themselves free of ideological coloring. In a review of my Faulkner book—rather favorable, so that no ego wounds prompt what follows—Robert Daniel writes that "Because of Mr. Howe's connections with . . . the *Partisan Review,* one might expect his literary judgments to be shaped by political and social preconceptions, but that does not happen often." Mr. Daniel is surprised that a critic whose politics happen to be radical should try to keep his literary views distinct from his non-literary ones. To be sure, this is sometimes very difficult, and perhaps no one entirely succeeds. But the one sure way of not succeeding is to write, as Mr. Daniel does, from no very pressing awareness that it is a problem for critics who appear in *The Sewanee Review* quite as much as for those who appear in *Partisan Review.*

cism is that these two contexts are either taken to be one or to be organically related, so that it becomes possible to assume that a sense of literary tradition necessarily involves and sanctions a "traditional" view of morality. There is a powerful inclination here—it is the doing of the impish *Zeitgeist*—to forget that literary traditions can be fruitfully seen as a series of revolts, literary but sometimes more than literary, of generation against generation, age against age. The emphasis on "tradition" has other contemporary implications: it is used as a not very courageous means of countering the experimental and the modern; it can enclose the academic assumption—and this is the curse of the Ph.D. system—that the whole of the literary past is at every point equally relevant to a modern intelligence; and it frequently includes the provincial American need to be more genteel than the gentry, more English than the English. Basically, it has served as a means of asserting conservative or reactionary moral-ideological views not, as they should be asserted, in their own terms, but through the refining medium of literary talk.

In general, there has been a tendency among critics to subsume literature under their own moral musings, which makes for a conspicuously humorless kind of criticism.* Morality is assumed to be a sufficient container for the floods of experience, and poems or novels that gain their richness from the complexity with which they dramatize the incommensurability between man's existence and his conceptualizing, are thinned, pruned, and allegorized into moral fables. Writers who spent—in both senses of the word—their lives wrestling with terrible private demons are elevated into literary dons and deacons. It is as if Stendhal had never come

* Writing about *Wuthering Heights* Mark Schorer solemnly declares that "the theme of the moral magnificence of unmoral passion is an impossible theme to sustain, and the needs of her temperament to the contrary, all personal longing and reverie to the contrary, Emily Brontë teaches herself that this was indeed not at all what her material must mean as art." What is more, if Emily Brontë had lived a little longer she would have been offered a Chair in Moral Philosophy.

forth, with his subversive wit, to testify how often life and literature find the whole moral apparatus irrelevant or tedious, as if Lawrence had never written *The Man Who Died*, as if Nietzsche had never launched his great attack on the Christian impoverishment of the human psyche. One can only be relieved, therefore, at knowing a few critics personally: how pleasant the discrepancy between their writings and their lives!

But it is Original Sin that today commands the highest prestige in the literary world. Like nothing else, it allows literary men to enjoy a sense of profundity and depth—to relish a disenchantment which allows no further risk of becoming enchanted—as against the superficiality of *mere* rationalism. It allows them to appropriate to the "tradition" the greatest modern writers, precisely those whose values and allegiances are most ambiguous, complex, and enigmatic, while at the same time generously leaving, as Leslie Fiedler once suggested, Dreiser and Farrell as the proper idols for that remnant benighted enough to maintain a naturalist philosophy. To hold, as Dickens remarks in *Bleak House*, "a loose belief that if the world go wrong, it was, in some offhand manner, never meant to go right," this becomes the essence of wisdom. (Liberals too have learned to cast a warm eye on "man's fallen nature," so that one gets the high comedy of Arthur Schlesinger, Jr. interrupting his quite worldly political articles with uneasy bows in the direction of Kierkegaard.) And with this latest dispensation come, of course, many facile references to the ideas supposedly held by Rousseau* and Marx, that man is "perfectible" and that progress moves in a steady upward curve.

I say, facile references, because no one who has troubled to read Rousseau or Marx could write such things. Exactly what the "perfectibility of man" is supposed to mean, if

* Randall Jarrell, who usually avoids fashionable cant: "Most of us know, now, that Rousseau was wrong; that man, when you knock his chains off, sets up the death camps." Which chains were knocked off in Germany to permit the setting-up of death camps? And which chains must be put up again to prevent a repetition of the death camps?

anything at all, I cannot say; but it is not a phrase intrinsic to the *kind* of thought one finds in the mature Marx or, most of the time, in Rousseau. Marx did not base his argument for socialism on any view that one could isolate a constant called "human nature"; he would certainly have agreed with Ortega that man has not a nature, but a history. Nor did he have a very rosy view of the human beings who were his contemporaries or recent predecessors: see in *Capital* the chapter on the Working Day, a grisly catalogue of human bestiality. Nor did he hold to a naïve theory of progress: he wrote that the victories of progress "seem bought by the loss of character. At the same pace that mankind masters nature, man seems to become enslaved to other men or to his own infamy."

As for Rousseau, the use of even a finger's-worth of historical imagination should suggest that the notion of "a state of nature" which modern literary people so enjoy attacking, was a political metaphor employed in a prerevolutionary situation, and not, therefore, to be understood outside its context. Rousseau explicitly declared that he did not suppose the "state of nature" to have existed in historical time; it was, he said, "a pure idea of reason" reached by abstraction from the observable state of society. As G. D. H. Cole remarks, "in political matters at any rate, the 'state of nature' is for [Rousseau] only a term of controversy . . . he means by 'nature' not the original state of a thing, nor even its reduction to the simplest terms; he is passing over to the conception of 'nature' as identical with the full development of [human] capacity. . . ." There are, to be sure, elements in Rousseau's thought which one may well find distasteful, but these are not the elements commonly referred to when he is used in literary talk as a straw man to be beaten with the cudgels of "orthodoxy."

What then is the significance of the turn to Original Sin among so many intellectuals? Surely not to inform us, at this late moment, that man is capable of evil. Or is it, as Cleanth Brooks writes, to suggest that man is a "limited" creature, limited in possibilities and capacities, and hence unable to achieve his salvation through social means? Yes, to be sure; but the problem of history is to determine, by action, how far those limits may go. Conservative critics like to say that "man's fallen nature" makes unrealistic the liberal-radical vision of the good society—apparently, when Eve bit the apple she predetermined, with one fatal crunch, that her progeny could work its way up to capitalism, and not a step further. But the liberal-radical vision of the good society does not depend upon a belief in the "unqualified goodness of man"; nor does it locate salvation in society: anyone in need of being saved had better engage in a private scrutiny. The liberal-radical claim is merely that the development of technology has now made possible—possible, not inevitable—a solution of those material problems that have burdened mankind for centuries. These problems solved, man is then on his own, to make of his self and his world what he can.

The literary prestige of Original Sin cannot be understood without reference to the current cultural situation; it cannot be understood except as an historical phenomenon reflecting, like the whole turn to religion and religiosity, the weariness of intellectuals in an age of defeat and their yearning to remove themselves from the bloodied arena of historical action and choice, which necessarily means, of secular action and choice. Much sarcasm and anger has been expended on the "failure of nerve" theory, usually by people who take it as a personal affront to be told that there is a connection between what happens in their minds and what happens in the world; but if one looks at the large-scale shifts in belief among intellectuals during the past twenty-five years, it becomes impossible to put *all* of them down to a simultaneous, and thereby miraculous, discovery of Truth, some at least must be seen as a consequence of those historical pressures which make this an age of conformism. Like other efforts to explain major changes in belief, the "failure of nerve" theory does not tell us why certain people believed in the thirties what was only to become popular in the fifties and why others still believe in the fifties what was popular in the thirties; but it does tell us something more important: why a complex of beliefs is dominant at one time and subordinate at another.

5.

I have tried to trace a rough pattern from social history through politics and finally into literary ideology, as a means of explaining the power of the conformist impulse in our time. But it is obvious that in each intellectual "world" there are impulses of this kind that cannot easily be shown to have their sources in social or historical pressures. Each intellectual world gives rise to its own patterns of obligation and preference. The literary world, being relatively free from the coarser kinds of social pressure, enjoys a considerable degree of detachment and autonomy. (Not as much as it likes to suppose, but a considerable degree.) That the general intellectual tendency is to acquiesce in what one no longer feels able to change or modify, strongly encourages the internal patterns of conformism in the literary world and intensifies the yearning, common to all groups but especially to small and insecure groups, to draw together in a phalanx of solidarity. Then too, those groups that live by hostility to the dominant values of society—in this case, cultural values—find it extremely difficult to avoid an inner conservatism as a way of balancing their public role of opposition; anyone familiar with radical politics knows this phenomenon only too well. Finally, the literary world, while quite powerless in relation to, say, the worlds of business and politics, disposes of a measurable amount of power and patronage within its own domain; which makes, again, for predictable kinds of influence.

Whoever would examine the inner life of the literary world should turn first not to the magazines or the dignitaries or famous writers but to the graduate students, for like it or not the graduate school has become the main recruiting ground for critics and sometimes even for writers. Here, in conversation with the depressed classes of the academy, one sees how the Ph.D. system—more powerful today than it has been for decades, since so few other choices are open to young literary men—grinds and batters personality into a mold of cautious routine. And what one finds among these young people, for all their intelligence and devotion and eagerness, is often appalling: a remarkable desire to be "critics," not as an accompaniment to the writing of poetry or the changing of the world or the study of man and God, but just critics—as if criticism were a *subject,* as if one could be a critic without having at least four nonliterary opinions, or as if criticism "in itself" could adequately engage an adult mind for more than a small part of its waking time. An equally astonishing indifference to the ideas that occupy the serious modern mind—Freud, Marx, Nietzsche, Frazer, Dewey are not great thinkers in their own right, but reservoirs from which one dredges up "approaches to criticism"—together with a fabulous knowledge of what Ransom said about Winters with regard to what Winters had said about Eliot. And a curiously humble discipleship—but also arrogant to those beyond the circle—so that one meets not fresh minds in growth but apostles of Burke or Trilling or Winters or Leavis or Brooks or neo-Aristotle.

Very little of this is the fault of the graduate students themselves, for they, like the distinguished figures I have just listed, are the victims of an unhappy cultural moment. What we have today in the literary world is a gradual bureaucratization of opinion and taste; not a dictatorship, not a conspiracy, not a coup, not a Machiavellian plot to impose a mandatory "syllabus"; but the inevitable result of outer success and inner hardening. Fourth-rate exercises in exegesis are puffed in the magazines while so remarkable and provocative a work as Arnold Hauser's *Social History of Art* is hardly reviewed, its very title indicating the reason. Learned young critics who have never troubled to open a novel by Turgenev can rattle off reams of Kenneth Burke, which gives them, understandably, a sensation of having enlarged upon literature. Literature itself becomes a raw material which critics work up into schemes of structure and symbol; to suppose that it is concerned with anything so gauche as human experience or so obsolete as human beings —"You mean," a student said to me, "that you're interested in the *characters* of novels!"—is to commit Mr. Elton alone knows how many heresies. (Cf. the *Glossary*, now in its fifth edition, which proves that bad reviews can't kill ponies.) Symbols clutter the literary landscape like the pots and pans a two-year-old strews over the kitchen floor; and what is wrong here is not merely the transparent absence of literary tact—the gift for saying when a pan is a pan and when a pan is a symbol—but far more important, a transparent lack of interest in represented experience. For Mr. Stallman the fact that Stephen Crane looking at the sun felt moved to compare it to a wafer is not enough, the existence of suns and wafers and their possible conjunction is not sufficiently marvelous; both objects must be absorbed into Christian symbolism (an ancient theory of literature developed by the Church fathers to prove that suns, moons, vulva, chairs, money, hair, pots, pans and words are really crucifixes). Techniques for reading a novel that have at best a limited relevance are frozen into dogmas: one might suppose from glancing at the more imposing literary manuals that "point of view" is the crucial means of judging a novel. (Willa Cather, according to Caroline Gordon, was "astonishingly ignorant of her craft," for she refrained from "using a single consciousness as a prism of moral reflection." The very mistake Tolstoy made, too!) Criticism itself, far from being the reflection of a solitary mind upon a work of art and therefore, like the solitary mind, incomplete and subjective, comes increasingly to be regarded as a problem in mechanics, the tools, methods, and trade secrets of which can be picked up, usually during the summer, from the more experienced operatives. In the mind of Stanley Hyman, who serves the indispensable function of reducing fashionable literary notions, criticism seems to resemble Macy's on bargain day: *First floor, symbols; Second floor, myths (rituals to the rear on your right); Third floor, ambiguities and paradoxes; Fourth floor, word counting; Fifth floor, Miss Harrison's antiquities; Attic, Marxist remnants; Basement, Freud; Sub-basement, Jung. Watch your step, please.*

What is most disturbing, however, is that writing about literature and writers has become an industry. The preposterous academic requirement that professors write books they don't want to write and no one wants to read, together with the obtuse assumption that piling up more and more irrelevant information about an author's life helps us understand his work—this makes for a vast flood of books that have little to do with literature, criticism, or even scholarship. Would you care to know the contents of the cargo (including one elephant) carried by the vessel of which Hawthorne's father was captain in 1795? Mr. Cantwell has an itemized list, no doubt as an aid to reading *The Scarlet Letter*. Mr. Leyda knows what happened to Melville day by day and it is hardly his fault that most days nothing very much happened. Mr. Johnson does as much for Dickens and adds plot summaries too, no doubt because he is dealing with a little-read author. Another American scholar has published a full book on *Mardi*, which is astonishing not because he wrote the book but because he managed to finish reading *Mardi* at all.

I have obviously chosen extreme examples and it would be silly to contend that they adequately describe the American literary scene; but like the distorting mirrors in Coney Island they help bring into sharper contour the major features. Or as Donald Davie writes in *Twentieth Century:*

> The professional poet has already disappeared from the literary scene, and the professional man of letters is following him into the grave. . . . It becomes more and more difficult, and will soon be impossible, for a man to make his living as a literary dilettante. . . . And instead of the professional man of letters we

> have the professional critic, the young don writing in the first place for other dons, and only incidentally for that supremely necessary fiction, the common reader. In other words, an even greater proportion of what is written about literature, and even of what literature is written, is "academic". . . . Literary standards are now in academic hands; for the free-lance man of letters, who once supplemented and corrected the don, is fast disappearing from the literary scene. . . .
>
> The pedant is as common as he ever was. And now that willy-nilly so much writing about literature is in academic hands, his activities are more dangerous than ever. But he has changed his habits. Twenty years ago he was to be heard asserting that his business was with hard facts, that questions of value and technique were not his affair, and that criticism could therefore be left to the impressionistic journalist. Now the pedant is proud to call himself a critic; he prides himself on evaluation and analysis; he aims to be penetrating, not informative. . . .
>
> The pedant is a very adaptable creature, and can be as comfortable with Mr. Eliot's "objective correlative," Mr. Empson's "ambiguities" and Dr. Leavis's "complexities" as in the older suit of critical clothes that he has now, for the most part, abandoned.

Mr. Davie has in mind the literary situation in England, but all one needs for applying his remarks to America is an ability to multiply.

6.

All of the tendencies toward cultural conformism come to a head in the assumption that the *avant-garde*, as both concept and intellectual grouping, has become obsolete or irrelevant. Yet the future quality of American culture, I would maintain, largely depends on the survival, and the terms of survival, of precisely the kind of dedicated group that the *avant-garde* has been.

The *avant-garde* first appeared on the American scene some twenty-five or thirty years ago, as a response to the need for absorbing the meanings of the cultural revolution that had taken place in Europe during the first two decades of the century. The achievements of Joyce, Proust, Schoenberg, Bartok, Picasso, Matisse, to mention only the obvious figures, signified one of the major turnings in the cultural history of the West, a turning made all the more crucial by the fact that it came not during the vigor of a society but during its crisis. To counter the hostility which the work of such artists met among all the official spokesmen of culture, to discover formal terms and modes through which to secure these achievements, to insist upon the continuity between their work and the accepted, because dead, artists of the past—this became the task of the *avant-garde.* Somewhat later a section of the *avant-garde* also became politically active, and not by accident; for precisely those aroused sensibilities that had responded to the innovations of the modern masters now responded to the crisis of modern society. Thus, in the early years of a magazine like *Partisan Review*—roughly between 1936 and 1941—these two radical impulses came together in an uneasy but fruitful union; and it was in those years that the magazine seemed most exciting and vital as a link between art and experience, between the critical consciousness and the political conscience, between the *avant-garde* of letters and the independent left of politics.

That union has since been dissolved, and there is no likelihood that it will soon be re-established. American radicalism exists only as an idea, and that barely; the literary *avant-garde*—it has become a stock comment for reviewers to make—is rapidly disintegrating, without function or spirit, and held together only by an inert nostalgia.

Had the purpose of the *avant-garde* been to establish the currency of certain names, to make the reading of *The Waste Land* and *Ulysses* respectable in the universities, there would be no further need for its continuance. But clearly this was not the central purpose of the *avant-garde,* it was only an unavoidable fringe of snobbery and fashion. The struggle for Joyce mattered only as it was a struggle for literary standards; the defense of Joyce was a defense not merely of modern innovation but of that traditional culture which was the source of modern innovation. And at its best it was a defense against those spokesmen for the genteel, the respectable, and the academic who had established a stranglehold over traditional culture. At the most serious level, the *avant-garde* was trying to face the problem of the quality of our culture, and when all is said and done, it faced that problem with a courage and honesty that no other group in society could match.

If the history of the *avant-garde* is seen in this way, there is every reason for believing that its survival is as necessary today as it was twenty-five years ago. To be sure, our immediate prospect is not nearly so exciting as it must then have seemed: we face no battle on behalf of great and difficult artists who are scorned by the official voices of culture. Today, in a sense, the danger is that the serious artists are not scorned enough. Philistinism has become very shrewd; it does not attack its enemies as much as it disarms them through reasonable cautions and moderate amendments. But this hardly makes the defense of those standards that animated the *avant-garde* during its best days any the less a critical obligation.

It has been urged in some circles that only the pressure of habit keeps serious writers from making "raids" upon the middle-brow world, that it is now possible to win substantial outposts in that world if we are ready to take risks. Perhaps. But surely no one desires a policy of high-brow isolation, and no one could oppose raids, provided that is what they really are. The precondition for successful raids, however, is that the serious writers themselves have a sense—not of belonging to an exclusive club—but of representing those cultural values which alone can sustain them while making their raids. Thus far the incursions of serious writers into the middle-brow world have not been remarkably successful: for every short-story writer who has survived *The New Yorker* one could point to a dozen whose work became trivial and frozen after they had begun to write for it. Nor do I advocate, in saying this, a policy of evading temptations. I advocate overcoming them. Writers today have no choice, often enough, but to write for magazines like *The New Yorker*—and worse, far worse. But what matters is the terms upon which the writer enters into such relationships, his willingness to understand with whom he is dealing, his readiness not to deceive himself that an unpleasant necessity is a desirable virtue.

It seems to me beyond dispute that, thus far at least, in the encounter between high and middle culture, the latter has come off by far the better. Every current of the *Zeitgeist*, every imprint of social power, every assumption of contemporary American life favors the safe and comforting patterns of middle-brow feeling. And then too the gloomier Christian writers may have a point when they tell us that it is easier for a soul to fall than to rise.*

Precisely at the time that the high-brows seem inclined to abandon what is sometimes called their "proud isolation," the middle-brows have become more intransigent in their opposition to everything that is serious and creative in our culture (which does not, of course, prevent them from exploiting and contaminating, for purposes of mass gossip, everything that is serious and creative in our culture). What else is the meaning of the coarse attack launched by the *Saturday Review* against the high-brows under the guise of discussing the Pound case? What, for that matter, is the meaning of the hostility with which the *Partisan Review* symposium on

* Thus Professor Gilbert Highet, the distinguished classicist, writing in *Harper's* finds André Gide "an abominably wicked man. His work seems to me to be either shallowly based symbolism, or else cheap cynicism made by inverting commonplaces or by grinning through them. . . . Gide had the curse of perpetual immaturity. But then I am always aware of the central fact about Gide—that he was a sexual pervert who kept proclaiming and justifying his perversion; and perhaps this blinds me to his merits . . . the garrulous, Pangloss-like, pimple-scratching, self-exposure of Gide."

I don't mean to suggest that many fall so low, but then not many philistines are so well educated as Mr. Highet.

"Our Country and Our Culture" was received in the popular press? It would take no straining of texts to see this symposium as a disconcerting sign of how far intellectuals have drifted in the direction of cultural adaptation, yet the middle-brows wrote of it with blunt enmity. And perhaps because they too sensed this drift in the symposium, the middle-brows, highly confident at the moment, became more aggressive, for they do not desire compromise, they know that none is possible. So genial a middle-brow as Elmer Davis, in a long review of the symposium, entitled with a characteristic smirk "The Care and Feeding of Intellectuals," ends upon a revealing note: "The highbrows seem to be getting around to recognizing what the middlebrows have known for the past thirty years. This is progress." It is also the best possible argument for the maintenance of the *avant-garde*, even if only as a kind of limited defense.

Much has been written about the improvement of cultural standards in America, though a major piece of evidence—the wide circulation of paper-bound books—is still an unweighed and unanalyzed quantity. The basic relations of cultural power remain unchanged, however: the middle-brows continue to dominate. In the leading American book supplement it is possible for the head of the largest American museum to refer, with egregious ignorance, to "the Spenglerian sterility which has possessed Europe for the past half century and [has] produced Proust, Gide and Picasso. . . ." Nothing here gives us cause for reassurance or relaxation; nothing gives us reason to dissolve that compact in behalf of critical intransigence known as the *avant-garde.*

No formal ideology or program is entirely adequate for coping with the problems that intellectuals face in the twentieth century. No easy certainties and no easy acceptance of uncertainty. All the forms of authority, the states and institutions and monster bureaucracies, that press in upon modern life—what have these shown us to warrant the surrender of independence?

The most glorious vision of the intellectual life is still that which is loosely called humanist: the idea of a mind committed yet dispassionate, ready to stand alone, curious, eager, skeptical. The banner of critical independence, ragged and torn though it may be, is still the best we have.

PART V *How It Started*

A MEMOIR OF THE THIRTIES

HERE is the point at which, for myself and others, the radical experience began. My intent in writing this sketch was to look back upon formative years without romanticizing or reviling; but that is a very hard thing to do, since memory is mischievous and the experience here evoked was in American terms very special, perhaps even exotic. Whether I have succeeded in capturing this segment of the past is something about which I am not at all certain. How can one be?

GROWING up in New York during the thirties meant, for me, the Jewish slums of the East Bronx, endless talk about Hitler, money worries of my parents migrating to my own psyche, public schools that really were schools and devoted teachers whose faces lived in memory longer than their names, fantasies of heroism drawn from Austria and Spain to excite my imagination, the certainty bordering on comfort that I would never find a regular job, and above all, the Movement. At the age of fourteen I wandered into the ranks of the socialist youth and from then on, all through my teens and twenties, the Movement was my home and passion, the Movement as it ranged through the various left-wing, anti-Communist groups.

From the chilling distance of time I now ask myself: what did it mean, what do I really feel about those years in New York? And to my dismay I hardly know, there does not seem to be a total and assured perspective upon the past. Annoyed by those who have made a virtue out of scoffing at the generosities of their youth, one part of me would cry out that despite all the fanaticism and absurdity, it was good, vibrant with hope, an opening to vision. Another part, involved beyond retreat with the style of the problematic, cannot help remembering in terms of uneasiness and dismay. As I rummage through the past, all I can find are bits and pieces of that chaos which forms the true substance of life.

1.

New York did not really exist for us as a city, a defined place we felt to be our own. Too many barriers intervened, too many kinds of anxiety. In the thirties New York was not merely the vital metropolis, brimming with politics and contention, that has since become a sentimental legend; it was also brutal, ugly, frightening, the foul-smelling jungle that Céline would later evoke in *Journey to the End of the Night.* New York was the embodiment of that alien world which every boy raised in a Jewish immigrant home had been taught, whether he realized it or not, to look upon with suspicion. It was "their" city in ways that one's parents could hardly have explained, and hardly needed to; and later, once I had absorbed the values of the Movement, it became "their" city in a new and, as it seemed to me, deeper sense.

If someone had asked me in 1939 what I thought of New York, I would have been puzzled, for that was not the kind of question one worried in those days. It was quite as if I had been asked what I thought about my family: there seemed no choice but to accept the one I had, lamentable as it may sometimes have been, and I no more imagined that I would ever live—or be able to live—anywhere but in New York than that I could find myself a more fashionable set of parents. Provinciality breeds a determinism of its own, and the provinciality of New York in the thirties, which tended to regard a temporary meeting of ethnic cultures and social crises as if it were an unalterable fact of history, led us to suppose that only here, in New York, could one bear to live at all, yet that unless one were in total revolt the life of the city was mean, constricted, intolerable. For the city in its own right, as it actually was, we had little concern or sensitivity. Only in the mythology of the Movement did New York figure significantly for us, and there it took on a glamorous cast: for New York was always "the party center," no matter which party it was; here you could listen to the leaders and intellectuals, and here it was possible, usually, to fill a fair-sized hall so as to soften our awareness of how small and futile we were.

Yet there were places I knew intimately. In our very distance from the city—caused, I suspect, less by a considered "alienation" than by a difficulty of access, a puritanical refusal of possibilities, and an unacknowledged shyness beneath our pose of bravado—we made for ourselves a kind of underground city consisting of a series of stopping places where we could ease the strain of restlessness and feel indifferent to our lack of money. In the winter there were the numberless "socials" given by branches of the Movement to raise funds for their headquarters, evenings I remember, perhaps inaccurately, as drab and awkward. There were the movies on Forty-second Street where amid clouds of steam and stench our political virtue was compromised by sophisticated European art films. There were the free concerts at the Metropolitan Museum where—it was a matter of pride to know—the music was poor but one found a sort of comfort in sitting on the marble floors, snuggling together in a chosen arc of relaxation, and allowing our romanticism to find a sanctioned outlet in Beethoven and Schubert.

In retrospect what strikes me as remarkable is that while we thought of ourselves as exposed to the coldest winds of the coldest capitalist city—and in many, many ways we were—we still lived in a somewhat sheltered world. Not only because the Movement had a way of turning in upon itself, becoming detached and self-contained, and finding a security in that isolation which all our speeches bemoaned. But more. Only now do I see the extent to which our life, for all that we had decided to cut ourselves off from official society, was shaped by the fact that many of us came from immigrant Jewish families and that in New York the Jews still formed a genuine community reaching half-unseen into a dozen neighborhoods and a multitude of institutions, within the shadows of which we found protection of a kind.

Attitudes of tolerance and permissiveness, feelings that one had to put up with and indulge one's cranks, eccentrics, idealists, and extremists, affected the Jewish community to an extent that those profiting from them did not always stop to appreciate. And the Jewish labor movement, ranging from the garment workers' unions to the large fraternal societies and small political groups, had established a tradition of protest, controversy, and freedom, so that even when such organizations violated this tradition, it still exerted an enormous moral power in the Jewish community and provided cover for the left-wing parties. Trotskyist street meetings were sometimes broken up, but only upon the decision of the Communist Party, which until the Popular Front prided itself on standing outside the spectrum of Jewish ideological life. In the garment center things were of course different, and there, in the bitter struggles between left and right unions, knives were wielded with a supreme indifference to race, creed, color, or size. But the Jewish neighborhood was prepared to listen to almost anyone, with its characteristic mixture of skepticism, interest, and amusement.

Even among the Stalinists the fact of Jewishness counted in surprising ways. I remember one evening when a street meeting was being harassed by a gang of Jewish Stalinists, and a screeching lady heckler jostled a friend of mine, causing her glasses to fall and break. My friend started bawling that her mother would berate her for breaking the glasses, and the Jewish lady, suddenly sympathetic, took the girl to a store and bought her a new pair. For the Communist lady my friend had a few minutes earlier been a "Fascist" but when trouble came and the glasses were broken, she also must have seemed like a nice Jewish girl. . . .

It was not only the Jewish labor movement that provided a protective aura; the Jewish community did the same thing, though less from political principle than from what I would hesitantly call ethnic shrewdness. In the thirties the ordinary New York Jew realized that Jewishness was not something one had much choice about, and in this respect his instincts were sounder, both morally and practically, than that of the radicals who chose for their "party names" almost anything that did not sound Jewish. You might be shouting at the top of your lungs against reformism or Stalin's betrayals, but for the middle-aged garment worker strolling along Southern Boulevard you were just a bright and cocky Jewish boy, a talkative little *pisher*.

The Jewish community enclosed one, not through choice as much as through experience and instinct, and often not very gently or with the most refined manners. What you believed, or said you believed, did not matter nearly as much as what you were, and what you were was not nearly so much a matter of choice as you might care to suppose. If you found a job, it was likely to be in a "Jewish industry" and if you went to college it was still within an essentially Jewish milieu. We did not realize then how sheltering it was to grow up in this world, just as we did not realize how the "bourgeois democracy" at which we railed was the medium making it possible for us to speak and survive. It was all part of our mania for *willing* a new life, our tacit wish to transform deracination from a plight into a program.

Thinking about it now, I am struck by how little I saw as a boy in the thirties of hunger and suffering, though surely there was no lack of either in New York and I was quite prepared to notice both. I knew, of course, the shacks of Hooverville on Riverside Drive, the lines of people waiting before store fronts rented by the welfare agencies, the piles of furniture on top of which sat the children of evicted tenants, the panhandlers slouching on Fourteenth Street, the idle men standing day after day near the rowboats of Crotona Park. But while the East Bronx was a place of poverty, it kept an inner discipline: Jews felt obligated to look after each other, they fought desperately to avoid going on relief, they would treat with the outer world only under extreme duress.

I have said that the movement was my home and passion. Yes; but the forces that shaped one, the subtle enveloping conditions that slowly did their work on character and disposition, were not really matters of choice. The world I never made, made me.

2.

There never seemed any place to go. The thought of bringing my friends home was inconceivable, for I would have been as ashamed to show them to my parents as to show my parents to them. I had enough imagination to suppose that each could see through the shams and limitations of the other, but not enough courage to defend one against the other. Besides, where would people sit in those cramped apartments? The worldly manner, the *savoir-faire* of Monroe High School and then of the city colleges, that was affected by some of my friends would have stirred flames of suspicion in the eyes of my father; the sullen immigrant kindliness of my parents would have struck my friends as all too similar to that of their own fathers and mothers; and my own self-consciousness, which in relation to my parents led me into a maze of superfluous lies and trivial deceptions, made it difficult for me to believe in the possibility of a life grounded in simple good faith. I could not imagine bringing together the life that was given, with its sweet poignancy and embittered conflicts, and the life one had chosen, with its secret fellowship and sectarian vocabulary.

So we walked the streets, never needing to tell one another why we chose this neutral setting for our escape at evening. In the winter, when the Bronx is gray and icy, there were cafeterias in which the older comrades, those who had jobs or were on WPA, bought coffee while the rest of us filled the chairs. In the summer, after meetings, we would parade across the middle bulge of the Bronx from the tenements on Wilkins Avenue in the East to the forbidding apartment houses of the Grand Concourse on the West. I remember those night walks as carefree and relaxed, away from the pressures of family and politics, though always with some secret anxiety that I would get home too late—for my parents, in their sweet blind innocence, were more distressed by my irregular hours than my irregular opinions.

The streets would be empty, the summer nights cool, a kind of expansiveness would come over us. Our enemies slept, the world was ours. We would listen with pleasure to our professional jokester, full of panting malice as he raked every friend who happened not to be along, or to the brilliant leader who warmed us with his confidence. We would glide away in our Melvillian freedom, away from the frustrations of the Movement and the dreary thought of the next morning when, with mama's quarter in my pocket for carfare and lunch, I would be taking the subway to City College, prepared once again to cut the classes that had, I was entirely confident, nothing to teach me.

3.

Someone always had a little money. I remember my friend M., who had a gift for picking up odd jobs and a passion for consuming ice cream sodas. Late one night, in the drab center of the Bronx, we passed by a little candy store whose owner had been sitting up in wait for a "sale." We went in, M. treated me to a soda and then returned to the storekeeper for a little more seltzer in his glass. The man stared at him in dismay, and M., no longer a budding Marxist theoretician but a nice roly-poly Jewish boy, said in great earnestness, "But I *always* get more seltzer with my sodas. . . ." The storekeeper turned wearily to his fountain, shrugging his Jewish shoulders as if his fragment of profit, the reward of his vigil, had just been dissolved in the bubbling glass.

4.

To be poor is something that happens; to experience poverty is to gain an idea as to what is happening. Once my father's grocery store went bankrupt in 1930 and he became a "customer peddler" trudging from door to door with sheets and linens, we were often very poor, living together with uncles, aunts, and grandmothers to save rent. Yet I had no very acute sense of being deprived, or any notions that I was the victim of social injustice. It was simply that, for reasons beyond my comprehension or probing, things had changed unpleasantly. Only after I had begun to go to high school did the idea of poverty start creeping into my consciousness, and I learned to regard it with the familiar blend of outrage, shame, and ambition. When I was thirteen or fourteen I began to buy a magazine that was printing Sherwood Anderson's reports about hunger in the North Carolina textile towns, and I would read these articles with tears of indignation, barely aware of the extent to which I was perhaps feeling sorry for myself. The realization of what it meant to be poor I had first to discover through writings about poverty; the sense of my own handicap became vivid to me only after I had learned about the troubles of people I did not know. And surely this experience was typical.

5.

Why did the Movement prove so attractive to young people? Or perhaps more to the point, why have those who left it found themselves romanticizing their youthful time as radicals?

It was not merely the power of ideology which bound one to the Movement. Ideology mattered, of course, but only the more ambitious among us really tried to master the intricacies of Marxist economics or Trotsky's critique of Soviet industrial policy. (In economics I was a complete bust, and to this day feel somewhat queasy when trying to remember the formulas of *Capital*, perhaps because they were taught in the Movement with the same talmudic rote which, years earlier, had characterized my disastrous Hebrew lessons. For a young Marxist in the thirties, the greatest ploy was a claim to be learned in economics, the science we faithfully praised as basic and secretly regarded as dismal.) Nor was it merely the magnetic pull of group life, with its enormous yet curiously satisfying demands upon our time and loyalty, that drew us so closely to the Movement. Almost all of us rebelled, at one point or another, against the exhausting routine of political activism—so much of it calculated to force upon us an awareness of our distance from American politics.

No, what I think held young people to the Movement was

the sense that they had gained, not merely a "purpose" in life but, far more important, a coherent perspective upon everything that was happening to us. And this perspective was something rather different from, a good deal more practical and immediate than, Marxist ideology; it meant the capacity for responding quickly and with a comforting assurance to events. The Movement gave us a language of response and gesture, the security of a set orientation—perhaps impossible to a political tendency that lacked an ideology but not quite to be identified with ideology as such. It felt good "to know." One revelled in the innocence and arrogance of knowledge, for even in our inexpert hands Marxism could be a powerful analytic tool and we could nurture the feeling that, whether other people realized it or not, we enjoyed a privileged relationship to history. The totalism of the Marxist system seemed attractive not merely because we wanted a key to all the doors of knowledge (most of which we never tried to open), but also because there was a keen pleasure in picking up a copy of *The New York Times* and reading it with that critical superiority, that presumptive talent for giving a "basic" interpretation to events, which our commitment enabled us to command. And if we were often mistaken, we were surely no more so than most other people.

But there is a more fundamental reason for the appeal of the Movement. Marxism involves a profoundly *dramatic* view of human experience. With its stress upon inevitable conflicts, apocalyptic climaxes, ultimate moments, hours of doom, and shining tomorrows, it appealed deeply to our imaginations. We felt that we were always on the rim of heroism, that the mockery we might suffer at the moment would turn to vindication in the future, that our loyalty to principle would be rewarded by the grateful masses of tomorrow. The principle of classic drama, peripeteia or the sudden reversal of fortune, we stood upon its head quite as Marx was supposed to have done to Hegel; and then it became for us a crux of our political system. The moment would come, our leaders kept assuring us and no doubt themselves, if only we did not flinch, if only we were ready to remain a tiny despised minority, if only we held firm to our sense of destiny. It was this pattern of drama which made each moment of our participation seem so rich with historical meaning.

6.

Were we so entirely wrong? The ways in which we were, are now obvious and if there is one middle-aged literary man or journalist who has failed to point them out I do not know his name. Our hopes and expectations were not realized, and concerning those that were crudely tainted by power-hunger it is perhaps just as well that they were not. But this is not at all to say that the radical outlook of the thirties was a mere fantasy or rested upon a failure to apprehend the realities of American society. There *were* millions of people desperate, hungry, hopeless; the society *was* sick and inhumane; people who cared nothing about ideology also shared the desire for profound social and moral change. When we fought against the Stalinist theory of "social Fascism" we were partly responding to ideological disputes in Russia but also trying to cope with a form of political adventurism that threatened to destroy the trade unions of New York. When we endlessly debated "the class nature of Soviet Russia" in Webster Hall and Irving Plaza we were partly succumbing to a Marxist scholasticism but also trying to cope with the problem of a new kind of society, a problem that still bedevils serious students of politics. And when we thought in terms of catastrophe and apocalypse . . . well, how many years did it take before catastrophe and apocalypse came to blacken the globe?

7.

A Movement that raises in the imagination of its followers the vision of historical drama, must find ways of realizing the dramatic in the course of history. And so we lived in hopes of a re-enactment that would be faithful to the severities of the Marxist myth and would embody once more in action the idea of October. Since we had, meanwhile, to suffer the awareness of our limitations, we found excitement —that poor substitute for drama—in the ceaseless round of faction fights.

Often enough these disputes concerned issues of genuine importance, in which the Movement found itself groping toward problems that most political analysts had not even begun to consider. Occasionally these disputes produced some vivid writing and speaking, in which the talents of the leaders, unable to find a public outlet, were expressed inwardly through polemic, wit, and invective. But I think the faction fights had another purpose that we could not then acknowledge: they were charades of struggle, substitute rituals for the battles we could not join, ceremonies of "acting out." Through them we created our own drama in our own world.

Once these dialectical tournaments began, the opposing factions would line up their squads of speakers, like knights arrayed at both ends of the field. They would then batter away at each other to the point of exhaustion and hoarseness, and continue to enact the whole combat-pageant even after everyone had firmly taken his stand. One's capacity for endurance played an extraordinary role in these political war games, and there were old-timers who prided themselves on battle scars from the legendary faction fights—the days of the titans—in the old days, just as there were party leaders whose prestige rested not on their achievements as organizers or gifts as writers but on their reputed shrewdness in faction maneuvers. It was a somewhat specialized skill.

If at a discussion meeting there happened to be a maverick who wished to speak apart from the lists of the two factions, the decorum of democracy required that he be given the floor. The sophisticated adherents of both sides shared, however, an impatience to get him out of the way, so that unless he were an important member whom it was advisable to court, the orderly buffeting of dispute could be resumed quite as if he had never spoken at all. Both sides gained a kind of pleasure from watching these disputes move forward step by step, from jocular argument to fierce attack, from amiable preparation to split or near-split—a drama in which the main fighters held to their fixed roles and seemed bound by the fatalities of an action quite as much as the protagonists of a classical play. Later it would all be repeated, a bit more crudely, in the local branches and then in the youth organization. One of my least happy recollections is that of meetings where eighteen- and nineteen-year-olds would hector each other with pat formulas as to whether Russia was "state capitalist" or "bureaucratic collectivist," hardly aware of the analytic difficulties in which they had become entangled, so puffed up were they with the vanity of rhetoric.

Years later, one hot night in Indiana, I had a bitter quarrel with Alfred Kazin about the intellectual quality of this life. He had used the phrase "sodden brilliance" to describe it and I had reacted with irritation, making the point that his phrase was a contradiction in terms. I must have been wounded by the accuracy of Kazin's thrust and by what I took to be his piety of manner; but now I cannot help seeing that "sodden brilliance" was really a good description. For while the debates were frequently brilliant, there was also a heavy-handed sarcasm, a nasty and unexamined personal violence, and a lumbering scholasticism that would warrant the qualifying "sodden."

8.

The Movement was a school in both politics and life, and much of what we know, both good and bad, we learned there. It made us sensitive to the decay and brutality of the modern world. It taught us to look upon social problems in terms extending beyond local or even national interests. It imbued us with an intense fascination for the *idea* of history, and if that brought intellectual dangers, they were probably worth facing. It trained us to think on our feet, and opened to us the pleasures of thrust and parry. And not entirely by intention, it led us to a strong feeling for democracy, if only because the harassments and persecutions to which we were subjected by the Communists persuaded us to value freedom of thought more than we quite knew we did.

Yes, the Movement taught us to think, but "only along too well-defined and predictable lines." (I repeat this phrase from a comment a City College teacher once wrote on a Marxistic composition of mine. The phrase burnt itself into my consciousness, and hearing it can still make me blush. Later, having become a teacher myself, I found it a consoling memory when dealing with narrow-minded students.) What passed for thought among us was often no more than facility: we were clever and fast in responding to familiar cues, especially in arguments with Communists, but had little capacity for turning back with a critical eye upon our own assumptions. Against opponents who shared our essential beliefs we could argue well—too often confusing arguing well with thinking well—but against those who dared question our essential beliefs we were not nearly so effective. We were trained in agility rather than reflection, dialectic rather than investigation. We had a strong sense of intellectual honor, but only a feeble appetite for intellectual risk. And that is why we seldom became disturbed when a member questioned a tactical or strategic "line" of the Movement, but felt uneasy, as if sensing the threat of heresy, when he began to wonder about the more abstract and fundamental Marxist tenets. In my own case, a fleeting encounter with Robert Michels's book on political parties left me with a permanent feeling of uneasiness, which time and exposure sharpened into doubt.

At least as crippling as its refusal to examine first principles was the attitude of the Movement toward what we called "bourgeois thought." Perhaps the most insidious doctrine afflicting the radical world was the Leninist theory of the "vanguard party," the notion that we possessed the political truth, held the key to the future, and had, so to say, signed a pact with history for a ninety-nine-year lease on the privilege. Pride in belonging to the "vanguard" was an expression of, as also an incitement toward, a naïve authoritarianism: I recall one youth leader riding on a Fifth Avenue bus and pointing to the skyscrapers with the remark: "Some day that will all belong to us. . . ." Such historic arrogance had its intellectual equivalents: a barely disguised contempt for the thought and learning of the past, an intolerance of divergent thought, a condescension toward "bourgeois scholars" who, it is true, occasionally accumulated valuable material but lacked the depth interpretation that "only Marxism" could provide. It was a heady brew for young people, and some suffered a hangover for years.

9.

Still, life had a way of asserting itself, and the reality was always far more complex and diverse than any possible description. Life would break through the crevices of our ideology and prompt us to unpolitical happiness and spontaneous feelings. It would tempt us with the delights of *avant-garde* writing—I read *Axel's Castle* at fifteen, understood little of it, and profited greatly—and lure us to the discoveries of romantic love. Some of the leaders were intellectuals *manqués*, full of pomp and pretension; others were serious and gifted men, at least as serious and gifted as the writers and professors I later came to know. When I try to summon an image of human goodness in its more public aspect, I still find myself remembering an ill-favored curmudgeon in the Bronx as selfless as he was grumpy, a girl in Brooklyn who poured the purity of her soul into the hope for socialism, a peculiarly mixed group of people whom I knew well or barely at all, yet who survive dimly as faces, those who enjoyed talking to "outsiders" about politics and those who were shy and would mail newspapers or fold leaflets in the office. For some the Movement was a mere steppingstone to careers, a training school for political advisors to trade-union leaders, academic sociologists, freewheeling literary critics; for most it was an experience both liberating and crippling, beautiful and ugly. . . .

10.

It is all gone, and we cannot have it back. There is nothing I desire more than a revival of American radicalism, but the past is done with, and I have no wish to re-create it nor any belief in the possibility of doing so. With time I hope that the past will yet settle into coherence for me—more coherence than these notes reveal—and that I will learn to look back with peace and good feeling. There are moments now and again when I recall the life of New York in the thirties, and see it through the lens of affection; and then it all seems pure in the light of time, I feel with pleasure the old stirrings of faith and conviction, that love for the unborn future which may yet redeem the past.